# Practical Business Analytics Using SAS

# Practical Business Analytics Using SAS

**Editor:**

Dr. Jovan Pehcevski, Ph.D.

ArclerPress

www.arclerpress.com

**Practical Business Analytics Using SAS**

*Editor: Dr. Jovan Pehcevski, Ph.D.*


**708 3rd Avenue, 6th Floor**
**New York**
**NY 10017**
**United States of America**
**www.arclerpress.com**

ISBN: 978-1-68094-486-0

Library of Congress Control Number: 2016951346

# About the Editor

## Dr. Jovan Pehcevski, Ph.D.

Jovan obtained his PhD in Computer Science from RMIT University in Melbourne, Australia in 2007. His research interests include big data, business intelligence and predictive analytics, data and information science, information retrieval, XML, web services and service-oriented architectures, and relational and NoSQL database systems. He has published over 30 journal and conference papers and he also serves as a journal and conference reviewer. He is currently working as a Dean and Associate Professor at European University in Skopje, Macedonia.

# Contents

# List of Contributors

**Silvia Bolohan**
SAS Analytical Solutions Romania

**Sebastian Ciobanu**
SAS Analytical Solutions Romania

**Silvia Bolohan**
SAS Analytical Solutions Romania

**Sebastian ciobanu**
SAS Analytical Solutions Romania

**David Shubert**
SAS Institute Inc., Cary NC

**Scott Sams**
SAS Institute Inc, Cary, NC

**Anca Ioana Andreescu**
Economic Informatics and Cybernetics Department, Academy of Economic Studies, Bucharest, Romania

**Anda Velicanu**
Economic Informatics and Cybernetics Department, Academy of Economic Studies, Bucharest, Romania

**Daniela Mitroescu**
Economic Informatics and Cybernetics Department, Academy of Economic Studies, Bucharest, Romania

# Preface

Big data and predictive analytics have become extremely relevant to all business domains, especially for the position of CEOs. Predictive analytics makes use of the variety and the volume of big data to provide analysis and understanding of what happened in the past, and, by taking advantage of the identified schemes and trends, it uses sophisticated algorithms to predict the future as accurately as possible. It is essentially a science about understanding customer behavior when making purchases on ecommerce sites, tracking and modeling market and price dynamics, and finding the correlation between internal and external financial factors. SAS, a software package recognized as an industry leader in analytics, provides the most comprehensive, integrated and easy-to-use reporting and analysis features on big data, either on a desktop computer or on the go. Its toolboxes for business analytics and business intelligence can mine, alter, manage and retrieve data from a variety of data sources. SAS performs statistical analysis and provides a graphical point-and-click user interface for non-technical users. It also offers more advanced options through the SAS programming language. SAS offers functions for descriptive statistics, such as calculating mean, standard deviation, correlation, regression and analysis of variance, and it represents data both in tabular and graphic formats. The main features that allow SAS users to perform business analytics tasks include: reading and accessing data, combining and manipulation of data, modeling and analytics with linear regression, SAS programs for repetitive analysis, presentation of output results in proper format, as well as interpretation of results and their connection with other (external) software tools. SAS allows business users to find relationships in data, by structuring and analyzing data stored in different IT systems within their company. Importantly, SAS also combines this data with external data sources, such as social networks and/or market research tools, to derive new knowledge relevant to the company business. This edition describes practical business analytics practices using SAS. It consists of three sections: basic SAS features, advanced data manipulation functions in SAS, and practical business analytics performed by SAS. Section 1 covers different statistic functions implemented in SAS, explaining descriptive statistics, frequencies, reading and accessing data, combining and manipulation of data, and modeling and analytics with linear regression. Section 2 covers advanced data manipulation and analytics with SAS, explaining creation and recording of variables, sub-setting variables and observations, labeling data, variables and values, using Proc sort and 'By' statement, concatenating (stacking) SAS data files, etc. Section 3 covers practical business analytics case studies using SAS, describing how to get meaningful information with SAS high-performance analytics, the SAS enterprise data integration server, data entry in the SAS Strategy Management tool, building interactive, data-driven dashboard applications with the SAS Business Intelligence Dashboard, and applications of spatial data using SAS business analytics.

**Editor**
**Dr. Jovan Pehcevski, Ph.D.**

# INTRODUCTION

Business analytics (BA) refers to the skills, technologies, practices for continuous iterative exploration and investigation of past business performance to gain insight and drive business planning. Business analytics focuses on developing new insights and understanding of business performance based on data and statistical methods. In contrast, business intelligence traditionally focuses on using a consistent set of metrics to both measure past performance and guide business planning, which is also based on data and statistical methods.

Business analytics makes extensive use of statistical analysis, including explanatory and predictive modeling, and fact-based management to drive decision making. It is therefore closely related to management science. Analytics may be used as input for human decisions or may drive fully automated decisions. Business intelligence is querying, reporting, online analytical processing (OLAP), and "alerts."

In other words, querying, reporting, OLAP, and alert tools can answer questions such as what happened, how many, how often, where the problem is, and what actions are needed. Business analytics can answer questions like why is this happening, what if these trends continue, what will happen next (that is, predict), what is the best that can happen (that is, optimize).

SAS is a leader in business analytics. Through innovative analytics it caters to business intelligence and data management software and services. SAS transforms data into insight which can give a fresh perspective on business.

Unlike other BI tools available in the market, SAS takes an extensive programming approach to data transformation and analysis rather than a pure drag drop and connect approach. That makes it stand out from the crowd as it gives much finer control over data manipulation. SAS has a very large number of components customized for specific industries and data analysis tasks.

### *Types of Analytics*

- Decision analytics: supports human decisions with visual analytics the user models to reflect reasoning.
- Descriptive analytics: gains insight from historical data with reporting, scorecards, clustering etc.
- Predictive analytics: employs predictive modeling using statistical and machine learning techniques
- Prescriptive analytics: recommends decisions using optimization, simulation, etc.

BA is used to gain insights that inform business decisions and can be used to automate and optimize business processes. Data-driven companies treat their data as a corporate asset and leverage it for competitive advantage. Successful business analytics depends on data quality, skilled analysts who understand the technologies and the business and an organizational commitment to data-driven decision making.

Examples of BA uses include:

- Exploring data to find new patterns and relationships (data mining)
- Explaining why a certain result occurred (statistical analysis, quantitative analysis)
- Experimenting to test previous decisions (A/B testing, multivariate testing)
- Forecasting future results (predictive modeling, predictive analytics)

Once the business goal of the analysis is determined, an analysis methodology is selected and data is acquired to support the analysis. Data acquisition often involves extraction from one or more business systems, cleansing, and integration into a single repository such as a data warehouse or data mart. The analysis is typically performed against a smaller sample set of data. Analytic tools range from spreadsheets with statistical functions to complex data mining and predictive modeling applications. As patterns and relationships in the data are uncovered, new questions are asked and the analytic process iterates until the business goal is met. Deployment of predictive models involves scoring data records (typically in a database) and using the scores to optimize real-time decisions within applications and business processes. BA also supports tactical decision making in response to unforeseen events, and in many cases the decision making is automated to support real-time responses.

While the terms business intelligence and business analytics are often used interchangeably, there are some key differences:

| BI vs BA | Business Intelligence | Business Analytics |
|---|---|---|
| Answers the questions: | What happened?<br>When?<br>Who?<br>How many? | Why did it happen?<br>Will it happen again?<br>What will happen if we change *x*?<br>What else does the data tell us that never thought to ask? |
| Includes: | Reporting (KPIs, metrics)<br>Automated Monitoring/Alerting (thresholds)<br>Dashboards<br>Scorecards<br>OLAP (Cubes, Slice & Dice, Drilling)<br>Ad hoc query | Statistical/Quantitative Analysis<br>Data Mining<br>Predictive Modeling<br>Multivariate Testing |

Recognizing the growing popularity of business analytics, business intelligence application vendors are including some BA functionality in their products. More recently, data warehouse appliance vendors have started to embed BA functionality within the appliance. Major enterprise system vendors are also embedding analytics, and the trend towards putting more analytics into memory is expected to shorten the time between a business event and decision/response.

### *What is a Statistical Analysis System?*

The term "statistical analysis system" is used to refer to software that allows the user to perform statistical analysis on data sets. Another commonly-used term for this type of software is statistical programming language. When capitalized, Statistical Analysis System (SAS) is also the proper name of one of the most well-known software packages of this type.

A statistical analysis system provides the automation and processing power needed to facilitate the manipulation and analysis of data sets. These packages facilitate computation of both descriptive and inductive statistics. Commonly-used descriptive statistical computations include calculation of central tendency, frequency distribution, and association. Inductive statistical analysis that can be performed with a statistical analysis system includes statistical hypothesis testing, such as the t-test, the z-test, and the chi-square test. Many statistical analysis systems also support other tests, such as analysis of variance (ANOVA) and its relatives, and various types of regression testing.

Statistical analysis systems are used in a wide variety of settings. Natural and social scientists in academic and commercial research settings are the most frequent users of these types of software packages. Businesses may also use a statistical analysis system for operations research, project management, and other business intelligence applications.

With some software packages, the command-line interface (CLI) is more often used, while others primarily feature a graphical user interface (GUI), often with drop-down menus. Most software packages provide both CLI and GUI capabilities, although the user may not be able to access all features from both interfaces. While a GUI is more familiar for non-technical users, using a CLI to create programs enables easier replication of analyses.

Many statistical software packages make use of fourth-generation programming languages (4GL). Due to their higher level of abstraction and more natural syntax, data manipulation and analysis in 4GL is quicker and easier than in lower-level programming languages. Before the development of 4GL, computer-assisted statistical analysis was cumbersome and required greater programming expertise.

A large number of statistical analysis software applications with varied interfaces, capabilities, and extensions are available. Proprietary software applications remain popular, but many open-source software applications are also widely used. Virtually all statistical software packages will run on Windows operating systems, and most also have Macintosh and Linux versions. A few applications are compatible with Unix operating systems as well.

## Using Statistical Analysis System in Business

In an effort to organize their data and predict future trends based on the information, many businesses rely on statistical analysis system. While organizations have lots of options on what to do with their big data, statistical analysis system is a way for it to be examined as a whole, as well as broken down into individual samples.

Statistical analysis examines every single data sample in a business population (the set of items from which samples can be drawn), rather than a cross sectional representation of samples as less sophisticated method.

SAS point to specific ways in which statistical analysis is completed in the business profits. There five steps are taken during the process, including:

- Describe the nature of the business data to be analyzed.
- Explore the relation of the business data.
- Create a model to summarize understanding of how the data relates to the business growth.
- Prove (or disprove) the validity of the business model.

Statistical data analysts interpret quantitative data and design statistical models for business researching problems or questions. They also maintain databases and ensure that their data are reliable. Most statistical analysts specialize in particular types of data, such as business, marketing, health and medicine, education or economics. Almost any field that relies on collecting and analyzing large amounts of data employs statistical data analysts.

# SECTION I: STATISTICS ANALYSES AND FUNCTIONS IN SAS

CHAPTER 1

# FUNDAMENTALS OF USING SAS

## BASIC FUNCTIONS

### Introduction

This chapter illustrates some of the features of the SAS System. SAS is a comprehensive package with very powerful data management tools, a wide variety of statistical analysis and graphical procedures. This is a very brief introduction and only covers just a fraction of all of the features of SAS. We use the following data file to illustrate the features of SAS. This data file contains information about 26 automobiles, namely their make, price, miles per gallon, repair rating (in 1978), weight in pounds, length in inches, and whether the car was foreign or **domestic**. Here is the data file.

```
make    price mpg rep78 weight length foreign

AMC      4099 22  3     2930   186     0
AMC      4749 17  3     3350   173     0
AMC      3799 22  3     2640   168     0
Audi     9690 17  5     2830   189     1
Audi     6295 23  3     2070   174     1
BMW      9735 25  4     2650   177     1
Buick    4816 20  3     3250   196     0
Buick    7827 15  4     4080   222     0
Buick    5788 18  3     3670   218     0
Buick    4453 26  3     2230   170     0
Buick    5189 20  3     3280   200     0
Buick   10372 16  3     3880   207     0
Buick    4082 19  3     3400   200     0
Cad.    11385 14  3     4330   221     0
Cad.    14500 14  2     3900   204     0
Cad.    15906 21  3     4290   204     0
Chev.    3299 29  3     2110   163     0
Chev.    5705 16  4     3690   212     0
Chev.    4504 22  3     3180   193     0
Chev.    5104 22  2     3220   200     0
Chev.    3667 24  2     2750   179     0
Chev.    3955 19  3     3430   197     0
Datsun   6229 23  4     2370   170     1
Datsun   4589 35  5     2020   165     1
Datsun   5079 24  4     2280   170     1
Datsun   8129 21  4     2750   184     1
```

**Citation:** Fundamentals of using SAS", Web Tutorial by UCLA: Statistical Consulting Group, 2016.

The program below reads the data and creates a temporary data file called **auto**. The descriptive statistics shown in this module are all performed on this data file called **auto**.

```
DATA auto ;
  INPUT make $ price mpg rep78 weight length foreign ;
DATALINES;
AMC      4099 22  3     2930   186     0
AMC      4749 17  3     3350   173     0
AMC      3799 22  3     2640   168     0
Audi     9690 17  5     2830   189     1
Audi     6295 23  3     2070   174     1
BMW      9735 25  4     2650   177     1
Buick    4816 20  3     3250   196     0
Buick    7827 15  4     4080   222     0
Buick    5788 18  3     3670   218     0
Buick    4453 26  3     2230   170     0
Buick    5189 20  3     3280   200     0
Buick   10372 16  3     3880   207     0
Buick    4082 19  3     3400   200     0
Cad.    11385 14  3     4330   221     0
Cad.    14500 14  2     3900   204     0
Cad.    15906 21  3     4290   204     0
Chev.    3299 29  3     2110   163     0
Chev.    5705 16  4     3690   212     0
Chev.    4504 22  3     3180   193     0
Chev.    5104 22  2     3220   200     0
Chev.    3667 24  2     2750   179     0
Chev.    3955 19  3     3430   197     0
Datsun   6229 23  4     2370   170     1
Datsun   4589 35  5     2020   165     1
Datsun   5079 24  4     2280   170     1
Datsun   8129 21  4     2750   184     1
;
RUN;

PROC PRINT DATA=auto(obs=10);
RUN;
```

The output of the **proc print** is shown below. You can compare the program to the output below.

| OBS | MAKE | PRICE | MPG | REP78 | WEIGHT | LENGTH | FOREIGN |
|---|---|---|---|---|---|---|---|
| 1 | AMC | 4099 | 22 | 3 | 2930 | 186 | 0 |
| 2 | AMC | 4749 | 17 | 3 | 3350 | 173 | 0 |
| 3 | AMC | 3799 | 22 | 3 | 2640 | 168 | 0 |
| 4 | Audi | 9690 | 17 | 5 | 2830 | 189 | 1 |
| 5 | Audi | 6295 | 23 | 3 | 2070 | 174 | 1 |
| 6 | BMW | 9735 | 25 | 4 | 2650 | 177 | 1 |
| 7 | Buick | 4816 | 20 | 3 | 3250 | 196 | 0 |
| 8 | Buick | 7827 | 15 | 4 | 4080 | 222 | 0 |
| 9 | Buick | 5788 | 18 | 3 | 3670 | 218 | 0 |
| 10 | Buick | 4453 | 26 | 3 | 2230 | 170 | 0 |

## Descriptive statistics in SAS

We can get descriptive statistics for all of the variables using **proc means** as shown below.

```
PROC MEANS DATA=auto;
RUN;
```

Here is the output produced by the **proc means** statements above.

| Variable | N | Mean | Std Dev | Minimum | Maximum |
|---|---|---|---|---|---|
| PRICE | 26 | 6651.73 | 3371.12 | 3299.00 | 15906.00 |
| MPG | 26 | 20.9230769 | 4.7575042 | 14.0000000 | 35.0000000 |
| REP78 | 26 | 3.2692308 | 0.7775702 | 2.0000000 | 5.0000000 |
| WEIGHT | 26 | 3099.23 | 695.0794089 | 2020.00 | 4330.00 |
| LENGTH | 26 | 190.0769231 | 18.1701361 | 163.0000000 | 222.0000000 |
| FOREIGN | 26 | 0.2692308 | 0.4523443 | 0 | 1.0000000 |

We can get descriptive statistics separately for foreign and domestic cars (i.e., broken down by **foreign**) as shown below.

```
PROC MEANS DATA=auto;
  CLASS foreign;
RUN;
```

The output from the above statements is shown below.

| FOREIGN | N Obs | Variable | N | Mean | Std Dev | Minimum |
|---|---|---|---|---|---|---|
| 0 | 19 | PRICE | 19 | 6484.16 | 3768.46 | 3299.00 |
| | | MPG | 19 | 19.7894737 | 4.0356598 | 14.0000000 |
| | | REP78 | 19 | 2.9473684 | 0.5242650 | 2.0000000 |
| | | WEIGHT | 19 | 3347.89 | 627.1769106 | 2110.00 |
| | | LENGTH | 19 | 195.4210526 | 17.9639014 | 163.0000000 |
| 1 | 7 | PRICE | 7 | 7106.57 | 2101.83 | 4589.00 |
| | | MPG | 7 | 24.0000000 | 5.5075705 | 17.0000000 |
| | | REP78 | 7 | 4.1428571 | 0.6900656 | 3.0000000 |
| | | WEIGHT | 7 | 2424.29 | 325.1593016 | 2020.00 |
| | | LENGTH | 7 | 175.5714286 | 8.4628038 | 165.0000000 |

| FOREIGN | N Obs | Variable | Maximum |
|---|---|---|---|
| 0 | 19 | PRICE | 15906.00 |
| | | MPG | 29.0000000 |
| | | REP78 | 4.0000000 |
| | | WEIGHT | 4330.00 |
| | | LENGTH | 222.0000000 |
| 1 | 7 | PRICE | 9735.00 |
| | | MPG | 35.0000000 |
| | | REP78 | 5.0000000 |
| | | WEIGHT | 2830.00 |
| | | LENGTH | 189.0000000 |

We can get detailed descriptive statistics for **price** using **proc univariate** as shown below.

```
PROC UNIVARIATE DATA=auto;
  VAR PRICE;
RUN;
```

The results are shown below.

```
 Univariate Procedure
Variable=PRICE

                 Moments
N                26  Sum Wgts          26
Mean       6651.731  Sum           172945
Std Dev     3371.12  Variance    11364449
Skewness   1.470727  Kurtosis    1.534672
USS        1.4345E9  CSS         2.8411E8
CV         50.68034  Std Mean     661.131
T:Mean=0   10.06114  Pr>|T|        0.0001
Num ^= 0         26  Num > 0           26
M(Sign)          13  Pr>=|M|       0.0001
Sgn Rank      175.5  Pr>=|S|       0.0001

           Quantiles(Def=5)

100% Max      15906         99%     15906
 75% Q3        8129         95%     14500
 50% Med     5146.5         90%     11385
 25% Q1        4453         10%      3799
  0% Min       3299          5%      3667
                             1%      3299
Range         12607
Q3-Q1          3676
Mode           3299

                 Extremes
   Lowest     Obs     Highest     Obs
    3299(      17)      9735(       6)
    3667(      21)     10372(      12)
    3799(       3)     11385(      14)
    3955(      22)     14500(      15)
    4082(      13)     15906(      16)
```

We can get a frequency distribution of **rep78** (the repair rating of the car) using **proc freq** as shown below.

```
PROC FREQ DATA=auto;
  TABLES rep78 ;
RUN;
```

The results are shown below.

```
                                    Cumulative  Cumulative
REP78   Frequency   Percent   Frequency    Percent
--------------------------------------------------------
   2          3       11.5           3        11.5
   3         15       57.7          18        69.2
   4          6       23.1          24        92.3
   5          2        7.7          26       100.0
```

We can make a two way table showing the frequencies for **rep78** for foreign and domestic cars as shown below.

```
PROC FREQ DATA=auto ;
  TABLES rep78 * foreign ;
RUN;
```

The output is shown below.

```
TABLE OF REP78 BY FOREIGN

REP78     FOREIGN

Frequency|
Percent  |
Row Pct  |
Col Pct  |       0|       1|  Total
---------+--------+--------+
       2 |      3 |      0 |      3
         |  11.54 |   0.00 |  11.54
         | 100.00 |   0.00 |
         |  15.79 |   0.00 |
---------+--------+--------+
       3 |     14 |      1 |     15
         |  53.85 |   3.85 |  57.69
         |  93.33 |   6.67 |
         |  73.68 |  14.29 |
---------+--------+--------+
       4 |      2 |      4 |      6
         |   7.69 |  15.38 |  23.08
         |  33.33 |  66.67 |
         |  10.53 |  57.14 |
---------+--------+--------+
       5 |      0 |      2 |      2
         |   0.00 |   7.69 |   7.69
         |   0.00 | 100.00 |
         |   0.00 |  28.57 |
---------+--------+--------+
Total          19        7      26
            73.08    26.92  100.00
```

## Making graphs in SAS

We can make a bar chart showing the frequencies of **rep78** as shown below.

```
TITLE 'Bar Chart with Discrete Option';
PROC GCHART DATA=auto;
      VBAR rep78/ DISCRETE;

RUN;
```

This program produces the following chart.

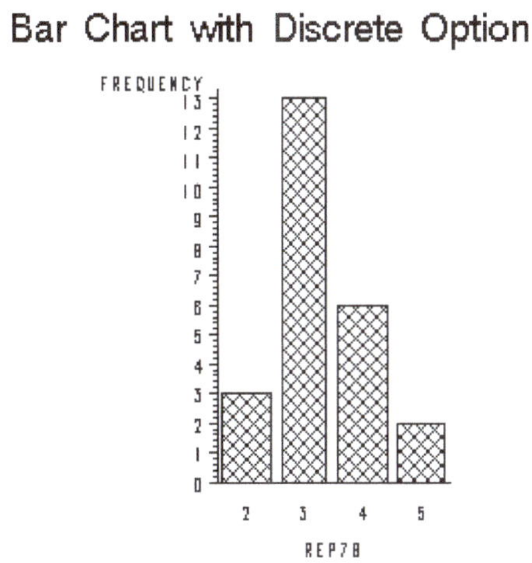


## Correlation, regression and analysis of variance

We can use **proc corr** to get correlations of **price mpg weight** and **length** as shown below.

```
PROC CORR DATA=auto ;
  VAR price mpg weight length ;
RUN;
```

The output is shown below.

```
                               Simple Statistics

Variable      N       Mean    Std Dev        Sum    Minimum    Maximum

PRICE        26       6652       3371     172945       3299      15906
MPG          26   20.92308    4.75750  544.00000   14.00000   35.00000
WEIGHT       26       3099  695.07941      80580       2020       4330
LENGTH       26  190.07692   18.17014       4942  163.00000  222.00000
```

Pearson Correlation Coefficients / Prob > |R| under Ho: Rho=0 / N = 26

```
               PRICE          MPG       WEIGHT       LENGTH

PRICE        1.00000     -0.43846      0.55607      0.43604
              0.0         0.0251       0.0032       0.0260

MPG         -0.43846      1.00000     -0.80816     -0.76805
              0.0251      0.0          0.0001       0.0001

WEIGHT       0.55607     -0.80816      1.00000      0.90654
              0.0032      0.0001       0.0          0.0001

LENGTH       0.43604     -0.76805      0.90654      1.00000
              0.0260      0.0001       0.0001       0.0
```

We can use **proc reg** to predict **mpg** from **weight length** and **foreign**, as shown below.

```
PROC REG DATA=auto;
  MODEL mpg = weight length foreign ;
RUN;
```

The output is shown below.

```
Model: MODEL1
Dependent Variable: MPG

Analysis of Variance

                          Sum of         Mean
Source           DF      Squares       Square       F Value       Prob>F

Model             3    378.69701    126.23234        14.839       0.0001
Error            22    187.14915      8.50678
C Total          25    565.84615

    Root MSE        2.91664     R-square       0.6693
    Dep Mean       20.92308     Adj R-sq       0.6242
    C.V.           13.93982
```

Parameter Estimates

```
                 Parameter      Standard     T for H0:
Variable  DF      Estimate         Error   Parameter=0    Prob > |T|

INTERCEP   1     44.968582    9.32267757         4.824        0.0001
WEIGHT     1     -0.005008    0.00218752        -2.289        0.0320
LENGTH     1     -0.043056    0.07692650        -0.560        0.5813
FOREIGN    1     -1.269211    1.63213395        -0.778        0.4451
```

We can use **proc glm** to do an ANOVA to test if the mean **mpg** is the same for foreign and domestic cars, as shown below.

```
PROC GLM DATA=auto;
  CLASS foreign ;
  MODEL mpg = foreign ;
RUN;
```

The output is shown below.

```
General Linear Models Procedure
Class Level Information

Class     Levels     Values

FOREIGN        2     0 1

Number of observations in data set = 26

General Linear Models Procedure

Dependent Variable: MPG
                                   Sum of           Mean
Source                DF          Squares         Square    F Value      Pr > F
Model                  1      90.68825911    90.68825911       4.58      0.0427
Error                 24     475.15789474    19.79824561
Corrected Total       25     565.84615385

                R-Square             C.V.       Root MSE                MPG Mean
                0.160270         21.26610      4.4495220               20.923077

Source                DF        Type I SS    Mean Square    F Value      Pr > F
FOREIGN                1      90.68825911    90.68825911       4.58      0.0427

Source                DF      Type III SS    Mean Square    F Value      Pr > F
FOREIGN                1      90.68825911    90.68825911       4.58      0.0427
```

## DESCRIPTIVE STATISTICS

### Introduction

This module illustrates how to obtain basic descriptive statistics using SAS. We illustrate this using a data file about 26 automobiles with their make, price, mpg, repair record, and whether the car was foreign or domestic. The data file is illustrated below

```
MAKE PRICE MPG REP78 FOREIGN
AMC     4099 22 3 0
AMC     4749 17 3 0
AMC     3799 22 3 0
Audi    9690 17 5 1
Audi    6295 23 3 1
BMW     9735 25 4 1
Buick  4816 20 3 0
Buick  7827 15 4 0
Buick  5788 18 3 0
Buick  4453 26 3 0
Buick  5189 20 3 0
Buick 10372 16 3 0
Buick  4082 19 3 0
Cad.  11385 14 3 0
Cad.  14500 14 2 0
Cad.  15906 21 3 0
Chev.  3299 29 3 0
Chev.  5705 16 4 0
Chev.  4504 22 3 0
Chev.  5104 22 2 0
Chev.  3667 24 2 0
Chev.  3955 19 3 0
Datsun 6229 23 4 1
Datsun 4589 35 5 1
Datsun 5079 24 4 1
Datsun 8129 21 4 1
```

The program below reads the data and creates a temporary data file called **auto**. The descriptive statistics shown in this module are all performed on this data file called **auto**.

```
DATA auto ;
  input MAKE $ PRICE MPG REP78 FOREIGN ;
DATALINES;
AMC     4099 22 3 0
AMC     4749 17 3 0
AMC     3799 22 3 0
Audi    9690 17 5 1
Audi    6295 23 3 1
BMW     9735 25 4 1
Buick   4816 20 3 0
Buick   7827 15 4 0
Buick   5788 18 3 0
Buick   4453 26 3 0
Buick   5189 20 3 0
Buick  10372 16 3 0
Buick   4082 19 3 0
Cad.   11385 14 3 0
Cad.   14500 14 2 0
Cad.   15906 21 3 0
Chev.   3299 29 3 0
Chev.   5705 16 4 0
Chev.   4504 22 3 0
Chev.   5104 22 2 0
Chev.   3667 24 2 0
Chev.   3955 19 3 0
Datsun 6229 23 4 1
Datsun 4589 35 5 1
Datsun 5079 24 4 1
Datsun 8129 21 4 1
;
RUN;

PROC PRINT DATA=auto(obs=10);
RUN;
```

The output of the **proc print** is shown below. You can compare the program above to the output below.

| OBS | MAKE | PRICE | MPG | REP78 | FOREIGN |
|---|---|---|---|---|---|
| 1 | AMC | 4099 | 22 | 3 | 0 |
| 2 | AMC | 4749 | 17 | 3 | 0 |
| 3 | AMC | 3799 | 22 | 3 | 0 |
| 4 | Audi | 9690 | 17 | 5 | 1 |
| 5 | Audi | 6295 | 23 | 3 | 1 |
| 6 | BMW | 9735 | 25 | 4 | 1 |
| 7 | Buick | 4816 | 20 | 3 | 0 |
| 8 | Buick | 7827 | 15 | 4 | 0 |
| 9 | Buick | 5788 | 18 | 3 | 0 |
| 10 | Buick | 4453 | 26 | 3 | 0 |

## Using proc freq for frequencies

We can use **proc freq** to produce frequency tables. Below, we use it to make frequency tables for **make**, **rep78** and **foreign**.

```
PROC FREQ DATA=auto;
  TABLES make ;
RUN;

PROC FREQ DATA=auto;
  TABLES rep78 ;
RUN;

PROC FREQ DATA=auto;
  TABLES foreign ;
RUN;
```

Here is the output produced by the proc freq statements above.

| MAKE | Frequency | Percent | Cumulative Frequency | Cumulative Percent |
|---|---|---|---|---|
| AMC | 3 | 11.5 | 3 | 11.5 |
| Audi | 2 | 7.7 | 5 | 19.2 |
| BMW | 1 | 3.8 | 6 | 23.1 |
| Buick | 7 | 26.9 | 13 | 50.0 |
| Cad. | 3 | 11.5 | 16 | 61.5 |
| Chev. | 6 | 23.1 | 22 | 84.6 |
| Datsun | 4 | 15.4 | 26 | 100.0 |

| REP78 | Frequency | Percent | Cumulative Frequency | Cumulative Percent |
|---|---|---|---|---|
| 2 | 3 | 11.5 | 3 | 11.5 |
| 3 | 15 | 57.7 | 18 | 69.2 |
| 4 | 6 | 23.1 | 24 | 92.3 |
| 5 | 2 | 7.7 | 26 | 100.0 |

| FOREIGN | Frequency | Percent | Cumulative Frequency | Cumulative Percent |
|---|---|---|---|---|
| 0 | 19 | 73.1 | 19 | 73.1 |
| 1 | 7 | 26.9 | 26 | 100.0 |

Instead of having three separate **proc freqs**, we could have done this all in one **proc freq** step as illustrated below. The output will be the same as shown above.

```
PROC FREQ DATA=auto;
  TABLES make rep78 foreign ;
RUN;
```

Let's use **proc freq** to look at a cross tabulation of the repair history of the cars (**rep78**) for foreign and domestic cars (**foreign**). The **proc freq**statements for this are shown below.

Note the asterisk (*) between the variables **rep78** and **foreign** on the **tables** statement.

```
PROC FREQ DATA=auto;
  TABLES rep78*foreign ;
RUN;
```

This is the output produced.

```
TABLE OF REP78 BY FOREIGN

REP78     FOREIGN

Frequency|
Percent  |
Row Pct  |
Col Pct  |       0|       1|  Total
---------+--------+--------+
       2 |      3 |      0 |      3
         |  11.54 |   0.00 |  11.54
         | 100.00 |   0.00 |
         |  15.79 |   0.00 |
---------+--------+--------+
       3 |     14 |      1 |     15
         |  53.85 |   3.85 |  57.69
         |  93.33 |   6.67 |
         |  73.68 |  14.29 |
---------+--------+--------+
       4 |      2 |      4 |      6
         |   7.69 |  15.38 |  23.08
         |  33.33 |  66.67 |
         |  10.53 |  57.14 |
---------+--------+--------+
       5 |      0 |      2 |      2
         |   0.00 |   7.69 |   7.69
         |   0.00 | 100.00 |
         |   0.00 |  28.57 |
---------+--------+--------+
Total          19        7       26
            73.08    26.92   100.00
```

We can show just the cell percentages to make the table easier to read by using the **norow**, **nocol** and **nofreq** options on the **tables** statement to suppress the printing of the row percentages, column percentages and frequencies (leaving just the cell percentages). Note that the options come after the forward slash ( / ) on the **tables** statement.

```
PROC FREQ DATA=auto;
  TABLES rep78*foreign / NOROW NOCOL NOFREQ ;
RUN;
```

The output is shown below.

```
TABLE OF REP78 BY FOREIGN

REP78     FOREIGN

Percent |       0|       1|  Total
--------+--------+--------+
      2 |  11.54 |   0.00 |  11.54
--------+--------+--------+
      3 |  53.85 |   3.85 |  57.69
--------+--------+--------+
      4 |   7.69 |  15.38 |  23.08
--------+--------+--------+
      5 |   0.00 |   7.69 |   7.69
--------+--------+--------+
Total         19        7       26
           73.08    26.92   100.00
```

The order of the options does not matter. We would have gotten the same output had we written the command like this.

```
PROC FREQ DATA=auto;
  TABLES rep78*foreign / NOFREQ NOROW NOCOL ;
RUN;
```

## Using proc means for summary statistics

**Proc means** can be used to produce summary statistics. Below, **proc means** is used to get descriptive statistics for the variable **mpg**.

```
PROC MEANS DATA=auto;
  VAR mpg;
RUN;
```

The results of the **proc means** are shown below.

```
Analysis Variable : MPG

 N         Mean        Std Dev        Minimum        Maximum
-------------------------------------------------------------
26   20.9230769      4.7575042     14.0000000     35.0000000
-------------------------------------------------------------
```

Suppose we would like to get the summary statistics separately for foreign and domestic cars (indicated by the variable **foreign**). We can use the **class**statement (shown below) to get separate results for the different values of **foreign**.

```
PROC MEANS DATA=auto;
  CLASS foreign ;
  VAR mpg;
RUN;
```

As you see below, the results of **proc means** are presented separately for the seven foreign cars (when **foreign** equals 1) and the 19 domestic cars (when **foreign** equals 0).

```
Analysis Variable : MPG

FOREIGN  N Obs   N    Mean       Std Dev     Minimum   Maximum
----------------------------------------------------------------
      0     19  19   19.78     4.0356598     14.0000     29.00
      1      7   7   24.00     5.5075705     17.0000     35.00
----------------------------------------------------------------
```

## Using proc univariate for detailed summary statistics

You can use **proc univariate** to get more detailed summary statistics, as shown below.

```
PROC UNIVARIATE DATA=auto;
  VAR mpg;
RUN;
```

And here are the results of **proc univariate**.

```
Univariate Procedure

Variable=MPG

                    Moments
 N                26  Sum Wgts          26
 Mean       20.92308  Sum              544
 Std Dev    4.757504  Variance    22.63385
 Skewness   0.935473  Kurtosis      1.7927
 USS           11948  CSS         565.8462
 CV         22.73807  Std Mean    0.933023
 T:Mean=0   22.42503  Pr>|T|        0.0001
 Num ^= 0         26  Num > 0           26
 M(Sign)          13  Pr>=|M|       0.0001
 Sgn Rank      175.5  Pr>=|S|       0.0001

          Quantiles(Def=5)
 100% Max         35        99%         35
  75% Q3          23        95%         29
  50% Med         21        90%         26
  25% Q1          17        10%         15
   0% Min         14         5%         14
                             1%         14

 Range            21
 Q3-Q1             6
 Mode             22

               Extremes
    Lowest    Obs     Highest    Obs
       14(        15)      24(        25)
       14(        14)      25(         6)
       15(         8)      26(        10)
       16(        18)      29(        17)
       16(        12)      35(        24)
```

We can use the **class** statement to obtain separate **univariate** results for foreign and domestic cars.

```
PROC UNIVARIATE DATA=auto;
  CLASS foreign;
  VAR mpg;
RUN;
```

As you see in the output below, you get a complete set of output for the case when **foreign** equals 0 and then another set of output when **foreign** equals 1.

```
The UNIVARIATE Procedure
Variable:  MPG
FOREIGN = 0

                            Moments

N                          19    Sum Weights                19
Mean               19.7894737    Sum Observations          376
Std Deviation      4.03565976    Variance           16.2865497
Skewness             0.477379    Kurtosis           0.04119835
Uncorrected SS           7734    Corrected SS       293.157895
Coeff Variation    20.3929616    Std Error Mean     0.92584385

                 Basic Statistical Measures

     Location                     Variability

Mean      19.78947     Std Deviation              4.03566
Median    20.00000     Variance                  16.28655
Mode      22.00000     Range                     15.00000
                       Interquartile Range        6.00000

               Tests for Location: Mu0=0

Test            -Statistic-      -----p Value------

Student's t     t  21.37453      Pr > |t|     <.0001
Sign            M       9.5      Pr >= |M|    <.0001
Signed Rank     S        95      Pr >= |S|    <.0001

Quantiles (Definition 5)

Quantile      Estimate

100% Max            29
99%                 29
95%                 29
90%                 26
75% Q3              22
50% Median          20
25% Q1              16
10%                 14
5%                  14
1%                  14
0% Min              14

Variable:  MPG
FOREIGN = 0

             Extreme Observations

----Lowest----          ----Highest---

Value      Obs          Value      Obs

   14       15             22       19
   14       14             22       20
   15        8             24       21
   16       18             26       10
   16       12             29       17

Variable:  MPG
FOREIGN = 1
                              Moments

N                           7    Sum Weights                 7
Mean                       24    Sum Observations          168
Std Deviation      5.50757055    Variance           30.3333333
Skewness           1.34081176    Kurtosis           3.28605241
Uncorrected SS           4214    Corrected SS              182
Coeff Variation    22.9482106    Std Error Mean       2.081666

                 Basic Statistical Measures

     Location                     Variability

Mean      24.00000     Std Deviation              5.50757
Median    23.00000     Variance                  30.33333
Mode      23.00000     Range                     18.00000
                       Interquartile Range        4.00000

               Tests for Location: Mu0=0

Test            -Statistic-      -----p Value------

Student's t     t  11.52923      Pr > |t|     <.0001
Sign            M       3.5      Pr >= |M|    0.0156
Signed Rank     S        14      Pr >= |S|    0.0156

Quantiles (Definition 5)

Quantile      Estimate

100% Max            35
99%                 35
95%                 35
90%                 35
75% Q3              25
50% Median          23
25% Q1              21
10%                 17
5%                  17
1%                  17
0% Min              17

Variable:  MPG
FOREIGN = 1
```

```
                Extreme Observations

     ----Lowest----          ----Highest---

     Value      Obs          Value      Obs

        17        4             23        5
        21       26             23       23
        23       23             24       25
        23        5             25        6
        24       25             35       24
```

## Problems to look out for

If you make a crosstab with **proc freq** and one of the variables has large number of values (say 10 or more) the crosstab table could be very hard to read. In such cases, try using the **list** option on the **tables** statement.

```
TABLES rep78*foreign / LIST ;
```

When using the **by** statement in **proc univariate,** if you choose a **by** variable with a large number of values (say 5, 10, or more) it will produce a very large amount of output. In such cases, you may try to use **proc means** with a **class** statement instead of **proc univariate.**

# AN OVERVIEW OF STATISTICAL TESTS IN SAS

## Introduction and description of data

We will illustrate doing some basic statistical tests in SAS, including t-tests, chi square, correlation, regression, and analysis of variance. We demonstrate this using the **auto** data file. The program below reads the data and creates a temporary data file called **auto**. (Please note that we have made the values of **mpg** to be missing for the **AMC** cars. This differs from the other example data files where the **AMC** cars have valid data for **mpg**.)

```
DATA auto ;
  LENGTH make $ 20 ;
  INPUT make $ 1-17 price mpg rep78 hdroom trunk weight
        length turn displ gratio foreign ;
CARDS;
AMC Concord        4099  . 3 2.5 11 2930 186 40 121 3.58 0
AMC Pacer          4749  . 3 3.0 11 3350 173 40 258 2.53 0
AMC Spirit         3799  . . 3.0 12 2640 168 35 121 3.08 0
Audi 5000          9690 17 5 3.0 15 2830 189 37 131 3.20 1
Audi Fox           6295 23 3 2.5 11 2070 174 36  97 3.70 1
BMW 320i           9735 25 4 2.5 12 2650 177 34 121 3.64 1
Buick Century      4816 20 3 4.5 16 3250 196 40 196 2.93 0
Buick Electra      7827 15 4 4.0 20 4080 222 43 350 2.41 0
Buick LeSabre      5788 18 3 4.0 21 3670 218 43 231 2.73 0
Buick Opel         4453 26 . 3.0 10 2230 170 34 304 2.87 0
Buick Regal        5189 20 3 2.0 16 3280 200 42 196 2.93 0
Buick Riviera     10372 16 3 3.5 17 3880 207 43 231 2.93 0
Buick Skylark      4082 19 3 3.5 13 3400 200 42 231 3.08 0
Cad. Deville      11385 14 3 4.0 20 4330 221 44 425 2.28 0
Cad. Eldorado     14500 14 2 3.5 16 3900 204 43 350 2.19 0
Cad. Seville      15906 21 3 3.0 13 4290 204 45 350 2.24 0
Chev. Chevette     3299 29 3 2.5  9 2110 163 34 231 2.93 0
Chev. Impala       5705 16 4 4.0 20 3690 212 43 250 2.56 0
Chev. Malibu       4504 22 3 3.5 17 3180 193 31 200 2.73 0
Chev. Monte Carlo  5104 22 2 2.0 16 3220 200 41 200 2.73 0
Chev. Monza        3667 24 2 2.0  7 2750 179 40 151 2.73 0
Chev. Nova         3955 19 3 3.5 13 3430 197 43 250 2.56 0
Datsun 200         6229 23 4 1.5  6 2370 170 35 119 3.89 1
Datsun 210         4589 35 5 2.0  8 2020 165 32  85 3.70 1
Datsun 510         5079 24 4 2.5  8 2280 170 34 119 3.54 1
Datsun 810         8129 21 4 2.5  8 2750 184 38 146 3.55 1
Dodge Colt         3984 30 5 2.0  8 2120 163 35  98 3.54 0
Dodge Diplomat     4010 18 2 4.0 17 3600 206 46 318 2.47 0
Dodge Magnum       5886 16 2 4.0 17 3600 206 46 318 2.47 0
Dodge St. Regis    6342 17 2 4.5 21 3740 220 46 225 2.94 0
Fiat Strada        4296 21 3 2.5 16 2130 161 36 105 3.37 1
Ford Fiesta        4389 28 4 1.5  9 1800 147 33  98 3.15 0
Ford Mustang       4187 21 3 2.0 10 2650 179 43 140 3.08 0
Honda Accord       5799 25 5 3.0 10 2240 172 36 107 3.05 1
Honda Civic        4499 28 4 2.5  5 1760 149 34  91 3.30 1
Linc. Continental 11497 12 3 3.5 22 4840 233 51 400 2.47 0
Linc. Mark V      13594 12 3 2.5 18 4720 230 48 400 2.47 0
Linc. Versailles  13466 14 3 3.5 15 3830 201 41 302 2.47 0
Mazda GLC          3995 30 4 3.5 11 1980 154 33  86 3.73 1
Merc. Bobcat       3829 22 4 3.0  9 2580 169 39 140 2.73 0
Merc. Cougar       5379 14 4 3.5 16 4060 221 48 302 2.75 0
Merc. Marquis      6165 15 3 3.5 23 3720 212 44 302 2.26 0
Merc. Monarch      4516 18 3 3.0 15 3370 198 41 250 2.43 0
Merc. XR-7         6303 14 4 3.0 16 4130 217 45 302 2.75 0
Merc. Zephyr       3291 20 3 3.5 17 2830 195 43 140 3.08 0
Olds 98            8814 21 4 4.0 20 4060 220 43 350 2.41 0
Olds Cutl Supr     5172 19 3 2.0 16 3310 198 42 231 2.93 0
Olds Cutlass       4733 19 3 4.5 16 3300 198 42 231 2.93 0
Olds Delta 88      4890 18 4 4.0 20 3690 218 42 231 2.73 0
Olds Omega         4181 19 3 4.5 14 3370 200 43 231 3.08 0
Olds Starfire      4195 24 1 2.0 10 2730 180 40 151 2.73 0
Olds Toronado     10371 16 3 3.5 17 4030 206 43 350 2.41 0
Peugeot 604       12990 14 . 3.5 14 3420 192 38 163 3.58 1
Plym. Arrow        4647 28 3 2.0 11 3260 170 37 156 3.05 0
Plym. Champ        4425 34 5 2.5 11 1800 157 37  86 2.97 0
Plym. Horizon      4482 25 3 4.0 17 2200 165 36 105 3.37 0
Plym. Sapporo      6486 26 . 1.5  8 2520 182 38 119 3.54 0
Plym. Volare       4060 18 2 5.0 16 3330 201 44 225 3.23 0
Pont. Catalina     5798 18 4 4.0 20 3700 214 42 231 2.73 0
Pont. Firebird     4934 18 1 1.5  7 3470 198 42 231 3.08 0
Pont. Grand Prix   5222 19 3 2.0 16 3210 201 45 231 2.93 0
Pont. Le Mans      4723 19 3 3.5 17 3200 199 40 231 2.93 0
Pont. Phoenix      4424 19 . 3.5 13 3420 203 43 231 3.08 0
Pont. Sunbird      4172 24 2 2.0  7 2690 179 41 151 2.73 0
Renault Le Car     3895 26 3 3.0 10 1830 142 34  79 3.72 1
Subaru             3798 35 5 2.5 11 2050 164 36  97 3.81 1
Toyota Celica      5899 18 5 2.5 14 2410 174 36 134 3.06 1
Toyota Corolla     3748 31 5 3.0  9 2200 165 35  97 3.21 1
Toyota Corona      5719 18 5 2.0 11 2670 175 36 134 3.05 1
Volvo 260         11995 17 5 2.5 14 3170 193 37 163 2.98 1
VW Dasher          7140 23 4 2.5 12 2160 172 36  97 3.74 1
VW Diesel          5397 41 5 3.0 15 2040 155 35  90 3.78 1
VW Rabbit          4697 25 4 3.0 15 1930 155 35  89 3.78 1
VW Scirocco        6850 25 4 2.0 16 1990 156 36  97 3.78 1
;
RUN;
```

### T-tests

We can use **proc ttest** to perform a t-test to determine whether the average **mpg** for domestic cars differ from the foreign cars.

```
PROC TTEST DATA=auto;
  CLASS foreign;
  VAR mpg;
RUN;
```

Here is the output produced by the **proc ttest**. The results show that foreign cars have significantly higher gas mileage ( **mpg** ) than domestic cars. Note that the overall N is 71 (not 74). This is because **mpg** was missing for 3 of the observations, so those observations were omitted from the analysis.

```
TTEST PROCEDURE

Variable: MPG

FOREIGN      N         Mean     Std Dev    Std Error      Minimum      Maximum
------------------------------------------------------------------------------
      0     49  19.79591837  4.85188791   0.69312684  12.00000000  34.00000000
      1     22  24.77272727  6.61118690   1.40950978  14.00000000  41.00000000

Variances        T       DF    Prob>|T|
---------------------------------------
Unequal    -3.1685     31.6      0.0034
Equal      -3.5597     69.0      0.0007

For H0: Variances are equal, F' = 1.86    DF = (21,48)    Prob>F' = 0.0776
```

Note that the output provides two t values, one assuming that the variances are **Unequal** and another assuming that the variances are **Equal**, and below that is shown a test of whether the variances are equal. The test for equal variances has an F value of 1.86, with a p value of 0.0776 indicating that the variances of the two groups do not significantly differ, therefore the **Equal** variance t-test would be the appropriate test to use. In this case, we would report a t value of -3.5597 with a p value of 0.0007, concluding that the mean **mpg** for foreign cars is significantly greater than the **mpg** for domestic cars.

Had the F test of equal variances been significant, then the **Unequal** variance t value (-3.1685) would have been the appropriate value to use. This is especially important when the sample sizes for the 2 groups differ, because when the variances of the two groups differ **and** the sample sizes of the two groups differ, then the results assuming **Equal**variances can be quite inaccurate and could differ from the **Unequal** variance result.

## Chi-square tests

We can use **proc freq** to examine the repair records of the cars (**rep78**, where 1 is the worst repair record, 5 is the best repair record) by **foreign** (foreign coded 1, domestic coded 0). Using the **chisq** option we can request a chi-square test that tests if these two variables are independent, as shown below.

```
PROC FREQ DATA=auto;
  TABLES rep78*foreign / CHISQ ;
RUN;
```

The results are shown below, first giving the crosstab and then the chi-square test.

```
TABLE OF REP78 BY FOREIGN

REP78     FOREIGN

Frequency|
Percent  |
Row Pct  |
Col Pct  |       0|       1|  Total
---------+--------+--------+
       1 |      2 |      0 |      2
         |   2.90 |   0.00 |   2.90
         | 100.00 |   0.00 |
         |   4.17 |   0.00 |
---------+--------+--------+
       2 |      8 |      0 |      8
         |  11.59 |   0.00 |  11.59
         | 100.00 |   0.00 |
         |  16.67 |   0.00 |
---------+--------+--------+
       3 |     27 |      3 |     30
         |  39.13 |   4.35 |  43.48
         |  90.00 |  10.00 |
         |  56.25 |  14.29 |
---------+--------+--------+
       4 |      9 |      9 |     18
         |  13.04 |  13.04 |  26.09
         |  50.00 |  50.00 |
         |  18.75 |  42.86 |
---------+--------+--------+
       5 |      2 |      9 |     11
         |   2.90 |  13.04 |  15.94
         |  18.18 |  81.82 |
         |   4.17 |  42.86 |
---------+--------+--------+
Total          48       21       69
            69.57    30.43   100.00

Frequency Missing = 5
```

```
STATISTICS FOR TABLE OF REP78 BY FOREIGN
Statistic                       DF     Value      Prob
------------------------------------------------------
Chi-Square                       4    27.264     0.001
Likelihood Ratio Chi-Square      4    29.912     0.001
Mantel-Haenszel Chi-Square       1    23.851     0.001
Phi Coefficient                        0.629
Contingency Coefficient                0.532
Cramer's V                             0.629

Effective Sample Size = 69
Frequency Missing = 5
WARNING: 40% of the cells have expected counts less
         than 5. Chi-Square may not be a valid test.
```

Notice the warning that SAS gave at the end of the results. The chi-square is not really valid when you have empty cells (or cells with expected values less than 5). In such cases, you can request Fisher's exact test (which is valid under such circumstances) with the **exact** option as shown below.

```
PROC FREQ DATA=auto;
  TABLES rep78*foreign / CHISQ EXACT ;
RUN;
```

The results are shown below (omitting the crosstab, which is exactly the same as the prior results). The Fisher's Exact Test is significant, showing that there is an association between **rep78** and **foreign**. In other words, the repair records for the domestic cars differ from the repair record of the foreign cars.

```
STATISTICS FOR TABLE OF REP78 BY FOREIGN

Statistic                      DF      Value       Prob
-------------------------------------------------------
Chi-Square                      4     27.264      0.001
Likelihood Ratio Chi-Square     4     29.912      0.001
Mantel-Haenszel Chi-Square      1     23.851      0.001
Fisher's Exact Test (2-Tail)                   6.27E-06
Phi Coefficient                        0.629
Contingency Coefficient                0.532
Cramer's V                             0.629
```

## Correlation

Let's use **proc corr** to examine the correlations among **price mpg** and **weight**.

```
PROC CORR DATA=auto;
  VAR price mpg weight ;
RUN;
```

The results of the **proc corr** are shown below.

```
Correlation Analysis
   3 'VAR' Variables:  PRICE    MPG      WEIGHT

                         Simple Statistics
Variable     N       Mean    Std Dev       Sum    Minimum    Maximum
PRICE       74       6165       2949    456229       3291      15906
MPG         71   21.33803    5.88447      1515   12.00000   41.00000
WEIGHT      74       3019  777.19357    223440       1760       4840

Pearson Correlation Coefficients / Prob > |R| under Ho: Rho=0/Number of Observations
                PRICE        MPG     WEIGHT
PRICE         1.00000   -0.47774    0.53861
              0.0         0.0001     0.0001
                   74         71         74

MPG          -0.47774    1.00000   -0.80749
               0.0001    0.0         0.0001
                   71         71         71

WEIGHT        0.53861   -0.80749    1.00000
               0.0001     0.0001    0.0
                   74         71         74
```

The top portion of the output shows simple descriptive statistics for the variables (note that the N for **mpg** is 71 because it has 3 missing observations). The second part of the output shows the correlation matrix for the **price**, **mpg**, and **weight** Each entry shows the correlation, and below that the 2 tailed p value for the hypothesis test that the correlation is 0, and below that is the sample size (N) on which the correlation is based.

By looking at the sample sizes, we can see how **proc corr** handled the missing values. Since **mpg** had 3 missing values, all the correlations that involved it have an N of 71, whereas the rest of the correlations were based on an N of 74. This is called **pairwise deletion of missing data** since SAS used the maximum number of non-missing values for each pair of variables. It is possible to ask SAS to only perform the correlations on the records which had complete data for all of the variables on the **var** statement. This is called **listwise deletion of missing data**, meaning that when any of the variables are missing, the entire record will be omitted from analysis. You can request **listwise deletion** with the **nomiss** option as illustrated below.

```
PROC CORR DATA=auto NOMISS ;
  VAR price mpg weight ;
RUN;
```

The results are shown below. Notice that the N for all the simple statistics is 71, and notice that the N is not displayed along with the correlations. That is because the N is 71 for all of them (as shown in the title, N = 71).

```
Correlation Analysis
   3 'VAR' Variables:  PRICE    MPG      WEIGHT

                              Simple Statistics
Variable          N        Mean     Std Dev         Sum     Minimum     Maximum
PRICE            71        6248        2983      443582        3291       15906
MPG              71    21.33803     5.88447        1515    12.00000    41.00000
WEIGHT           71        3021   791.31589      214520        1760        4840

Pearson Correlation Coefficients / Prob > |R| under Ho: Rho=0 / N = 71
                 PRICE              MPG              WEIGHT
PRICE          1.00000         -0.47774             0.54176
                 0.0             0.0001              0.0001

MPG           -0.47774          1.00000            -0.80749
                0.0001           0.0                 0.0001

WEIGHT         0.54176         -0.80749             1.00000
                0.0001           0.0001              0.0
```

## Regression

Let's perform a regression analysis where we predict **price** from **mpg** and **weight**. The **proc reg** example below does just this.

```
PROC REG DATA=auto;
  MODEL price = mpg weight ;
RUN;
```

The results are shown below. Two interesting things to note are:

- Only 71 observations are used (not all 74) because **mpg** had three missing values. **Proc reg** deletes missing cases using **listwise deletion**. If you have lots of missing data, this is important to notice
- Looking at the predictors, the results show that **weight** is the only variable that significantly predicts **price** (with a t-value of 2.603 and a p-value of 0.0113).

```
NOTE: 74 observations read.
NOTE: 3 observations have missing values.
NOTE: 71 observations used in computations.

Model: MODEL1
Dependent Variable: PRICE

Analysis of Variance
                       Sum of         Mean
Source           DF   Squares        Square        F Value       Prob>F

Model             2 185670655.62 92835327.809       14.444       0.0001
Error            68 437038564.86 6427037.7185
C Total          70 622709220.48

    Root MSE     2535.16029     R-square       0.2982
    Dep Mean     6247.63380     Adj R-sq       0.2775
    C.V.           40.57793

Parameter Estimates
                   Parameter       Standard    T for H0:
Variable   DF       Estimate          Error  Parameter=0     Prob > |T|
INTERCEP    1    2394.284967   3647.8753623        0.656         0.5138
MPG         1     -58.668896    87.29400011       -0.672         0.5038
WEIGHT      1       1.689685     0.64914497        2.603         0.0113
```

## Analysis of variance (and analysis of covariance)

Let's compare the average miles per gallon (**mpg**) among the cars in the different repair groups using Analysis of Variance. You might think to use **proc anova** for such an analysis, but **proc anova** assumes that the sample sizes for all groups are equal, an assumption that is frequently untrue. Instead, we will use **proc glm**to perform an ANOVA comparing the prices among the repair groups. Since there are so few cars with a repair record (**rep78**) of 1 or 2, we will use a **where**statement to omit them, allowing us to concentrate on the cars with repair records of 3, 4 and 5. The **proc glm** below performs an Analysis of Variance testing whether the average **mpg** for the 3 repair groups (**rep78**) are the same. It also produces the means for the 3 repair groups.

```
PROC GLM DATA=auto;
  WHERE (rep78 = 3) OR (rep78 = 4) OR (rep78 = 5);
  CLASS rep78;
  MODEL mpg = rep78 ;
  MEANS rep78 ;
RUN;
```

The results of the **proc glm** are shown below. SAS informs us that it used only 57 observations (due to the missing values of **mpg**). The results suggest that there are significant differences in **mpg** among the three repair groups (based on the F value of 8.08 with a p value of 0.009). The means for groups 3, 4 and 5 were 19.43, 21.67, and 27.36 .

```
General Linear Models Procedure
Class Level Information

Class     Levels    Values
REP78          3    3 4 5

Number of observations in data set = 59
NOTE: Due to missing values, only 57 observations can be used in this analysis.
General Linear Models Procedure

Dependent Variable: MPG
                                         Sum of            Mean
Source                      DF          Squares          Square   F Value      Pr > F
Model                        2      497.26406926    248.63203463      8.08      0.0009
Error                       54     1661.40259740     30.76671477
Corrected Total             56     2158.66666667

                      R-Square             C.V.        Root MSE                MPG Mean
                      0.230357         25.60050       5.5467752               21.666667

Source                      DF        Type I SS     Mean Square   F Value      Pr > F
REP78                        2     497.26406926    248.63203463      8.08      0.0009

Source                      DF      Type III SS     Mean Square   F Value      Pr > F
REP78                        2     497.26406926    248.63203463      8.08      0.0009

Level of          -------------MPG-------------
REP78        N         Mean              SD

3           28     19.4285714      4.23764934
4           18     21.6666667      4.93486992
5           11     27.3636364      8.73238487
```

You can use the **tukey** option on the **means** statement to request Tukey tests for pairwise comparisons among the three means.

```
PROC GLM DATA=auto;
  WHERE (rep78 = 3) OR (rep78 = 4) OR (rep78 = 5);
  CLASS rep78;
  MODEL mpg = rep78 ;
  MEANS rep78 / TUKEY ;
RUN;
```

The results just for the Tukey tests are shown below (the rest of the output is identical). The Tukey comparisons that are significant are indicated by "***". The group with **rep78** of 5 is significantly different from 3 and significantly different from 4. However, the group with **rep78** of 3 is not significantly different from **rep78**of 4.

```
Tukey's Studentized Range (HSD) Test for variable: MPG

NOTE: This test controls the type I experimentwise error rate.

Alpha= 0.05  Confidence= 0.95  df= 54  MSE= 30.76671
Critical Value of Studentized Range= 3.408

Comparisons significant at the 0.05 level are indicated by '***'.

                   Simultaneous                Simultaneous
                       Lower     Difference       Upper
     REP78          Confidence     Between     Confidence
   Comparison          Limit        Means         Limit

5     - 4              0.581        5.697        10.813    ***
5     - 3              3.178        7.935        12.692    ***

4     - 5            -10.813       -5.697        -0.581    ***
4     - 3             -1.800        2.238         6.277

3     - 5            -12.692       -7.935        -3.178    ***
3     - 4             -6.277       -2.238         1.800
```

# GRAPHING DATA IN SAS

## Introduction and description of data

This module demonstrates how to obtain basic high resolution graphics using SAS 9.3. This example uses a data file about 26 automobiles with their make, mpg, repair record, weight, and whether the car was foreign or domestic. The program below reads the data and creates a temporary data file called **auto**. The graphs shown in this module are all performed on this data file called **auto**.

```
DATA auto ;
  INPUT make $  mpg rep78 weight foreign ;
CARDS;
AMC     22 3 2930 0
AMC     17 3 3350 0
AMC     22 . 2640 0
Audi    17 5 2830 1
Audi    23 3 2070 1
BMW     25 4 2650 1
Buick   20 3 3250 0
Buick   15 4 4080 0
Buick   18 3 3670 0
Buick   26 . 2230 0
Buick   20 3 3280 0
Buick   16 3 3880 0
Buick   19 3 3400 0
Cad.    14 3 4330 0
Cad.    14 2 3900 0
Cad.    21 3 4290 0
Chev.   29 3 2110 0
Chev.   16 4 3690 0
Chev.   22 3 3180 0
Chev.   22 2 3220 0
Chev.   24 2 2750 0
Chev.   19 3 3430 0
Datsun  23 4 2370 1
Datsun  35 5 2020 1
Datsun  24 4 2280 1
Datsun  21 4 2750 1
;
RUN;
```

## Creating charts with proc gchart

We create vertical Bar Charts with **proc gchart** and the **vbar** statement. The program below creates a vertical bar chart for **mpg**.

```
TITLE 'Simple Vertical Bar Chart ';
PROC GCHART DATA=auto;
     VBAR mpg;
RUN;
```

This program produces the following chart.

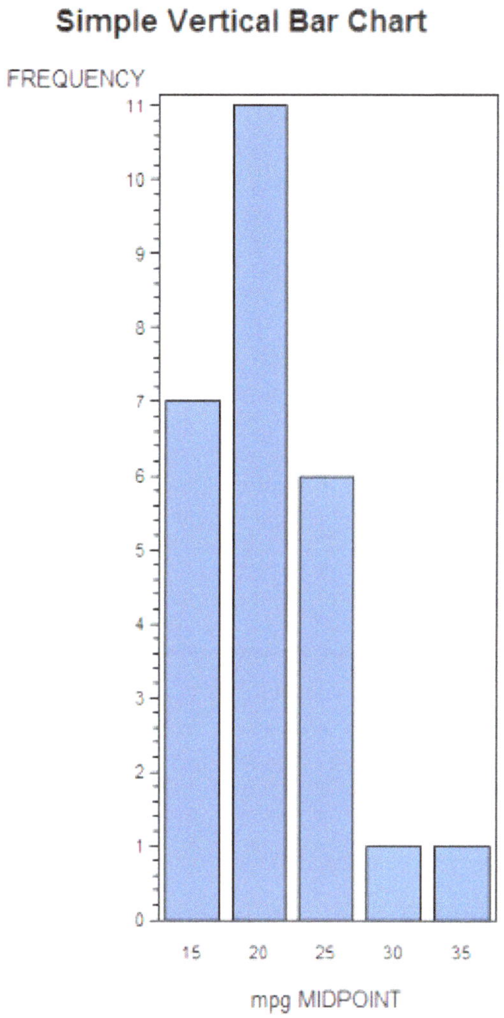


The **vbar** statement produces a vertical bar chart, and while optional the **title** statement allows you to label the chart. Since **mpg** is a continuous variable the automatic "binning" of the data into five groups yields a readable chart. The midpoint of each bin labels the respective bar.

You can control the number of bins for a continuous variable with the **level=** option on the **vbar** statement. The program below creates a vertical bar chart with seven bins for **mpg**.

```
TITLE 'Bar Chart - Control Number of Bins';
PROC GCHART DATA=auto;
     VBAR mpg/LEVELS=7;
RUN;
```

This program produces the following chart.

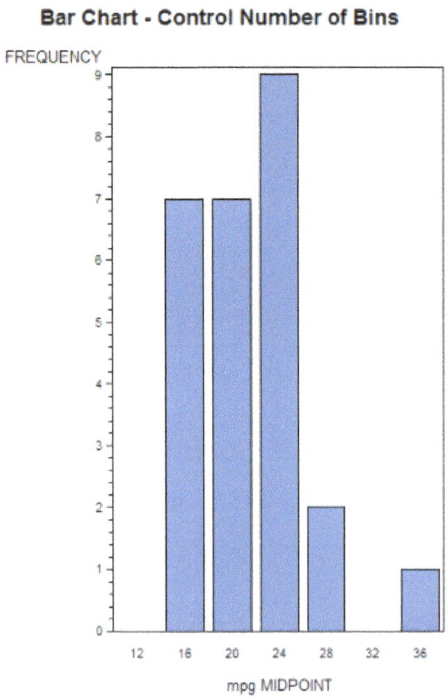


On the other hand, **rep78** has only four categories and SAS's tendency to bin into five categories and use midpoints would not do justice to the data. So when you want to use the actual values of the variable to label each bar you will want to use the **discrete** option on the **vbar** statement.

```
TITLE 'Bar Chart with Discrete Option';
PROC GCHART DATA=auto;
      VBAR rep78/ DISCRETE;
RUN;
```

This program produces the following chart.

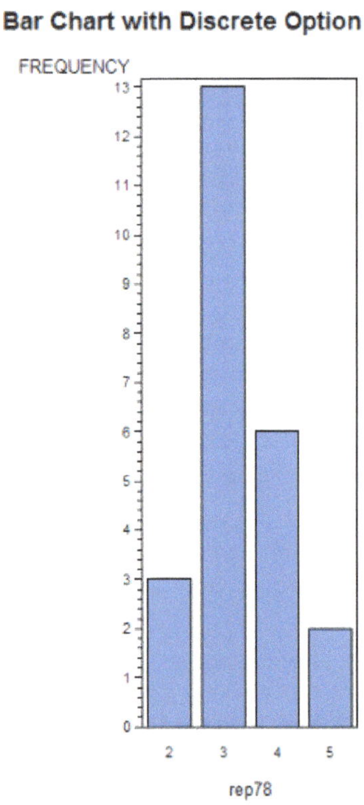


Notice that only the values in the dataset for **rep78** appear in the bar chart.

Other charts may be easily produced simply by changing **vbar**. For example, you can produce a horizontal bar chart by replacing **vbar** with **hbar**.

```
TITLE 'Horizontal Bar Chart with Discrete';
PROC GCHART DATA=auto;
      HBAR rep78/ DISCRETE;
RUN;
```

This program produces the following horizontal bar chart.

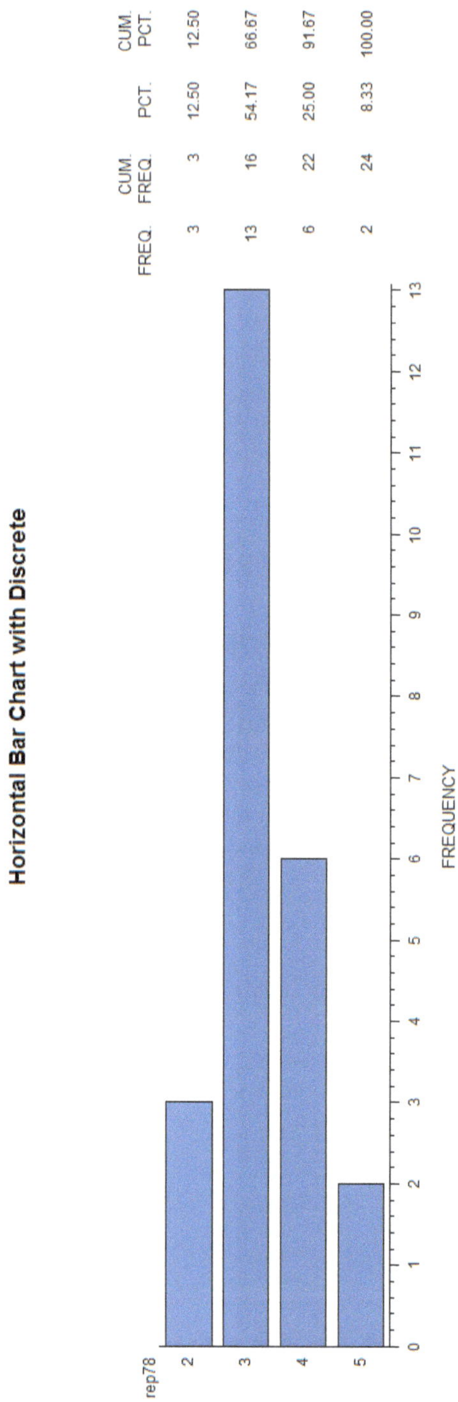


Use the **discrete** option to insure that only the values in the dataset for **rep78** label bars in the bar chart. With **hbar** you automatically obtain frequency, cumulative frequency, percent, and cumulative percent to the right of each bar.

You can produce a pie chart by replacing **hbar** in the above example with **pie**. The **value=**, **percent=**, and **slice=** options control the location of each of those labels.

```
TITLE 'Pie Chart with Discrete';
PROC GCHART DATA=auto;
     PIE rep78/ DISCRETE VALUE=INSIDE
                PERCENT=INSIDE SLICE=OUTSIDE;
RUN;
```

This program produces the following pie chart.

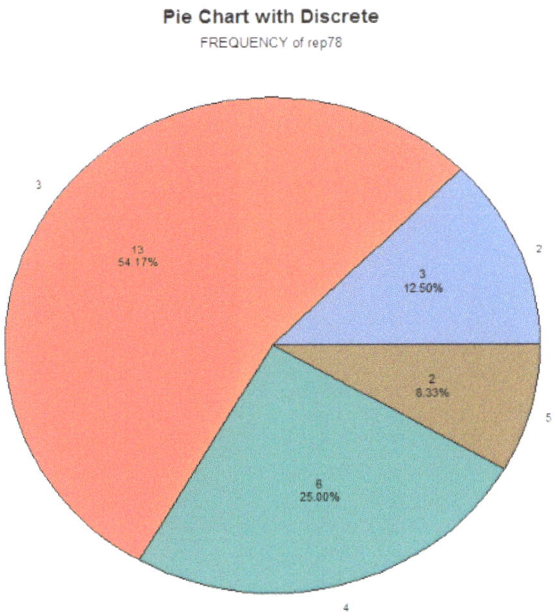


Use the **discrete** option to insure that only the values in the dataset for **rep78** label slices in the pie chart.

**value=inside** causes the frequency count to be placed inside the pie slice.

**percent=inside** causes the percent to be placed inside the pie slice.

**slice=outside** causes the label (value of **rep78**) to be placed outside the pie slice.

We have shown only some of the charts and options available to you. Additionally you can create city block charts (**block**) and star charts (**star**), and use options and statements to further control the look of charts.

## Creating Scatter plots with proc gplot

To examine the relationship between two continuous variables you will want to produce a scattergram using **proc gplot**, and the **plot** statement. The program below creates a scatter plot for **mpg*weight**. This means that **mpg** will be plotted on the vertical axis, and **weight** will be plotted on the horizontal axis.

```
TITLE 'Scatterplot - Two Variables';
PROC GPLOT DATA=auto;
     PLOT mpg*weight ;
RUN;
```

This program produces the following scattergram.

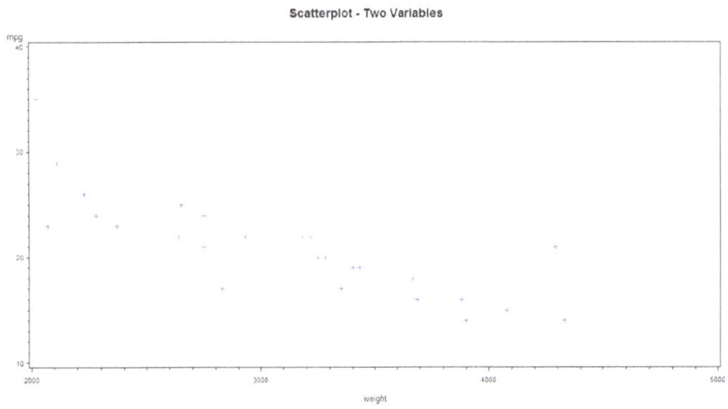


You can easily tell that there is a negative relationship between **mpg** and **weight**. As **weight** increases **mpg** decreases.

You may want to examine the relationship between two continuous variables and see which points fall into one or another category of a third variable. The program below creates a scatter plot for **mpg*weight** with each level of **foreign** marked. You specify **mpg*weight=foreign** on the **plot** statement to have each level of foreign identified on the plot.

```
TITLE 'Scatterplot - Foreign/Domestic Marked';
PROC GPLOT DATA=auto;
     PLOT mpg*weight=foreign;
RUN;
```

This program produces the following scattergram with each foreign and domestic marked.

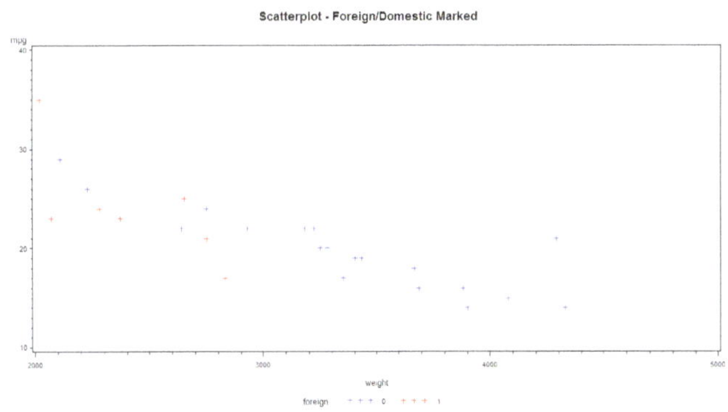


You can easily tell which level of **foreign** you are looking at, as values of zero are in black and values of 1 are in red. Since the default symbol is plus for both, if this graph is printed in black and white you will not be able to tell the levels of **foreign** apart. The next example demonstrates how to use different symbols in scattergrams.

## Customizing with proc gplot and symbol statements

The program below creates a scatter plot for **mpg*weight** with each level of **foreign** marked. The **proc gplot** is specified exactly the same as in the previous example. The only difference is the inclusion of **symbol** statements to control the look of the graph through the use of the operands **V=**, **I=**, and **C=**.

```
SYMBOL1 V=circle C=black I=none;
SYMBOL2 V=star   C=red   I=none;

TITLE 'Scatterplot - Different Symbols';
PROC GPLOT DATA=auto;
    PLOT mpg*weight=foreign;
RUN;
QUIT;
```

**Symbol1** is used for the lowest value of **foreign** which is zero (domestic cars), and **symbol2** is used for the next lowest value which is one (foreign cars) in this case.

**V=** controls the type of point to be plotted. We requested a **circle** to be plotted for domestic cars, and a **star** (asterisk) for foreign cars.

**I= none** causes SAS not to plot a line joining the points.

**C=** controls the color of the plot. We requested black for domestic cars, and red for foreign cars. (Sometimes the **C=** option is needed for any options to take effect.)

This program produces the following scatter plot with each foreign and domestic marked and with different symbols.

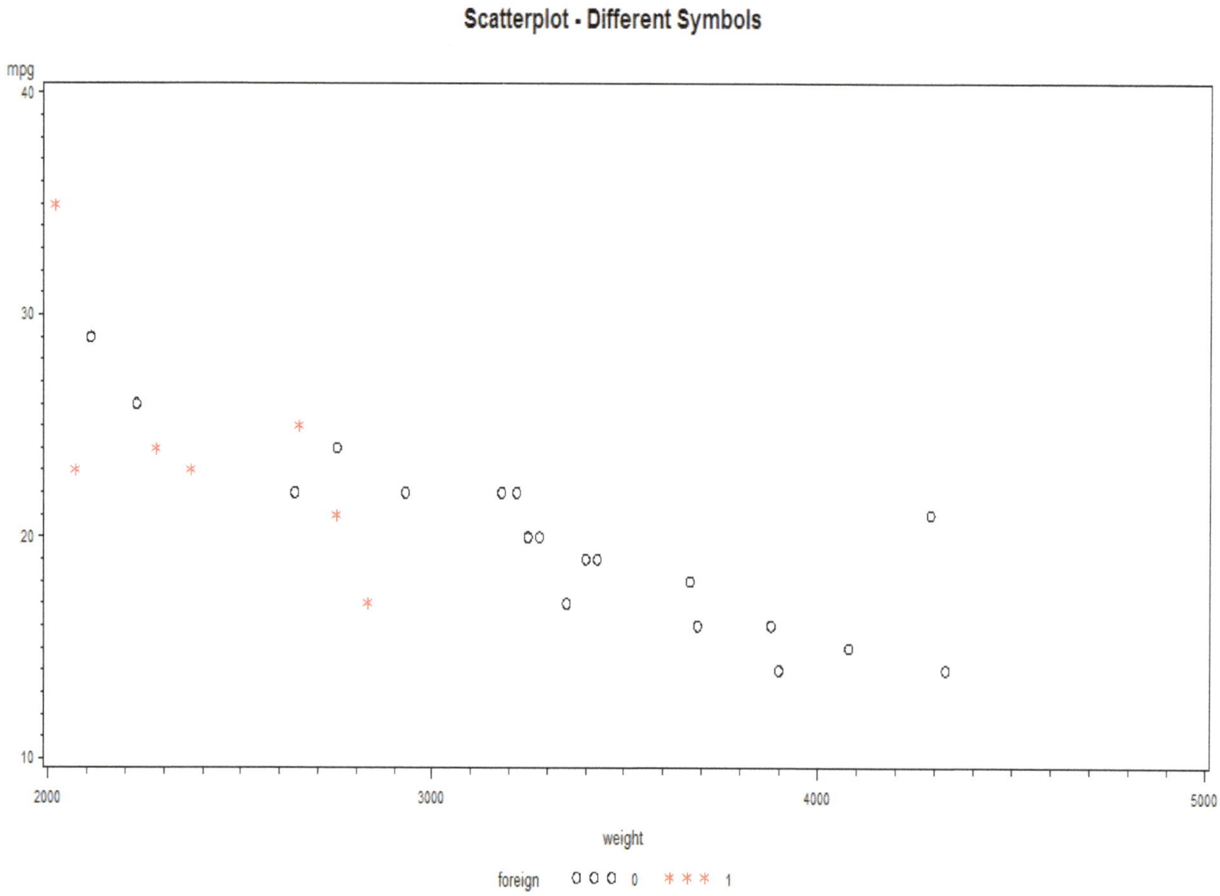


You can easily tell which level of **foreign** you are looking at, as values of zero are marked with circles in black and values of 1 are marked with asterisks in red. Now if this graph is printed in black and white you will be able to tell the levels of **foreign** apart.

At times it is useful to plot a regression line along with the scatter gram of points. The program below creates a scatter plot for **mpg*weight** with such a regression line. The regression line is produced with the **I=R** operand on the **symbol** statement.

```
SYMBOL1 V=circle C=blue I=r;

TITLE 'Scatterplot - With Regression Line ';
PROC GPLOT DATA=auto;
    PLOT mpg*weight ;
RUN;
QUIT;
```

The **symbol** statement controls color, the shape of the points, and the production of a regression line.

**I=R** causes SAS to plot a regression line.

**V=circle** causes a circle to be plotted for each case.

**C=blue** causes the points and regression line to appear in blue. Always specify the **C=** option to insure that the symbol statement takes effect.

This program produces the following scattergram with using blue circles and plotting a regression line.

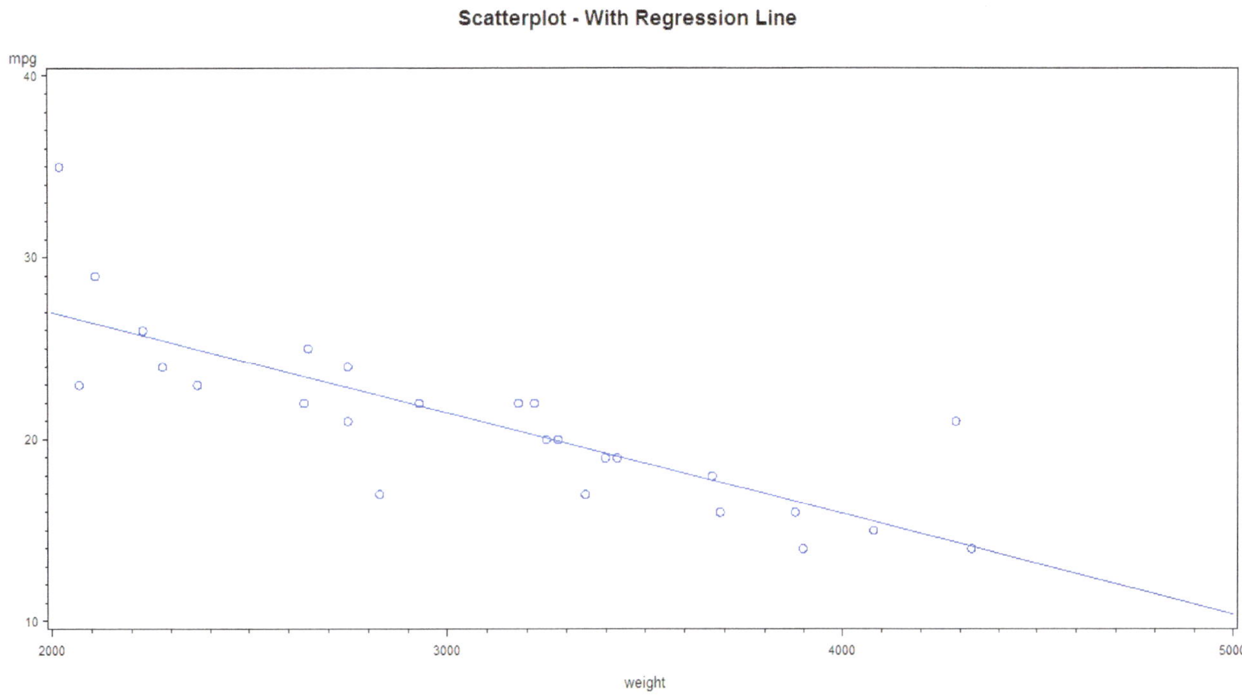


## USING WHERE WITH SAS PROCEDURES

### Introduction

This program builds a SAS file called **auto**, which we will use to demonstrate the use of the **where** statement. (For information about creating SAS files from raw data, see the SAS Learning Module titled Inputting Raw Data into SAS.

```
DATA auto ;
  INPUT make $ 1-17 price mpg rep78 hdroom trunk weight length turn
        displ gratio foreign ;
DATALINES;
AMC Concord        4099 22 3 2.5 11 2930 186 40 121 3.58 0
AMC Pacer          4749 17 3 3.0 11 3350 173 40 258 2.53 0
AMC Spirit         3799 22 . 3.0 12 2640 168 35 121 3.08 0
Audi 5000          9690 17 5 3.0 15 2830 189 37 131 3.20 1
Audi Fox           6295 23 3 2.5 11 2070 174 36  97 3.70 1
BMW 320i           9735 25 4 2.5 12 2650 177 34 121 3.64 1
Buick Century      4816 20 3 4.5 16 3250 196 40 196 2.93 0
Buick Electra      7827 15 4 4.0 20 4080 222 43 350 2.41 0
Buick LeSabre      5788 18 3 4.0 21 3670 218 43 231 2.73 0
Buick Opel         4453 26 . 3.0 10 2230 170 34 304 2.87 0
Buick Regal        5189 20 3 2.0 16 3280 200 42 196 2.93 0
Buick Riviera     10372 16 3 3.5 17 3880 207 43 231 2.93 0
Buick Skylark      4082 19 3 3.5 13 3400 200 42 231 3.08 0
Cad. Deville      11385 14 3 4.0 20 4330 221 44 425 2.28 0
Cad. Eldorado     14500 14 2 3.5 16 3900 204 43 350 2.19 0
Cad. Seville      15906 21 3 3.0 13 4290 204 45 350 2.24 0
Chev. Chevette     3299 29 3 2.5  9 2110 163 34 231 2.93 0
Chev. Impala       5705 16 4 4.0 20 3690 212 43 250 2.56 0
Chev. Malibu       4504 22 3 3.5 17 3180 193 31 200 2.73 0
Chev. Monte Carlo  5104 22 2 2.0 16 3220 200 41 200 2.73 0
Chev. Monza        3667 24 2 2.0  7 2750 179 40 151 2.73 0
Chev. Nova         3955 19 3 3.5 13 3430 197 43 250 2.56 0
Datsun 200         6229 23 4 1.5  6 2370 170 35 119 3.89 1
Datsun 210         4589 35 5 2.0  8 2020 165 32  85 3.70 1
Datsun 510         5079 24 4 2.5  8 2280 170 34 119 3.54 1
Datsun 810         8129 21 4 2.5  8 2750 184 38 146 3.55 1
Dodge Colt         3984 30 5 2.0  8 2120 163 35  98 3.54 0
Dodge Diplomat     4010 18 2 4.0 17 3600 206 46 318 2.47 0
Dodge Magnum       5886 16 2 4.0 17 3600 206 46 318 2.47 0
Dodge St. Regis    6342 17 2 4.5 21 3740 220 46 225 2.94 0
Fiat Strada        4296 21 3 2.5 16 2130 161 36 105 3.37 1
Ford Fiesta        4389 28 4 1.5  9 1800 147 33  98 3.15 0
Ford Mustang       4187 21 3 2.0 10 2650 179 43 140 3.08 0
Honda Accord       5799 25 5 3.0 10 2240 172 36 107 3.05 1
Honda Civic        4499 28 4 2.5  5 1760 149 34  91 3.30 1
Linc. Continental 11497 12 3 3.5 22 4840 233 51 400 2.47 0
Linc. Mark V      13594 12 3 2.5 18 4720 230 48 400 2.47 0
Linc. Versailles  13466 14 3 3.5 15 3830 201 41 302 2.47 0
Mazda GLC          3995 30 4 3.5 11 1980 154 33  86 3.73 1
Merc. Bobcat       3829 22 4 3.0  9 2580 169 39 140 2.73 0
Merc. Cougar       5379 14 4 3.5 16 4060 221 48 302 2.75 0
Merc. Marquis      6165 15 3 3.5 23 3720 212 44 302 2.26 0
Merc. Monarch      4516 18 3 3.0 15 3370 198 41 250 2.43 0
Merc. XR-7         6303 14 4 3.0 16 4130 217 45 302 2.75 0
Merc. Zephyr       3291 20 3 3.5 17 2830 195 43 140 3.08 0
Olds 98            8814 21 4 4.0 20 4060 220 43 350 2.41 0
```

```
Olds Cutl Supr     5172 19 3 2.0 16 3310 198 42 231 2.93 0
Olds Cutlass       4733 19 3 4.5 16 3300 198 42 231 2.93 0
Olds Delta 88      4890 18 4 4.0 20 3690 218 42 231 2.73 0
Olds Omega         4181 19 3 4.5 14 3370 200 43 231 3.08 0
Olds Starfire      4195 24 1 2.0 10 2730 180 40 151 2.73 0
Olds Toronado     10371 16 3 3.5 17 4030 206 43 350 2.41 0
Peugeot 604       12990 14 . 3.5 14 3420 192 38 163 3.58 1
Plym. Arrow        4647 28 3 2.0 11 3260 170 37 156 3.05 0
Plym. Champ        4425 34 5 2.5 11 1800 157 37  86 2.97 0
Plym. Horizon      4482 25 3 4.0 17 2200 165 36 105 3.37 0
Plym. Sapporo      6486 26 . 1.5  8 2520 182 38 119 3.54 0
Plym. Volare       4060 18 2 5.0 16 3330 201 44 225 3.23 0
Pont. Catalina     5798 18 4 4.0 20 3700 214 42 231 2.73 0
Pont. Firebird     4934 18 1 1.5  7 3470 198 42 231 3.08 0
Pont. Grand Prix   5222 19 3 2.0 16 3210 201 45 231 2.93 0
Pont. Le Mans      4723 19 3 3.5 17 3200 199 40 231 2.93 0
Pont. Phoenix      4424 19 . 3.5 13 3420 203 43 231 3.08 0
Pont. Sunbird      4172 24 2 2.0  7 2690 179 41 151 2.73 0
Renault Le Car     3895 26 3 3.0 10 1830 142 34  79 3.72 1
Subaru             3798 35 5 2.5 11 2050 164 36  97 3.81 1
Toyota Celica      5899 18 5 2.5 14 2410 174 36 134 3.06 1
Toyota Corolla     3748 31 5 3.0  9 2200 165 35  97 3.21 1
Toyota Corona      5719 18 5 2.0 11 2670 175 36 134 3.05 1
Volvo 260         11995 17 5 2.5 14 3170 193 37 163 2.98 1
VW Dasher          7140 23 4 2.5 12 2160 172 36  97 3.74 1
VW Diesel          5397 41 5 3.0 15 2040 155 35  90 3.78 1
VW Rabbit          4697 25 4 3.0 15 1930 155 35  89 3.78 1
VW Scirocco        6850 25 4 2.0 16 1990 156 36  97 3.78 1
;
RUN;
```

## Basic use of the where statement

The **where** statement allows us to run procedures on a subset of records. For example, instead of printing all records in the file, the following program prints only cars where the value for **rep78** is 3 or greater.

```
PROC PRINT DATA=auto;
 WHERE rep78 >= 3;
 VAR make rep78;
RUN;
```

Here is the output from the **proc print**. Note that we have directed SAS to print only two variables: **make** and **rep78**.

| Obs | make | rep78 |
|---|---|---|
| 1 | AMC Concord | 3 |
| 2 | AMC Pacer | 3 |
| 4 | Audi 5000 | 5 |
| 5 | Audi Fox | 3 |
| 6 | BMW 320i | 4 |
| 7 | Buick Century | 3 |
| 8 | Buick Electra | 4 |
| 9 | Buick LeSabre | 3 |
| 11 | Buick Regal | 3 |
| 12 | Buick Riviera | 3 |
| 13 | Buick Skylark | 3 |
| 14 | Cad. Deville | 3 |
| 16 | Cad. Seville | 3 |
| 17 | Chev. Chevette | 3 |
| 18 | Chev. Impala | 4 |
| 19 | Chev. Malibu | 3 |
| 22 | Chev. Nova | 3 |
| 23 | Datsun 200 | 4 |
| 24 | Datsun 210 | 5 |
| 25 | Datsun 510 | 4 |
| 26 | Datsun 810 | 4 |
| 27 | Dodge Colt | 5 |
| 31 | Fiat Strada | 3 |
| 32 | Ford Fiesta | 4 |
| 33 | Ford Mustang | 3 |
| 34 | Honda Accord | 5 |
| 35 | Honda Civic | 4 |
| 36 | Linc. Continental | 3 |
| 37 | Linc. Mark V | 3 |

| | | |
|---|---|---|
| 38 | Linc. Versailles | 3 |
| 39 | Mazda GLC | 4 |
| 40 | Merc. Bobcat | 4 |
| 41 | Merc. Cougar | 4 |
| 42 | Merc. Marquis | 3 |
| 43 | Merc. Monarch | 3 |
| 44 | Merc. XR-7 | 4 |
| 45 | Merc. Zephyr | 3 |
| 46 | Olds 98 | 4 |
| 47 | Olds Cutl Supr | 3 |
| 48 | Olds Cutlass | 3 |
| 49 | Olds Delta 88 | 4 |
| 50 | Olds Omega | 3 |
| 52 | Olds Toronado | 3 |
| 54 | Plym. Arrow | 3 |
| 55 | Plym. Champ | 5 |
| 56 | Plym. Horizon | 3 |
| 59 | Pont. Catalina | 4 |
| 61 | Pont. Grand Prix | 3 |
| 62 | Pont. Le Mans | 3 |
| 65 | Renault Le Car | 3 |
| 66 | Subaru | 5 |
| 67 | Toyota Celica | 5 |
| 68 | Toyota Corolla | 5 |
| 69 | Toyota Corona | 5 |
| 70 | Volvo 260 | 5 |
| 71 | VW Dasher | 4 |
| 72 | VW Diesel | 5 |
| 73 | VW Rabbit | 4 |
| 74 | VW Scirocco | 4 |

Consider the following program which compares repair records for foreign and domestic cars by creating a table of repairs (**rep78**) for each separately.

```
PROC FREQ DATA=auto;
  TABLES rep78*foreign ;
RUN;
```

```
Table of rep78 by foreign

rep78     foreign

Frequency|
Percent  |
Row Pct  |
Col Pct  |       0|       1|  Total
---------+--------+--------+
       1 |      2 |      0 |      2
         |   2.90 |   0.00 |   2.90
         | 100.00 |   0.00 |
         |   4.17 |   0.00 |
---------+--------+--------+
       2 |      8 |      0 |      8
         |  11.59 |   0.00 |  11.59
         | 100.00 |   0.00 |
         |  16.67 |   0.00 |
---------+--------+--------+
       3 |     27 |      3 |     30
         |  39.13 |   4.35 |  43.48
         |  90.00 |  10.00 |
         |  56.25 |  14.29 |
---------+--------+--------+
       4 |      9 |      9 |     18
         |  13.04 |  13.04 |  26.09
         |  50.00 |  50.00 |
         |  18.75 |  42.86 |
---------+--------+--------+
       5 |      2 |      9 |     11
         |   2.90 |  13.04 |  15.94
         |  18.18 |  81.82 |
         |   4.17 |  42.86 |
---------+--------+--------+
Total          48       21       69
            69.57    30.43   100.00
```

Using the **where** statement, we restrict the analysis to only cars with a repair rating of 3 or more (**rep78** >= **3**):

```
PROC FREQ DATA=auto;
  WHERE rep78 >= 3;
  TABLES rep78*foreign ;
RUN;
```

```
Table of rep78 by foreign

rep78     foreign

Frequency|
Percent  |
Row Pct  |
Col Pct  |       0|       1|  Total
---------+--------+--------+
       3 |     27 |      3 |     30
         |  45.76 |   5.08 |  50.85
         |  90.00 |  10.00 |
         |  71.05 |  14.29 |
---------+--------+--------+
       4 |      9 |      9 |     18
         |  15.25 |  15.25 |  30.51
         |  50.00 |  50.00 |
         |  23.68 |  42.86 |
---------+--------+--------+
       5 |      2 |      9 |     11
         |   3.39 |  15.25 |  18.64
         |  18.18 |  81.82 |
         |   5.26 |  42.86 |
---------+--------+--------+
Total          38       21      59
            64.41    35.59  100.00
```

The **where** statement works with most SAS procedures. The following program prints only records for which the car has a repair rating of 2 or less:

```
PROC PRINT DATA=auto;
  WHERE rep78 <= 2;
  VAR make price rep78 ;
RUN;
```

| Obs | make | price | rep78 |
|---|---|---|---|
| 3 | AMC Spirit | 3799 | . |
| 10 | Buick Opel | 4453 | . |
| 15 | Cad. Eldorado | 14500 | 2 |
| 20 | Chev. Monte Carlo | 5104 | 2 |
| 21 | Chev. Monza | 3667 | 2 |
| 28 | Dodge Diplomat | 4010 | 2 |
| 29 | Dodge Magnum | 5886 | 2 |
| 30 | Dodge St. Regis | 6342 | 2 |
| 51 | Olds Starfire | 4195 | 1 |
| 53 | Peugeot 604 | 12990 | . |
| 57 | Plym. Sapporo | 6486 | . |
| 58 | Plym. Volare | 4060 | 2 |
| 60 | Pont. Firebird | 4934 | 1 |
| 63 | Pont. Phoenix | 4424 | . |
| 64 | Pont. Sunbird | 4172 | 2 |

**Missing values and the where statement**

In the example above, note that some of the records print a '.' instead of a value for **rep78**. These are records where **rep78** is missing. SAS stores missing values for numeric variables as '.' and treats them as negative infinity, or the lowest number possible. To exclude missing values, modify the where statement as follows (the **rep78** ^= . indicates **rep78** is not equal to missing).

```
PROC PRINT DATA=auto;
  WHERE rep78 <= 2 and rep78 ^= . ;
  VAR make price rep78 ;
RUN;
```

Note that there are no missing values in the listing.

| Obs | make | price | rep78 |
|---|---|---|---|
| 15 | Cad. Eldorado | 14500 | 2 |
| 20 | Chev. Monte Carlo | 5104 | 2 |
| 21 | Chev. Monza | 3667 | 2 |
| 28 | Dodge Diplomat | 4010 | 2 |
| 29 | Dodge Magnum | 5886 | 2 |
| 30 | Dodge St. Regis | 6342 | 2 |
| 51 | Olds Starfire | 4195 | 1 |
| 58 | Plym. Volare | 4060 | 2 |
| 60 | Pont. Firebird | 4934 | 1 |
| 64 | Pont. Sunbird | 4172 | 2 |

Similarly, this where statement yields the same result:

```
PROC PRINT DATA=auto;
  WHERE . < rep78 <= 2;
  VAR make price rep78 ;
RUN;
```

**More complex where statements**

This program generates summary statistics for **price**, but only for cars with repair histories of 1 or 2:

```
PROC MEANS DATA=auto;
  WHERE rep78 = 1 OR rep78 = 2 ;
  VAR price ;
RUN;
```

Here is the output from the **proc means**. By default, **proc means** will generate the following statistics: mean, minimum and maximum values, standard deviation, and the number of non-missing values for the analysis variable (in this case price).

| Analysis Variable : price | | | | |
|---|---|---|---|---|
| N | Mean | Std Dev | Minimum | Maximum |
| 10 | 5687.00 | 3216.38 | 3667.00 | 14500.00 |

To see summary statistics for price for cars with repair histories of 3, 4 or 5, modify the **where** statement accordingly:

```
PROC MEANS DATA=auto;
  WHERE rep78 = 3 or rep78 = 4 or rep78 = 5 ;
  VAR price ;
RUN;
```

Or:

```
PROC MEANS DATA=auto;
  WHERE 3 <= rep78 <= 5 ;
  VAR price ;
RUN;
```

Or: The where statement also works with the **in** operator.

```
PROC MEANS DATA=auto;
  WHERE rep78 in (3,4,5) ;
  VAR price ;
RUN;
```

| Analysis Variable : price | | | | |
|---|---|---|---|---|
| N | Mean | Std Dev | Minimum | Maximum |
| 59 | 6223.85 | 2880.45 | 3291.00 | 15906.00 |

## Taking a random sample

It is also possible to randomly sample observations from your dataset. This information can be found on our SAS FAQ page: How do I do simple random sampling with or without replacement using proc survey select?

# MISSING DATA IN SAS

## Introduction

This module will explore missing data in SAS, focusing on numeric missing data. It will describe how to indicate missing data in your raw data files, how missing data are handled in SAS procedures, and how to handle missing data in a SAS **data step**. Suppose we did a reaction time study with six subjects, and the subjects reaction time was measured three times. The data file is shown below.

```
DATA times ;
  INPUT id trial1 trial2 trial3 ;
CARDS ;
1 1.5 1.4 1.6
2 1.5  .  1.9
3  .  2.0 1.6
4  .   .  2.2
5 2.1 2.3 2.2
6 1.8 2.0 1.9
;
RUN ;

PROC PRINT DATA=times ;
RUN ;
```

You might notice that some of the reaction times are coded using a single dot. For example, for subject 2, the second trial is coded just as a dot. Well, the person measuring response time for that trial did not measure the response time properly so the data for that trial was missing.

| OBS | ID | TRIAL1 | TRIAL2 | TRIAL3 |
|---|---|---|---|---|
| 1 | 1 | 1.5 | 1.4 | 1.6 |
| 2 | 2 | 1.5 | . | 1.9 |
| 3 | 3 | . | 2.0 | 1.6 |
| 4 | 4 | . | . | 2.2 |
| 5 | 5 | 2.1 | 2.3 | 2.2 |
| 6 | 6 | 1.8 | 2.0 | 1.9 |

In your raw data, missing data are generally coded using a single. to indicate a missing value. SAS recognizes a single. as a missing value and knows to interpret it as missing and handles it in special ways. Let's examine how SAS handles missing data in procedures.

## How SAS handles missing data in SAS procedures

As a general rule, SAS procedures that perform computations handle missing data by omitting the missing values. (We say **procedures that perform computations** to indicate that we are not addressing procedures like **proc contents**). The way that missing values are eliminated is not always the same among SAS procedures, so let's us look at some examples. First, let's do a **proc means** on our data file and see how SAS **proc means** handles the missing values.

```
PROC MEANS DATA=times ;
  VAR trial1 trial2 trial3 ;
RUN ;
```

As you see in the output below, **proc means** computed the means using 4 observations for **trial1** and **trial2** and 6 observations for **trial3**. In short, **proc means** used all of the valid data and performed the computations on all of the available data.

```
Variable  N        Mean        Std Dev       Minimum       Maximum
--------------------------------------------------------------------
TRIAL1    4   1.7250000    0.2872281    1.5000000    2.1000000
TRIAL2    4   1.9250000    0.3774917    1.4000000    2.3000000
TRIAL3    6   1.9000000    0.2683282    1.6000000    2.2000000
--------------------------------------------------------------------
```

As you see below, **proc freq** likewise performed its computations using just the available data. Note that the percentages are computed based on just the total number of non-missing cases.

```
PROC FREQ DATA=times ;
  TABLES trial1 trial2 trial3 ;
RUN ;
```

```
                                  Cumulative   Cumulative
TRIAL1   Frequency     Percent     Frequency      Percent
----------------------------------------------------------
   1.5          2        50.0             2         50.0
   1.8          1        25.0             3         75.0
   2.1          1        25.0             4        100.0

Frequency Missing = 2


                                  Cumulative   Cumulative
TRIAL2   Frequency     Percent     Frequency      Percent
----------------------------------------------------------
   1.4          1        25.0             1         25.0
     2          2        50.0             3         75.0
   2.3          1        25.0             4        100.0

Frequency Missing = 2


                                  Cumulative   Cumulative
TRIAL3   Frequency     Percent     Frequency      Percent
----------------------------------------------------------
   1.6          2        33.3             2         33.3
   1.9          2        33.3             4         66.7
   2.2          2        33.3             6        100.0
```

It is possible that you might want the percentages to be computed out of the total number of values, and even report the percentage missing right in the table itself. You can request this using the **missing** option on the **tables** statement of **proc freq** as shown below (just for **trial1**).

```
PROC FREQ DATA=times ;
  TABLES trial1 / MISSING ;
RUN ;
```

As you see, now the percentages are computed out of the total number of observations, and the percentage missing are shown right in the table as well.

```
                                   Cumulative  Cumulative
TRIAL1   Frequency   Percent   Frequency    Percent
----------------------------------------------------
   .          2        33.3          2        33.3
 1.5          2        33.3          4        66.7
 1.8          1        16.7          5        83.3
 2.1          1        16.7          6       100.0
```

Let's look at how **proc corr** handles missing data. We would expect that it would do the computations based on the available data, and omit the missing values. Here is an example program.

```
PROC CORR DATA=times ;
  VAR trial1 trial2 trial3 ;
RUN ;
```

The output of this program is shown below. Note how the missing values were excluded. For each **pair** of variables, **proc corr** used the number of pairs that had valid data. For the pair formed by **trial1** and **trial24**, there were 3 pairs with valid data. For the pairing of **trial1** and **trial3** there were 4 valid pairs, and likewise there were 4 valid pairs for **trial2** and **trial3**. Since this used all of the valid **pairs** of data, this is often called **pairwise deletion of missing data**.

```
Correlation Analysis
  3 'VAR' Variables:  TRIAL1    TRIAL2    TRIAL3
                      Simple Statistics
Variable  N       Mean    Std Dev        Sum    Minimum    Maximum
TRIAL1    4   1.725000   0.287228   6.900000   1.500000   2.100000
TRIAL2    4   1.925000   0.377492   7.700000   1.400000   2.300000
TRIAL3    6   1.900000   0.268328  11.400000   1.600000   2.200000

Pearson Correlation Coefficients / Prob > |R| under Ho: Rho=0 / Number of Observations

              TRIAL1      TRIAL2      TRIAL3
TRIAL1       1.00000     0.98198     0.85280
             0.0         0.1210      0.1472
                   4           3           4

TRIAL2       0.98198     1.00000     0.76089
             0.1210      0.0         0.2391
                   3           4           4

TRIAL3       0.85280     0.76089     1.00000
             0.1472      0.2391      0.0
                   4           4           6
```

It is possible to ask SAS to only perform the correlations on the observations that had complete data for all of the variables on the **var** statement. For example, you might want the correlations of the reaction times just for the observations that had non-missing data on all of the trials. This is called **listwise deletion of missing data** meaning that when any of the variables are missing, the entire observation is omitted from the analysis. You can request listwise deletion within **proc corr** with the **nomiss** option as illustrated below.

```
PROC CORR DATA=times NOMISS ;
  VAR trial1 trial2 trial3 ;
RUN ;
```

As you see in the results below, the N for all the simple statistics is the same, 3, which corresponds to the number of cases with complete non-missing data for trial1 trial2 and trial3. Since the N is the same for all of the correlations (i.e., 3), the N is not displayed along with the correlations.

```
Correlation Analysis
  3 'VAR' Variables:  TRIAL1    TRIAL2    TRIAL3
                      Simple Statistics
Variable  N       Mean    Std Dev        Sum    Minimum    Maximum
TRIAL1    3   1.800000   0.300000   5.400000   1.500000   2.100000
TRIAL2    3   1.900000   0.458258   5.700000   1.400000   2.300000
TRIAL3    3   1.900000   0.300000   5.700000   1.600000   2.200000

Pearson Correlation Coefficients / Prob > |R| under Ho: Rho=0 / N = 3

              TRIAL1      TRIAL2      TRIAL3
TRIAL1       1.00000     0.98198     1.00000
             0.0         0.1210      0.0001

TRIAL2       0.98198     1.00000     0.98198
             0.1210      0.0         0.1210

TRIAL3       1.00000     0.98198     1.00000
             0.0001      0.1210      0.0
```

## Summary of how missing values are handled in SAS procedures

- \- **proc means:** For each variable, the number of non-missing values are used
- **proc freq:** By default, missing values are excluded and percentages are based on the number of non-missing values. If you use the **missing** option on the **tables** statement, the percentages are based on the total number of observations (non-missing and missing) and the percentage of missing values are reported in the table.
- **proc corr:** By default, correlations are computed based on the number of pairs with non-missing data (**pairwise deletion of missing data**). The **nomiss** option can be used on the **proc corr** statement to request that correlations be computed only for observations that have non-missing data for all variables on the **var** statement (**listwise deletion of**

**missing data**).

- **proc reg:** If any of the variables on the **model** or **var** statement are missing, they are excluded from the analysis (i.e., **listwise deletion of missing data)**

- **proc factor:** Missing values are deleted **listwise**, i.e., observations with missing values on any of the variables in the analysis are omitted from the analysis.

- **proc glm:** The handling of missing values in **proc glm** can be complex to explain. If you have an analysis with just one variable on the left side of the model statement (just one outcome or dependent variable), observations are eliminated if any of the variables on the model statement are missing. Likewise, if you are performing a **repeated measures ANOVA** or a **MANOVA**, then observations are eliminated if any of the variables in the model statement are missing. For other situations, see the SAS/STAT manual about **proc glm**.

- For other procedures, see the SAS manual for information on how missing data are handled.

## Missing values in assignment statements

It is important to understand how missing values are handled in assignment statements. Consider the example shown below.

```
DATA times2 ;
  SET times ;
  avg = (trial1 + trial2 + trial3) / 3 ;
RUN ;

PROC PRINT DATA=times2 ;
RUN ;
```

The **proc print** below illustrates how missing values are handled in assignment statements. The variable **avg** is based on the variables **triall trial2** and**trial3**. If any of those variables were missing, the value for **avg** was set to missing. This meant that **avg** was missing for observations 2, 3 and 4.

| OBS | ID | TRIAL1 | TRIAL2 | TRIAL3 | AVG |
|---|---|---|---|---|---|
| 1 | 1 | 1.5 | 1.4 | 1.6 | 1.5 |
| 2 | 2 | 1.5 | . | 1.9 | . |
| 3 | 3 | . | 2.0 | 1.6 | . |
| 4 | 4 | . | . | 2.2 | . |
| 5 | 5 | 2.1 | 2.3 | 2.2 | 2.2 |
| 6 | 6 | 1.8 | 2.0 | 1.9 | 1.9 |

In fact, SAS included a **NOTE**: in the Log to let you know about the missing values that were created. The Log entry from this example is shown below.

```
222        DATA times2 ;
223          SET times ;
224          avg = (trial1 + trial2 + trial3) / 3 ;
225        RUN ;
NOTE: Missing values were generated as a result of performing an operation on
      missing values.
      Each place is given by: (Number of times) at (Line):(Column).
      3 at 224:17   3 at 224:26   3 at 224:36
NOTE: The data set WORK.TIMES2 has 6 observations and 5 variables.
```

This note tells us that three missing values were created in the program at line 224. This makes sense, we know that 3 missing values were created for **avg**and that **avg** is created on line 224.

As a general rule, computations involving missing values yield missing values. For example,

```
2 + 2 yields 4
2 + . yields .
2 / 2 yields 1
. / 2 yields .
2 * 3 yields 6
2 * . yields .
```

whenever you add, subtract, multiply, divide, etc., values that involve missing data, the result is missing.

In our reaction time experiment, the average reaction time **avg** is missing for three out of six cases. We could try just averaging the data for the non-missing trials by using the **mean** function as shown in the example below.

```
DATA times3 ;
  SET times ;
  avg = MEAN(trial1, trial2, trial3) ;
RUN ;

PROC PRINT DATA=times3 ;
RUN ;
```

The results below show that **avg** now contains the average of the non-missing trials.

| OBS | ID | TRIAL1 | TRIAL2 | TRIAL3 | AVG |
|---|---|---|---|---|---|
| 1 | 1 | 1.5 | 1.4 | 1.6 | 1.5 |
| 2 | 2 | 1.5 | . | 1.9 | 1.7 |
| 3 | 3 | . | 2.0 | 1.6 | 1.8 |
| 4 | 4 | . | . | 2.2 | 2.2 |
| 5 | 5 | 2.1 | 2.3 | 2.2 | 2.2 |
| 6 | 6 | 1.8 | 2.0 | 1.9 | 1.9 |

Had there been a large number of trials, say 50 trials, then it would be annoying to have to type

avg = mean(trial1, trial2, trial3 .... trial50)

Here is a shortcut you could use in this kind of situation

avg = mean(of trial1-trial50)

Also, if we wanted to get the sum of the times instead of the average, then we could just use the **sum** function instead of the **mean** function. The syntax of the **sum** function is just like the **mean** function, but it returns the sum of the non-missing values.

Finally, you can use the **N** function to determine the number of non-missing values in a list of variables, as illustrated below.

```
DATA times4 ;
  SET times ;
  n = N(trial1, trial2, trial3) ;
RUN ;

PROC PRINT DATA=times4 ;
RUN ;
```

As you see below, observations 1, 5 and 6 had three valid values, observations 2 and 3 had two valid values, and observation 4 had only one valid value.

| OBS | ID | TRIAL1 | TRIAL2 | TRIAL3 | N |
|---|---|---|---|---|---|
| 1 | 1 | 1.5 | 1.4 | 1.6 | 3 |
| 2 | 2 | 1.5 | . | 1.9 | 2 |
| 3 | 3 | . | 2.0 | 1.6 | 2 |
| 4 | 4 | . | . | 2.2 | 1 |
| 5 | 5 | 2.1 | 2.3 | 2.2 | 3 |
| 6 | 6 | 1.8 | 2.0 | 1.9 | 3 |

You might feel uncomfortable with the variable **avg** for observation 4 since it is not really an average at all. We can use the variable **n** to create **avg** only when there are two or more valid values, but if the number of non-missing values is 1 or less, then make **avg** to be missing. This is illustrated below.

```
DATA times5 ;
  SET times ;
  n = N(trial1, trial2, trial3) ;
  IF n >= 2 THEN avg = MEAN(trial1, trial2, trial3) ;
  IF n <= 1 THEN avg=. ;
RUN ;

PROC PRINT DATA=times5 ;
RUN ;
```

In the output below, you see that **avg** now contains the average reaction time for the non-missing values, except for observation 4 where the value is assigned to missing because it had only 1 valid observation.

| OBS | ID | TRIAL1 | TRIAL2 | TRIAL3 | N | AVG |
|---|---|---|---|---|---|---|
| 1 | 1 | 1.5 | 1.4 | 1.6 | 3 | 1.5 |
| 2 | 2 | 1.5 | . | 1.9 | 2 | 1.7 |
| 3 | 3 | . | 2.0 | 1.6 | 2 | 1.8 |
| 4 | 4 | . | . | 2.2 | 1 | . |
| 5 | 5 | 2.1 | 2.3 | 2.2 | 3 | 2.2 |
| 6 | 6 | 1.8 | 2.0 | 1.9 | 3 | 1.9 |

## Missing values in logical statements

It is important to understand how missing values are handled in logical statements. For example, say that you want to create a 0/1 value for **trial1** that is 0 if it is 1.5 or less, and 1 if it is over 1.5. We show this below (incorrectly, as you will see).

```
DATA times2 ;
  SET times ;
  if (trial1 <= 1.5) then trial1a = 0; else trial1a = 1 ;
RUN ;

proc print data=times2;
  var id trial1 trial1a;
run;
```

And as you can see in the output, the values for **trial1a** are wrong when **id** is 3 or 4, when **trial1** is missing. This is because SAS treats a missing value as the smallest possible value (e.g., negative infinity) and that value is less than 1.5, so then the value for **trial1a** becomes 0.

| Obs | id | trial1 | trial1a |
|---|---|---|---|
| 1 | 1 | 1.5 | 0 |
| 2 | 2 | 1.5 | 0 |
| 3 | 3 | . | 0 |
| 4 | 4 | . | 0 |
| 5 | 5 | 2.1 | 1 |
| 6 | 6 | 1.8 | 1 |

Instead, we will explicitly exclude missing values to make sure they are treated properly, as shown below.

```
DATA times2 ;
  SET times ;
  trial1a = .;
  if (trial1 <= 1.5) and (trial1 > .) then trial1a = 0;
  if (trial1 > 1.5) then trial1a = 1 ;
RUN ;

proc print data=times2;
  var id trial1 trial1a;
run;
```

And now we get the results that we wish. The value for **trial1a** is only 0 when it is less than or equal to 1.5 and it is not missing. The value for **trial1a** is only 1 when it is over 1.5, as shown below.

| Obs | id | trial1 | trial1a |
|---|---|---|---|
| 1 | 1 | 1.5 | 0 |
| 2 | 2 | 1.5 | 0 |
| 3 | 3 | . | . |
| 4 | 4 | . | . |
| 5 | 5 | 2.1 | 1 |
| 6 | 6 | 1.8 | 1 |

## Problems to look out for

When creating or recoding variables that involve missing values, always pay attention to the SAS log to detect when you are creating missing values.

## SAS SYSTEM OPTIONS

This module will illustrate some of the system options offered by the SAS system.

## SAS system options

System options are global instructions that affect the entire SAS session and control the way SAS performs operations. SAS system options differ from SAS data set options and statement options in that once you invoke a system option, it remains in effect for all subsequent **data** and **proc** steps in a SAS job, unless you specify them.

In order to view which options are available and in effect for your SAS session, use **proc options**.

```
PROC OPTIONS;
RUN;
```

Here is some sample output produced by the **proc options** statement above.

```
PORTABLE OPTIONS:

NOCAPS           Translate quoted strings and titles to upper case?
CENTER           Center SAS output?
DATE             Date printed in title?
ERRORS=20        Maximum number of observations with error messages
FIRSTOBS=1       First observation of each data set to be processed
FMTERR           Treat missing format or informat as an error?
LABEL            Allow procedures to use variable labels?
LINESIZE=96      Line size for printed output
MISSING=.        Character printed to represent numeric missing values
NOTES            Print SAS notes on log?
NUMBER           Print page number on each page of SAS output?
OBS=MAX          Number of last observation to be processed
PAGENO=1         Resets the current page number on the print file
PAGESIZE=54      Number of lines printed per page of output
PROBSIG=0        Number of significant figures guaranteed when printing P-values
REPLACE          Allow replacement of permanent SAS data sets?
SOURCE           List SAS source statements on log?
NOSOURCE2        List included SAS source statements on log?
YEARCUTOFF=1900  Cutoff year for DATE7. informat
```

Not every SAS system option is listed above, but many of the most common options are listed. Of course, it is not necessary to understand every SAS option in order to run a SAS job. This module will discuss some of the more common SAS system options that the typical user would use to customize their SAS sessions.

## Log, output and procedure options

Log, output and procedure options specify the ways in which SAS output is written to the SAS log and procedure output file.

Below are some commonly used log, output, and procedure options:

**center** controls whether SAS procedure output is centered. By default, output is always centered. To specify not centered, use **nocenter**, which will print results to the output window as left justified.

**date** prints the date and time to the log and output window. By default, the date and time is always printed. To suppress the printing of the date, use**nodate**.

**label** allows SAS procedures to use labels with variables. By default, labels are permitted. To suppress the printing of labels, use **nolabel**.

**notes** controls whether notes are printed to the SAS log. By default, notes are printed. To suppress the printing of notes, use **nonotes**.

**number** controls whether page numbers are printed on the first title line of each page of printed output. By default, page numbers are printed. To suppress the printing of page numbers, use **nonumber**.

**linesize=** specifies the line size (printer line width) for the SAS log and the SAS procedure output file used by the **data** step and procedures.

**pagesize=** specifies the number of lines that can be printed per page of SAS output.

**missing=** specifies the character to be printed for missing numeric variable values.

**formchar=** specifies the list of graphics characters that define table boundaries.

Below is sample syntax for setting some of these options.

```
OPTIONS NOCENTER NODATE NONOTES LINESIZE=80 MISSING=.
        FORMCHAR = '|----|+|---+=|-/<>*';
```

## SAS data set control options

SAS data set control options specify how SAS data sets are input, processed, and output.

Below are some commonly used SAS data set control options:

**firstobs=** causes SAS to begin reading at a specified observation in a data set. If SAS is processing a file of raw data, this option forces SAS to begin reading at a specified line of data. The default is **firstobs=1**.

**obs=** specifies the last observation from a data set or the last record from a raw data file that SAS is to read. To return to using all observations in a data set use **obs=all.**

**replace** specifies whether permanently stored SAS data sets are to be replaced. By default, the SAS system will over-write existing SAS data sets if the SAS data set is re-specified in a **data** step. To suppress this option, use **noreplace**.

Below is sample syntax for invoking some of these options.

```
OPTIONS OBS=100 NOREPLACE;
```

## Error handling options

Error handling options specify how the SAS System reports on and recovers from error conditions.

Below are two commonly used error handling options:

**errors=** controls the maximum number of observations for which complete error messages are printed. The default maximum number of complete error messages is **errors=20**

**fmterr** (which is in effect by default if not specified) controls whether the SAS System generates an error message when the system cannot find a format to associate with a variable. Turning this option **off** is useful when you have a SAS system data set with custom formats, but you do not have the corresponding SAS format library. In this situation, SAS will generate an ERROR message for every unknown format it encounters and will terminate the SAS job without running any following **data** and **proc** steps. Thus, in order to override this default option and read a SAS system data set without requiring a SAS format library, use **nofmterr**

Below is sample syntax for invoking these options.

```
OPTIONS ERRORS=100 NOFMTERR;
```

## Reading and writing data options

Reading and writing data options control the ways in which data are input to, and output from, the SAS system.

Below are some commonly used reading and writing data options:

**caps** specifies whether lowercase characters input to the SAS System are translated to uppercase. The default is **nocaps**.

**probsig=** controls the number of significant digits of p-values in some statistical procedures.

**yearcutoff=** specifies the first year of a 100-year span used as the default by various informats and functions. (For more information, see Using dates in SAS).

Below is sample syntax for invoking these options.

```
OPTIONS CAPS PROBSIG=3 YEARCUTOFF=1900;
```

It should also be noted that these data set options are global options, as opposed to local data set options that are specified within a **data** or **proc** step, and remain in effect until the **data** or **proc** step ends. For more information on local data set options, such as **obs, keep and drop**, see Subsetting data in SAS.

## AN OVERVIEW OF THE SYNTAX OF SAS PROCEDURES

### Introduction

This module will illustrate the general syntax of SAS procedures. We will use the auto data file, shown below, to illustrate the syntax of SAS procedures.

```
DATA auto ;
  input MAKE $ PRICE MPG REP78 FOREIGN ;
DATALINES;
AMC    4099 22 3 0
AMC    4749 17 3 0
AMC    3799 22 3 0
Audi   9690 17 5 1
Audi   6295 23 3 1
BMW    9735 25 4 1
Buick  4816 20 3 0
Buick  7827 15 4 0
Buick  5788 18 3 0
Buick  4453 26 3 0
Buick  5189 20 3 0
Buick 10372 16 3 0
Buick  4082 19 3 0
Cad.  11385 14 3 0
Cad.  14500 14 2 0
Cad.  15906 21 3 0
Chev.  3299 29 3 0
Chev.  5705 16 4 0
Chev.  4504 22 3 0
Chev.  5104 22 2 0
Chev.  3667 24 2 0
Chev.  3955 19 3 0
Datsun 6229 23 4 1
Datsun 4589 35 5 1
Datsun 5079 24 4 1
Datsun 8129 21 4 1
;
RUN;
```

### Using a procedure with no options

Now, lets have a look at the use of SAS procedures using **proc means** as an example. Here we show that it is possible to use **proc means** with no options at all. By default,SAS uses the last data file created (i.e., **auto**) and it provides means for all of the numeric variables in the data file.

```
PROC MEANS ;
RUN;
```

Here you see the results of the means procedure from the **auto** data file. SAS displays the sample size (N), mean, standard deviation , minimum and maximum for all of the numeric variables.

| Variable | N | Mean | Std Dev | Minimum | Maximum |
|---|---|---|---|---|---|
| PRICE | 26 | 6651.73 | 3371.12 | 3299.00 | 15906.00 |
| MPG | 26 | 20.9230769 | 4.7575042 | 14.0000000 | 35.0000000 |
| REP78 | 26 | 3.2692308 | 0.7775702 | 2.0000000 | 5.0000000 |
| FOREIGN | 26 | 0.2692308 | 0.4523443 | 0 | 1.0000000 |

### Using options on the PROC statement

We can use the **data=** option to tell **proc means** to tell SAS what data file will be used to perform the **means** procedure. The **data=** option comes right after **proc means**. Even though the **data=** option is optional, we strongly recommend using it every time because it avoids errors of omission when you revise your programs.

```
PROC MEANS DATA=auto;
RUN;
```

As you see, the results are identical to those above.

| Variable | N | Mean | Std Dev | Minimum | Maximum |
|---|---|---|---|---|---|
| PRICE | 26 | 6651.73 | 3371.12 | 3299.00 | 15906.00 |
| MPG | 26 | 20.9230769 | 4.7575042 | 14.0000000 | 35.0000000 |
| REP78 | 26 | 3.2692308 | 0.7775702 | 2.0000000 | 5.0000000 |
| FOREIGN | 26 | 0.2692308 | 0.4523443 | 0 | 1.0000000 |

We can use the **n**, **mean** and **std** options to tell **proc means** that we just want the N, mean and standard deviation for the data.

```
PROC MEANS DATA=auto N MEAN STD ;
RUN;
```

The output, shown below, shows just the N, mean, and standard deviation, just as we requested.

| Variable | N | Mean | Std Dev |
|---|---|---|---|
| PRICE | 26 | 6651.73 | 3371.12 |
| MPG | 26 | 20.9230769 | 4.7575042 |
| REP78 | 26 | 3.2692308 | 0.7775702 |
| FOREIGN | 26 | 0.2692308 | 0.4523443 |

These examples have shown us that you can have options on the **proc** statement, for example after **proc means** we used the **data= , n, mean** and **std**options.

### Using additional statements

**Proc means** also supports additional statements. Here we use the **var** statement to say which variable(s) we want SAS to produce means for.

```
PROC MEANS DATA=auto;
  VAR price ;
RUN;
```

As you would expect, the output shows the results just for the variable **price**.

Analysis Variable : PRICE

| N | Mean | Std Dev | Minimum | Maximum |
|---|---|---|---|---|
| 26 | 6651.73 | 3371.12 | 3299.00 | 15906.00 |

Here we also use the **class** statement to request means broken down by the variable **foreign** (i.e., foreign and domestic cars).

```
PROC MEANS DATA=auto;
  CLASS foreign ;
  VAR price ;
RUN;
```

As we requested, the means of **price** are shown for the two levels of **foreign**.

```
Analysis Variable : PRICE

                   N
     FOREIGN     Obs     N          Mean       Std Dev       Minimum       Maximum
----------------------------------------------------------------------------------
           0      19    19       6484.16       3768.46       3299.00      15906.00

           1       7     7       7106.57       2101.83       4589.00       9735.00
----------------------------------------------------------------------------------
```

These examples have shown that you can have additional statements with a **proc** (for example, the **var** and **class** statements). Each **proc** has its own set of additional statements that are valid for that **proc**.

## Options on additional statements

It is also possible to have options on the additional statements lines (the statements after the **proc** statement). We will illustrate this using **proc reg**.

Here we use **proc reg** to predict **price** from **mpg**. We use the **model** statement to tell **proc reg** that we want to predict **price** from **mpg.**

```
PROC REG DATA=auto ;
  MODEL price = mpg ;
RUN;
QUIT;
```

Here is the output from the **proc reg**.

```
Model: MODEL1
Dependent Variable: PRICE

Analysis of Variance

                          Sum of          Mean
Source          DF       Squares        Square       F Value       Prob>F

Model            1 54620027.581 54620027.581        5.712        0.0251
Error           24 229491191.53 9562132.9806
C Total         25 284111219.12

    Root MSE    3092.26988       R-square      0.1922
    Dep Mean    6651.73077       Adj R-sq      0.1586
    C.V.          46.48820

Parameter Estimates

                Parameter        Standard    T for H0:
Variable  DF     Estimate           Error  Parameter=0     Prob > |T|

INTERCEP   1        13152    2786.6930753        4.720         0.0001
MPG        1  -310.689641    129.99546608       -2.390         0.0251
```

Notice that we don't get standardized estimates (betas). We have to ask **proc reg** to give those to us. In particular, we use the **stb** option on the **model**statement, as shown below. Note that the **stb** option comes after a forward slash ( / ). Options on a **proc** statement come right after the name of the**proc**, but options for subsequent statements must follow a forward slash.

```
PROC REG DATA=auto ;
  MODEL price = mpg / STB;
RUN;
```

The output is the same as the output above, except that it also includes the portion shown below that has the standardized estimates (betas).

```
               Standardized
Variable  DF       Estimate

INTERCEP   1     0.00000000
MPG        1    -0.43846180
```

## More examples

We have illustrated the general syntax of SAS procedures using **proc means** and **proc reg**. Let's look at a few more examples, this time using **proc freq**. As you may imagine, **proc freq** is used for generating frequency tables. From what we have learned, we would expect that **proc freq** would have:

- Options on the **proc freq** statement that would influence the way that the tables look.

- Additional statements that would specify what tables to produce.
- Options on the additional statements lines that would influence how those particular tables look.

Let's examine some examples.

First, consider the program below. As you might expect, the program below would generate frequency tables for every variable in the **auto** data file.

```
PROC FREQ DATA=auto;
RUN;
```

If we use the **page** option, **proc freq** will start every table on a new page. Note that this influences all of the tables produced in that **proc freq** procedure.

```
PROC FREQ DATA=auto PAGE;
RUN;
```

We have also seen that a SAS procedure can have one or more optional statements. Below we show that we can have one or more **tables** statements to specify the frequency tables we want, in this case, tables for **rep78** and **price**. Because we used the **page** option, each table will start on a new page. This influences both the tables made for **rep78** and **price**. (Note that we could have specified **tables rep78 price,** and gotten the same result, but we wanted to illustrate having more than one **tables** statement.)

```
PROC FREQ DATA=auto PAGE;
  TABLES rep78 ;
  TABLES price ;
RUN;
```

As we might expect, we could supply options on each of the **tables** statements to determine how those particular tables are to be shown. The example below requests frequency tables for **rep78** and price, but the table for **rep78** will omit percentages because it used the **nopercent** option. Both tables will appear on a new page (because the **page** option influences all of the tables) but only **rep78** will suppress the printing of percentages because the**nopercent** option only applies to that one **tables** statement.

```
PROC FREQ DATA=auto PAGE;
  TABLES rep78 / NOPERCENT ;
  TABLES price ;
RUN;
```

## Problems to look out for

When you use options, it is easy to confuse an option that goes on the **proc** statement with options that follow on subsequent statements.

## COMMON ERROR MESSAGES IN SAS

When a SAS program is executed, SAS generates a log. The log echoes program statements, provides information about computer resources and provides diagnostic information.

Understanding the log enables you to identify and correct errors in your program. The log contains three types of messages: **Notes**, **Warnings** and**Errors**. Although notes and warnings will not cause the program to terminate, they are worthy of your attention, since they may alert you to potential problems. An error message is more serious, since it indicates that the program has failed and stopped execution.

Most of the errors can be easily corrected and this page discusses how some common errors occur and how to correct them.

Strategies in finding and correcting errors

### *1. Start at the beginning*

Do not become alarmed if your program has several errors in it. Sometimes there is a single error in the beginning of the program that causes the others. Correcting this error may eliminate all those that follow. Start at the beginning of your program and work down.

### *2. Debug your programs one step at a time*

SAS executes programs in steps, so even if you have an error in a step written in the beginning of your program, SAS will try to execute all subsequent steps, which wastes not only your time, but computer resources as well. Simplify your work. Correct your programs one step at a time, before proceeding to the next step. As mentioned above, often a single error in the beginning of the program can create a cascading error effect. Correcting an error in a previous step may eliminate other errors.

Look at the statements immediately above and immediately following the line with the error. SAS will underline the error **where it detects it**, but sometimes the actual error is in a different place in your program, typically the preceding line.

### *3. Look for common errors first*

Most errors are caused by a few very common mistakes.

## Common errors

### *1. Missing semicolon*

This is by far the most common error. A missing semicolon will cause SAS to misinterpret not only the statement where the semicolon is missing, but possibly several statements that follow. Consider the following program, which is correct, except for the missing semicolon:

```
proc print data =  auto
    var make mpg;
run;
```

The missing semicolon causes SAS to read the two statements as a single statement. As a result, the **var** statement is read as an option to the procedure. Since there is no **var** option in **proc print**, the program fails.

```
      proc print data = auto
44        var make mpg;
          ------------
          202 202  202
45        run;

ERROR 202-322: The option or parameter is not recognized.
NOTE: The SAS System stopped processing this step because of errors.
```

The syntax for the following program is absolutely correct, **except** for the missing semicolon on the comment:

```
* Build a file named auto2

data auto2;
      set auto;
      ratio=mpg/weight;
run;
```

```
34     * Build a file named auto2
35
36       data auto2;
37         set auto;
           -------
           180
ERROR 180-322: Statement is not valid or it is used out of proper order.
38         ratio=mpg/weight;
           -------
           180
ERROR 180-322: Statement is not valid or it is used out of proper order.
39       run;
```

Taken out of the context of the program, both statements are correct.

```
set auto;
 ratio=mpg/weight;
```

However, SAS flags them as errors because it fails to read the **data** statement correctly. Instead, it reads this statement as part of the comment.

```
* Build a file named auto2       data auto2;
```

Why? Because the first semicolon it encounters is after the word **auto2**. Consequently the two correct statements are now errors.

## *2. Misspellings*

Sometimes SAS will correct your spelling mistakes for you by making its best guess at what you meant to do. When this happens, SAS will continue execution and issue a warning explaining the assumption it has made. Consider for example, the following program:

```
DAT auto ;
  INPUT make $  mpg rep78 weight foreign ;
CARDS;
AMC      22 3 2930 0
AMC      17 3 3350 0
AMC      22 . 2640 0
;
run;
```

Note that the word "DATA" is misspelled. If we were to run this program, SAS would correct the spelling and run the program but issue a warning.

```
68    DAT auto ;
      ----
14 69 INPUT make $ mpg rep78 weight foreign ;
   70 CARDS; WARNING 14-169: Assuming the symbol DATA was misspelled as DAT.
NOTE: The data set WORK.AUTO has 26 observations and 5 variables.
```

Sometimes SAS identifies a spelling error in a note, which does not cause the program to fail. Never assume that a program that has run without errors is correct! Always review the SAS log for notes and warning as well as errors.

The following program runs successfully, but is it correct?

```
data auto2;
  set auto;
  ratio = mpg/wieght;
run;
```

A careful review of the SAS log reveals that it is not.

```
75   data auto2;
76      set auto;
77      ratio = mpg/wieght;
78   run;

NOTE: Variable WIEGHT is uninitialized.
NOTE: Missing values were generated as a result of performing an
      operation on missing values.
      Each place is given by:
      (Number of times) at (Line):(Column).     6 at 77:15
NOTE: The data set WORK.AUTO2 has 26 observations and 7 variables.
```

Sometimes missing values are legitimate. However, when a variable is missing for every record in the file, there may be a problem with the program, as illustrated above. More often, when your program contains spelling errors, the step will terminate and SAS will issue an error statement or a note underlining the word, or words, it does not recognize.

```
65   proc print
66   var make mpg weight;
     ----
     76
67   run;

ERROR 76-322: Syntax error, statement will be ignored.
NOTE: The SAS System stopped processing this step because of errors.
```

In this example, there is nothing wrong with the **var** statement. Adding a semicolon to the **proc print** solves the problem.

```
proc print;
   var make mpg weight;
run;
```

The following code will successfully create a new dataset **auto2**.

```
data auto2;
  set uato;
  ratio = mpg/weight;
run;
```

However, because we misspelled the dataset name in the **set** statement, the new dataset contains 0 observations.

```
2     data auto2;
3       set uato;
ERROR: File WORK.UATO.DATA does not exist.
4       ratio = mpg/weight;
5     run;

NOTE: The SAS System stopped processing this step because of errors.
WARNING: The data set WORK.AUTO2 may be incomplete.  When this step was stopped there were 0
         observations and 7 variables.
```

The error message indicates that no dataset exists with the name **uato** and the warning message hints that the new dataset may be problematic. Correcting the spelling solves the problem.

## *3. Wrong data type*

Consider the following data step. It runs without an error message. But does it give us the intended result?

```
data test;
  input a b;
cards;
john  1
megan 2
;
run;

proc print data = test;
run;
```

```
Obs    a    b

 1     .    1
 2     .    2
```

Obviously, variable "**a**" has not been created as desired. This is because that "**a**" should be created as a character variable using the dollar sign specification for character variables. Instead, since the dollar sign is missing, SAS assumes that "**a**" is of numeric type, such as an integer or a real number and SAS expects to encounter a numeric value whenever it is ready to read in something for "**a**". Now, let's take a look at the log and see how SAS reacts to not seeing a number for "**a**":

```
2308  data test;
2309   input a b;
2310  cards;

NOTE: Invalid data for a in line 2311 1-4.
RULE:       ----+----1----+----2----+----3----+----4----+----5----+----6----+----7----+----8----+-
2311        john 1
a=. b=1 _ERROR_=1 _N_=1
NOTE: Invalid data for a in line 2312 1-5.
2312        megan 2
a=. b=2 _ERROR_=1 _N_=2
NOTE: The data set WORK.TEST has 2 observations and 2 variables.
NOTE: DATA statement used (Total process time):
      real time           0.01 seconds
      cpu time            0.01 seconds


2313  ;
2314  run;
2315  proc print data = test;
2316  run;

NOTE: There were 2 observations read from the data set WORK.TEST.
NOTE: PROCEDURE PRINT used (Total process time):
      real time           0.00 seconds
      cpu time            0.00 seconds
```

Indeed, there are no error messages in red. But each NOTE offers some detailed information. The first NOTE says that the data for variable "**a**" is invalid in line 2311 position 1-4. Since line 2310 is the line corresponding to the statement «**cards;**", line 2311 corresponds to the first line of data which starts with input **john**. So the NOTE is basically saying that "john" is not a valid numeric value. Once we understand the message, correcting our code is usually simple enough and in this case, we just need to add a dollar sign after variable "**a**" in the **input** statement as shown below.

```
data test;
 input a $ b;
cards;
john 1
megan 2
;
run;
```

## 4. Unmatched quotes/comments

Unclosed quotes and unclosed comments will result in a variety of errors because SAS will fail to read subsequent statements correctly. If you are running interactively, your program may appear to be doing nothing, because SAS is waiting for the end of the quoted string or comment before continuing. For example, if we were to run the following program,

```
proc print data = hsb2 (obs=10);
  var write math;
  title "printing first ten observations';
run;
```

SAS would not execute the **run** statement. Instead it reads it as part of the title statement, because the title statement is missing the closing double quotes. When this block of code is run, the program would appear to be doing nothing. System messages would indicate that it is running, which in fact it is. However, SAS is reading the rest of the program, waiting the double quote that will end the step it is currently stuck on.

Nothing appears in the output window (not shown). If we check the log, it does not have any blue notes indicating that the code has been executed.

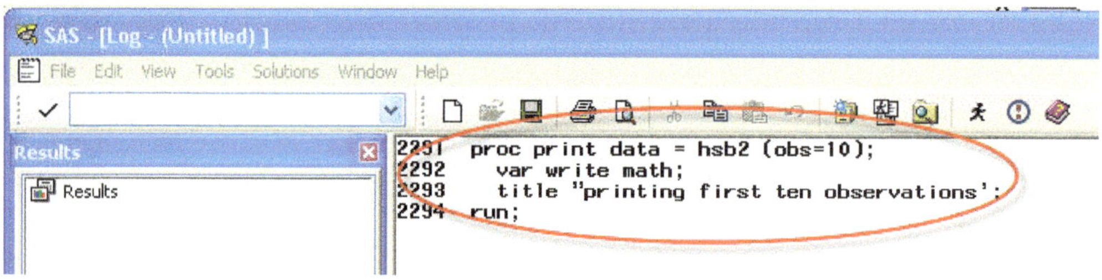


In the program editor window, the font color offers a hint that something is amiss. Everything appearing after the opening double quote of the title appears in purple. If we correct the program by replacing the single quote with a double quote, as follows,

```
proc print data = hsb2 (obs=10);
  var write math;
  title "printing first ten observations";
run;
```

the program will now run successfully and here is what we should see in the output:

printing first ten observations

| Obs | write | math |
|---|---|---|
| 1 | 31 | 44 |
| 2 | 40 | 43 |
| 3 | 65 | 48 |
| 4 | 44 | 49 |
| 5 | 57 | 50 |
| 6 | 41 | 43 |
| 7 | 52 | 41 |
| 8 | 49 | 43 |
| 9 | 59 | 63 |
| 10 | 37 | 42 |

### *5. Mixing proc and data statements*

Since the **data** and **proc** steps perform very different functions in SAS, statements that are valid for one will probably cause an error when used in the other. Although a program may include several steps, these steps are processed separately.

A step ends in one of three ways:

1. SAS encounters a keyword that begins a new step (either **proc** or **data**)
2. SAS encounters the **run** statement, which instructs it to run the previous step(s)
3. SAS encounters the end of the program.

Each **data**, **proc** and **run** statement causes the previous step to execute. Consequently, once a new step has begun, you may not go back and add statements to an earlier step. Consider this program, for example.

```
data auto2;
   set auto;
proc sort; by make;
   ratio = mpg/weight;
run;
```

SAS creates the new file **auto2** when it reaches the end of the **data** step. This occurs when it encounters the beginning of a new step (in this example**proc sort**). Consequently, the assignment statement (**ratio = mpg/weight;**) is invalid because the data step has been terminated, and an assignment statement cannot be used in a procedure.

```
40    data auto2;
41       set auto;

NOTE: The data set WORK.AUTO2 has 26 observations and 5 variables.
NOTE: The DATA statement used 0.12 seconds.

42    proc sort; by make;
43       ratio = mpg/weight;
         ------
         180
44    run;

ERROR 180-322: Statement is not valid or it is used out of proper order.
NOTE: The SAS System stopped processing this step because of errors.
```

Simply moving the assignment statement solves the problem.

```
data auto2;
   set auto;
   ratio = mpg/weight;
proc sort; by make;
run;
```

### *7. Using options with the wrong proc*

Similarly, although many options work with a variety of procedures, some are only valid when used with a particular procedure. Remember to evaluate all errors in context. A perfectly correct statement or option may cause an error not because it is written incorrectly, but because it is being used in the wrong place.

```
88    proc freq data = auto2;
89    var make;
      ---
      180
90    run;

ERROR 180-322: Statement is not valid or it is used out of proper order.
NOTE: The SAS System stopped processing this step because of errors.
```

The **var** statement is not valid when used with **proc freq**. Change the statement to **tables** and the program runs successfully.

```
proc freq data = auto2;
  tables make;
run;
```

Conversely, the **tables** statement may not work with other procedures.

```
92    proc means data = auto2;
93          tables make;
            ------
            180
94          run;

ERROR 180-322: Statement is not valid or it is used out of proper order.
NOTE: The SAS System stopped processing this step because of errors.
```

In this example, the **var** statement is correct:

```
proc means data = auto2;
  var make;
run;
```

*8. Logic errors*

Consider the log generated when the following program is run:

```
106  data auto2;
107     set auto;
108     if tons > .5;
109     tons = weight/2000;
110  run;

NOTE: The data set WORK.AUTO2 has 0 observations
```

Although the program ran with no errors, the new data set has no observations in it. Since we would expect most cars to weigh more than half a ton, there is probably an error in the program logic. In this case, we are subsetting on a variable that has not yet been defined.

Changing the order of the programming statements yields a different result:

```
118  data auto2;
119     set auto;
120     tons = weight/2000;
121     if tons > .5;
122  run;

NOTE: The data set WORK.AUTO2 has 26 observations.
```

*9. Missing options when dealing with missing data*

Consider following data stored in a text file called test.txt and the data step for reading the data.

```
john  11
megan 22 4
```

```
data test;
 infile 'd:\temp\test.txt';
 input a $ age y;
run;
proc print data = test;
run;
```

Here is the output from **proc print**:

```
Obs     a      age     y

 1     john     11     .
```

This is obviously not what we have intended. There should be two observations and there is only one. Most likely this is due to missing data and this is the case for this example. The value for the variable "**y**" is missing from row 1. In this case, we need to use the option "missover" of the **infile** statement to instruct SAS not to go a new input line if it does not find valid values in the current input line. Here is corrected version of the code together with the output.

```
data test;
 infile 'd:\temp\test.txt' missover;
 input a $ age y;
run;
proc print data = test;
run;

Obs     a       age     y

 1     john      11     .
 2     megan     22     4
```

*10. Not sorting data before using statements that require sort*

Although steps are executed independent of each other, some steps require a previous step in order to be carried out properly. A common example is the use of a **by** statement in a data step. This requires that the data has either been sorted by the variable(s) in the by statement or that the data was read in already sorted. If the code below is run without a previous sort on type,

```
data auto2; set auto;
  by type;
  retain types 0;
  if first.type then types = types + 1;
run;
```

the log indicates the omission of this step and prints the first line in the dataset that suggests non-sorted order of the variable(s).

```
70   data auto2; set auto;
71       by type;
72       retain types 0;
73       if first.type then types = types + 1;
74   run;

ERROR: BY variables are not properly sorted on data set WORK.AUTO.
Make=Acura Model=NSX coupe 2dr manual S Type=Sports Origin=Asia DriveTrain=Rear MSRP=$89,765
Invoice=$79,978 EngineSize=3.2 Cylinders=6 Horsepower=290 MPG_City=17 MPG_Highway=24 Weight=3153
Wheelbase=100 Length=174 FIRST.Type=0 LAST.Type=1 types=2 _ERROR_=1 _N_=7
NOTE: The SAS System stopped processing this step because of errors.
NOTE: There were 8 observations read from the data set WORK.AUTO.
WARNING: The data set WORK.AUTO2 may be incomplete.  When this step was stopped there were 6
         observations and 16 variables.
WARNING: Data set WORK.AUTO2 was not replaced because this step was stopped.
```

Adding a proc sort before this data step corrects this problem.

## INPUTTING DATA INTO SAS

This module will show how to input raw data into SAS, showing how to read instream data and external raw data files using some common raw data formats. Section 3 shows how to read external raw data files on a PC, UNIX/AIX, and Macintosh, while sections 4-6 give examples showing how to read the external raw data files on a PC, however these examples are easily converted to work on UNIX/AIX or a Macintosh based on the examples shown in section 3.

### Reading free formatted data instream

One of the most common ways to read data into SAS is by reading the data instream in a **data step** - that is, by typing the data directly into the syntax of your SAS program. This approach is good for relatively small datasets. Spaces are usually used to "delimit" (or separate) free formatted data. For example:

```
DATA cars1;
 INPUT make $ model $ mpg weight price;
CARDS;
AMC Concord 22 2930 4099
AMC Pacer   17 3350 4749
AMC Spirit  22 2640 3799
Buick Century 20 3250 4816
Buick Electra 15 4080 7827
;
RUN;
```

After reading in the data with a data step, it is usually a good idea to print the first few cases of your dataset to check that things were read correctly.

```
title "cars1 data";
PROC PRINT DATA=cars1(obs=5);
RUN;
```

Here is the output produced by the **proc print** statement above.

cars1 data

```
cars1 data

OBS   MAKE    MODEL     MPG   WEIGHT   PRICE
1     AMC     Concord    22    2930     4099
2     AMC     Pacer      17    3350     4749
3     AMC     Spirit     22    2640     3799
4     Buick   Century    20    3250     4816
5     Buick   Electra    15    4080     7827
```

## Reading fixed formatted data instream

Fixed formatted data can also be read instream. Usually, because there are no delimiters (such as spaces, commas, or tabs) to separate fixed formatted data, column definitions are required for every variable in the dataset. That is, you need to provide the beginning and ending column numbers for each variable. This also requires the data to be in the same columns for each case. For example, if we rearrange the cars data from above, we can read it as fixed formatted data:

```
DATA cars2;
  INPUT make $ 1-5 model $ 6-12 mpg 13-14 weight 15-18 price 19-22;
CARDS;
AMC  Concord2229304099
AMC  Pacer  1733504749
AMC  Spirit 2226403799
BuickCentury2032504816
BuickElectra1540807827
;
RUN;

TITLE "cars2 data";
PROC PRINT DATA=cars2(obs=5);
RUN;
```

The benefit of fixed formatted data is that you can fit more information on a line when you do not use delimiters such as spaces or commas.

Here is the output produced by the **proc print** statement above.

```
cars2 data

OBS    MAKE     MODEL     MPG    WEIGHT    PRICE
1      AMC      Concord   22     2930      4099
2      AMC      Pacer     17     3350      4749
3      AMC      Spirit    22     2640      3799
4      Buick    Century   20     3250      4816
5      Buick    Electra   15     4080      7827
```

## Reading fixed formatted data from an external file

Suppose you are using a PC and you have a file named **cars3.dat**, that is stored in the **c:\carsdata** directory of your computer. Here's what the data in the file **cars3.dat** look like:

```
AMC  Concord2229304099
AMC  Pacer  1733504749
AMC  Spirit 2226403799
BuickCentury2032504816
BuickElectra1540807827
```

To read the file **cars3.dat**, use the following syntax.

```
DATA cars3;
  INFILE "c:\carsdata\cars3.dat";
  INPUT make $ 1-5 model $ 6-12 mpg 13-14 weight 15-18 price 19-22;
RUN;

TITLE "cars3 data";
PROC PRINT DATA=cars3(obs=5);
RUN;
```

Here is the output produced by the **proc print** statement above.

```
cars3 data

OBS    MAKE      MODEL      MPG    WEIGHT    PRICE
1     AMC      Concord     22     2930      4099
2     AMC      Pacer       17     3350      4749
3     AMC      Spirit      22     2640      3799
4     Buick    Century     20     3250      4816
5     Buick    Electra     15     4080      7827
```

Suppose you were working on UNIX. The UNIX version of this program, assuming the file **cars3.dat** is located in the directory ~/ **carsdata**, would use the syntax shown below. (Note that the "~" in the UNIX pathname above refers to the user's HOME directory. Hence, the directory called **carsdata** that is located in the users HOME directory.)

```
DATA cars3;
  INFILE "~/carsdata/cars3.dat";
  INPUT make $ 1-5 model $ 6-12 mpg 13-14 weight 15-18 price 19-22;
RUN;

TITLE "cars3 data";
PROC PRINT DATA=cars3(obs=5);
RUN;
```

Likewise, suppose you were working on a Macintosh. The Macintosh version of this program, assuming **cars3.dat** is located on your hard drive (called**Hard Drive**) in a folder called **carsdata** would look like this.

```
DATA cars3;
  INFILE 'Hard Drive:carsdata:cars3.dat';
  INPUT make $ 1-5 model $ 6-12 mpg 13-14 weight 15-18 price 19-22;
RUN;

TITLE "cars3 data";
PROC PRINT DATA=cars3(OBS=5);
RUN;
```

In examples 4, 5 and 6 below, you can change the **infile** statement as these examples have shown to make the programs appropriate for UNIX or for the Macintosh.

### Reading free formatted (space delimited) data from an external file

Free formatted data that is **space** delimited can also be read from an external file. For example, suppose you have a space delimited file named**cars4.dat**, that is stored in the **c:\carsdata** directory of your computer.

Here›s what the data in the file **cars4.dat** look like:

```
AMC Concord 22 2930 4099
AMC Pacer   17 3350 4749
AMC Spirit  22 2640 3799
Buick Century 20 3250 4816
Buick Electra 15 4080 7827
```

To read the data from **cars4.dat** into SAS, use the following syntax:

```
DATA cars4;
  INFILE "c:\carsdata\cars4.dat";
  INPUT make $ model $ mpg weight price;
RUN;

TITLE "cars4 data";
PROC PRINT DATA=cars4(OBS=5);
RUN;
```

Here is the output produced by the **proc print** statement above.

```
cars4 data

OBS   MAKE    MODEL    MPG   WEIGHT   PRICE
1     AMC     Concord  22    2930     4099
2     AMC     Pacer    17    3350     4749
3     AMC     Spirit   22    2640     3799
4     Buick   Century  20    3250     4816
5     Buick   Electra  15    4080     7827
```

## Reading free formatted (comma delimited) data from an external file

Free formatted data that is **comma** delimited can also be read from an external file. For example, suppose you have a comma delimited file named**cars5.dat**, that is stored in the **c:\carsdata** directory of your computer.

Here›s what the data in the file **cars5.dat** look like:

```
AMC,Concord,22,2930,4099
AMC,Pacer,17,3350,4749
AMC,Spirit,22,2640,3799
Buick,Century,20,3250,4816
Buick,Electra,15,4080,7827
```

To read the data from **cars5.dat** into SAS, use the following syntax:

```
DATA cars5;
  INFILE "c:\carsdata\cars5.dat" delimiter=',';
  INPUT make $ model $ mpg weight price;
RUN;

TITLE "cars5 data";
PROC PRINT DATA=cars5(OBS=5);
RUN;
```

Here is the output produced by the **proc print** statement above.

```
cars5 data

OBS   MAKE    MODEL    MPG   WEIGHT   PRICE
1     AMC     Concord  22    2930     4099
2     AMC     Pacer    17    3350     4749
3     AMC     Spirit   22    2640     3799
4     Buick   Century  20    3250     4816
5     Buick   Electra  15    4080     7827
```

## Reading free formatted (tab delimited) data from an external file

Free formatted data that is **TAB** delimited can also be read from an external file. For example, suppose you have a tab delimited file named **cars6.dat**, that is stored in the **c:\carsdata** directory of your computer.

Here›s what the data in the file **cars6.dat** look like:

```
AMC     Concord 22      2930    4099
AMC     Pacer   17      3350    4749
AMC     Spirit  22      2640    3799
Buick   Century 20      3250    4816
Buick   Electra 15      4080    7827
```

To read the data from **cars6.dat** into SAS, use the following syntax:

```
DATA cars6;
  INFILE "c:\carsdata\cars6.dat" DELIMITER='09'x;
  INPUT make $ model $ mpg weight price;
RUN;

TITLE "cars6 data";
PROC PRINT DATA=cars6(OBS=5);
RUN;
```

Here is the output produced by the **proc print** statement above.

```
cars6 data

OBS   MAKE     MODEL     MPG   WEIGHT   PRICE
1     AMC      Concord   22    2930     4099
2     AMC      Pacer     17    3350     4749
3     AMC      Spirit    22    2640     3799
4     Buick    Century   20    3250     4816
5     Buick    Electra   15    4080     7827
```

## Problems to look out for

If you read a file that is wider than 80 columns, you may need to use the **lrecl=** parameter on the **infile** statement.

# USING DATES IN SAS

## Reading dates in data

This module will show how to read date variables, use date functions, and use date display formats in SAS. You are assumed to be familiar with **data** steps for reading data into SAS, and assignment statements for computing new variables. If any of the concepts are completely new, you may want to look at **For more information** below for directions to other learning modules. The data file used in the first example is presented next.

```
John  1 Jan 1960
Mary 11 Jul 1955
Kate 12 Nov 1962
Mark  8 Jun 1959
```

The program below reads the data and creates a temporary data file called **dates**. Note that the dates are read in the **data step**, and the format **date11.**is used to read the date.

```
DATA dates;
   INPUT  name $ 1-4 @6 bday date11.;
CARDS;
John  1 Jan 1960
Mary 11 Jul 1955
Kate 12 Nov 1962
Mark  8 Jun 1959
;
RUN;
PROC PRINT DATA=dates;
RUN;
```

The output of the **proc print** is presented below. Compare the dates in the data to the values of **bday**. Note that for **John** the date is **1 Jan 1960** and the value for **bday** is **0**. This is because dates are stored internally in SAS as the number of days from Jan 1,1960. Since **Mary** was born before 1960 the value of **bday** for her is negative **(-1635)**.

```
OBS    NAME     BDAY

1      John        0
2      Mary    -1635
3      Kate     1046
4      Mark     -207
```

In order to see the dates in a way that we understand you would have to format the output. We use the **date9.** format to see dates in the form**ddmmmyyyy.** This is specified on a **format** statement.

```
PROC PRINT DATA=dates;
  FORMAT bday date9. ;
RUN;
```

Here is the output produced by the **proc print** statement above.

```
OBS    NAME       BDAY

1      John    01JAN1960
2      Mary    11JUL1955
3      Kate    12NOV1962
4      Mark    08JUN1959
```

Let's look at the following data. At first glance it looks like the dates are so different that they couldn't be read. They do have two things in common:

1) they all have numeric months,

2) they all are ordered month, day, and then year.

```
John 1 1 1960
Mary 07/11/1955
Joan 07-11-1955
Kate 11.12.1962
Mark 06081959
```

These dates can be read with the same format, **mmddyy11.** An example of the use of that format in a **data step** follows.

```
DATA dates;
   INPUT  name $ 1-4 @6 bday mmddyy11.;
CARDS;
John 1 1 1960
Mary 07/11/1955
Joan 07-11-1955
Kate 11.12.1962
Mark 06081959
;
RUN;
PROC PRINT DATA=dates;
   FORMAT bday date9. ;
RUN;
```

The results of the above **proc print** show that all of the dates are read correctly.

```
OBS    NAME       BDAY

1      John    01JAN1960
2      Mary    11JUL1955
3      Joan    11JUL1955
4      Kate    12NOV1962
5      Mark    08JUN1959
```

There is a wide variety of **formats** available for use in reading dates into SAS. The following is a sample of some of those formats.

| Informat | Description | Range | Width | Sample |
|---|---|---|---|---|
| JULIANw. | Julian date YYDDD | 5-32 | 5 | 65001 |
| DDMMYYw. | date values | 6-32 | 6 | 14/8/1963 |
| MONYYw. | month and year | 5-32 | 5 | JUN64 |
| YYMMDDw. | date values | 6-32 | 8 | 65/4/29 |
| YYQw. | year and quarter | 4-32 | 4 | 65/1 |

Consider the following data in which the order is **month**, **year**, and **day**.

```
 7 1948 11
 1 1960  1
10 1970 15
12 1971 10
```

You may read these data with each portion of the date in a separate variable as in the **data step** that follows.

```
DATA dates;
   INPUT  month 1-2 year 4-7 day 9-10;
   bday=MDY(month,day,year);
CARDS;
 7 1948 11
 1 1960  1
10 1970 15
12 1971 10
;
RUN;

PROC PRINT DATA=dates;
   FORMAT bday date9. ;
RUN;
```

Notice the function **mdy(month,day,year)** in the **data step**. This function is used to create a date value from the individual components. The result of the**proc print** follows.

```
OBS  MONTH  YEAR  DAY       BDAY

 1      7   1948   11  11JUL1948
 2      1   1960    1  01JAN1960
 3     10   1970   15  15OCT1970
 4     12   1971   10  10DEC1971
```

## Two digit dates

Consider the following data, which are the same as above except that only two digits are used to signify the year, and year appears last.

```
 7 11 18
 7 11 48
 1  1 60
10 15 70
12 10 71
```

Reading the data is the same as we just did.

```
DATA dates;
   INPUT  month day year ;
   bday=MDY(month,day,year);
CARDS;
 7 11 18
 7 11 48
 1  1 60
10 15 70
12 10 71
;
RUN;

PROC PRINT DATA=dates;
   FORMAT bday date9. ;
RUN;
```

The results of the **proc print** are shown below.

```
OBS  MONTH  DAY   YEAR        BDAY

 1      7    11    18    11JUL1918
 2      7    11    48    11JUL1948
 3      1     1    60    01JAN1960
 4     10    15    70    15OCT1970
 5     12    10    71    10DEC1971
```

Two digit years work here because SAS assumes a cutoff (**yearcutoff**) before which value two digit years are interpreted as the year **2000** and above and after which they are interpreted as **1999** and below. The default **yearcutoff** differs for different versions of SAS:

```
SAS 6.12 and before (YEARCUTOFF=1900)
SAS 7 and 8         (YEARCUTOFF=1920)
```

The **options** statement in the program that follows changes the **yearcutoff** value to **1920**. This causes in two digit years lower than **20** to be read as after the year **2000**. Running the same program then will yield different results when this option is set.

```
OPTIONS YEARCUTOFF=1920;

DATA dates;
   INPUT  month day year ;
   bday=MDY(month,day,year);
CARDS;
 7 11 18
 7 11 48
 1  1 60
10 15 70
12 10 71
;
RUN;

PROC PRINT DATA=dates;
   FORMAT bday date9. ;
RUN;
```

The results of the **proc print** are shown below. The first observation is now read as occurring in 2018 instead of 1918.

```
OBS    MONTH    DAY   YEAR        BDAY

 1        7      11    18    11JUL2018
 2        7      11    48    11JUL1948
 3        1       1    60    01JAN1960
 4       10      15    70    15OCT1970
 5       12      10    71    10DEC1971
```

## Computations with elapsed dates

SAS date variables make computations involving dates very convenient. For example, to calculate everyone's age on **January 1, 2000** use the following conversion in the **data step**.

```
age2000=(mdy(1,1,2000)-bday)/365.25 ;
```

The program with this calculation in context follows.

```
OPTIONS YEARCUTOFF=1900; /* sets the cutoff back to the default */

DATA dates;
   INPUT  name $ 1-4 @6 bday mmddyy11.;
   age2000 = (MDY(1,1,2000)-bday)/365.25 ;
CARDS;
John 1 1 1960
Mary 07/11/1955
Joan 07-11-1955
Kate 11.12.1962
Mark 06081959
;
RUN;

PROC PRINT DATA=dates;
   FORMAT bday date9. ;
RUN;
```

The results of the **proc print** are shown below. The variable **AGE2000** now contains the age in years as of **January 1, 2000**.

```
OBS    NAME        BDAY      AGE2000

 1     John     01JAN1960    40.0000
 2     Mary     11JUL1955    44.4764
 3     Joan     11JUL1955    44.4764
 4     Kate     12NOV1962    37.1362
 5     Mark     08JUN1959    40.5667
```

## OTHER USEFUL DATE FUNCTIONS

There are a number of useful **functions** for use with date variables. The following is a list of some of those functions.

```
Function   Description            Sample
--------   ---------------------  -----------------
month()    Extracts Month         m=MONTH(bday);
day()      Extracts Day           d=DAY(bday) ;
year()     Extracts Year          y=YEAR(bday);
weekday()  Extracts Day of Week   wk_d=WEEKDAY(bday);
qtr()      Extracts Quarter       q=QTR(bday);
```

The following program demonstrates the use of these functions.

```
DATA dates;
   INPUT  name $ 1-4 @6 bday mmddyy11.;
   m=MONTH(bday);
   d=DAY(bday) ;
   y=YEAR(bday);
   wk_d=WEEKDAY(bday);
   q=QTR(bday);
CARDS;
John 1 1 1960
Mary 07/11/1955
Joan 07-11-1955
Kate 11.12.1962
Mark 06081959
;
RUN;

PROC PRINT DATA=dates;
   VAR bday m d y;
   FORMAT bday date9. ;
RUN;

PROC PRINT DATA=dates;
   VAR bday wk_d q;
   FORMAT bday date9. ;
RUN;
```

The **proc print** results are shown below. The new variables contain the month, day, year, day of the week and quarter.

```
OBS       BDAY      M     D      Y

 1     01JAN1960    1     1    1960
 2     11JUL1955    7    11    1955
 3     11JUL1955    7    11    1955
 4     12NOV1962   11    12    1962
 5     08JUN1959    6     8    1959

OBS       BDAY     WK_D   Q

 1     01JAN1960    6     1
 2     11JUL1955    2     3
 3     11JUL1955    2     3
 4     12NOV1962    2     4
 5     08JUN1959    2     2
```

## SUMMARY

- Dates are read with date formats, most commonly **date9.** and **mmddyy11.**
- Date functions can be used to create date values from their components **(mdy(m,d,y))**, and to extract the components from a date value**(month(),day(), etc.)**.
- The **yearcutoff** option may be used if you have to read two digit years.

## PROBLEMS TO LOOK OUT FOR

- Dates are mixed within a field such that no single date format can read them. **Solution:** Read the field as a character field, test the string, and use the **input** function and appropriate format to read the value into the date variable.
- There is no format capable of reading the date. **Solution:** read the date as components and use a function to produce a date value.
- Sometimes the default for **yearcutoff** is not the default for the version of the package mentioned above. **Solution:** to determine the current setting for **yearcutoff** simply run a program containing **PROC OPTIONS OPTION=YEARCUTOFF; RUN;** This will result in output containing the current value of **yearcutoff**.

# SECTION II: ADVANCED DATA MANIPULATION AND ANALYTICS IN SAS

# CHAPTER 2 BASIC AND ADVANCED DATA MANAGEMENT WITH SAS

## CREATING AND RECODING VARIABLES IN SAS

### Creating and replacing variables in SAS

We will illustrate creating and replacing variables in SAS using a data file about 26 automobiles with their **make**, **price**, **mpg**, repair record in 1978 (**rep78**), and whether the car was foreign or domestic (**foreign**). The program below reads the data and creates a temporary data file called "**auto**". Please note that there are two missing values for **mpg** in the data file (coded as a single period).

```
DATA auto;
  INPUT make $ price mpg rep78 foreign;
  cost = ROUND( price / 1000 );
  mpgptd = mpg / price;
DATALINES;
AMC     4099 22 3 0
AMC     4749 17 3 0
AMC     3799 22 3 0
Audi    9690  . 5 1
Audi    6295 23 3 1
BMW     9735 25 4 1
Buick   4816 20 3 0
Buick   7827 15 4 0
Buick   5788 18 3 0
Buick   4453 26 3 0
Buick   5189 20 3 0
Buick  10372 16 3 0
Buick   4082 19 3 0
Cad.   11385 14 3 0
Cad.   14500 14 2 0
Cad.   15906 21 3 0
Chev.   3299 29 3 0
Chev.   5705 16 4 0
Chev.   4504  . 3 0
Chev.   5104 22 2 0
Chev.   3667 24 2 0
Chev.   3955 19 3 0
Datsun  6229 23 4 1
Datsun  4589 35 5 1
Datsun  5079 24 4 1
Datsun  8129 21 4 1
;
RUN;

PROC PRINT DATA=auto;
RUN;
```

**Citation:** Basic and Advanced Data management with SAS", Web Tutorial by UCLA: Statistical Consulting Group, 2016.

We will create one new variable to go along with the existing ones. First, we will create **cost** so that it gives us the price in thousands of dollars. Then we will create **mpgpd** which will stand for miles per gallon per thousand dollars. In each case, we just type the variable name, followed by an equal sign, followed by an expression for the value.

Here is the output of the **proc print**. You can compare the output to the original data.

| OBS | MAKE | PRICE | MPG | REP78 | FOREIGN | COST | MPGPTD |
|---|---|---|---|---|---|---|---|
| 1 | AMC | 4099 | 22 | 3 | 0 | 4 | .0053672 |
| 2 | AMC | 4749 | 17 | 3 | 0 | 5 | .0035797 |
| 3 | AMC | 3799 | 22 | 3 | 0 | 4 | .0057910 |
| 4 | Audi | 9690 | . | 5 | 1 | 10 | . |
| 5 | Audi | 6295 | 23 | 3 | 1 | 6 | .0036537 |
| 6 | BMW | 9735 | 25 | 4 | 1 | 10 | .0025681 |
| 7 | Buick | 4816 | 20 | 3 | 0 | 5 | .0041528 |
| 8 | Buick | 7827 | 15 | 4 | 0 | 8 | .0019164 |
| 9 | Buick | 5788 | 18 | 3 | 0 | 6 | .0031099 |
| 10 | Buick | 4453 | 26 | 3 | 0 | 4 | .0058388 |
| 11 | Buick | 5189 | 20 | 3 | 0 | 5 | .0038543 |
| 12 | Buick | 10372 | 16 | 3 | 0 | 10 | .0015426 |
| 13 | Buick | 4082 | 19 | 3 | 0 | 4 | .0046546 |
| 14 | Cad. | 11385 | 14 | 3 | 0 | 11 | .0012297 |
| 15 | Cad. | 14500 | 14 | 2 | 0 | 15 | .0009655 |
| 16 | Cad. | 15906 | 21 | 3 | 0 | 16 | .0013203 |
| 17 | Chev. | 3299 | 29 | 3 | 0 | 3 | .0087905 |
| 18 | Chev. | 5705 | 16 | 4 | 0 | 6 | .0028046 |
| 19 | Chev. | 4504 | . | 3 | 0 | 5 | . |
| 20 | Chev. | 5104 | 22 | 2 | 0 | 5 | .0043103 |
| 21 | Chev. | 3667 | 24 | 2 | 0 | 4 | .0065449 |
| 22 | Chev. | 3955 | 19 | 3 | 0 | 4 | .0048040 |
| 23 | Datsun | 6229 | 23 | 4 | 1 | 6 | .0036924 |
| 24 | Datsun | 4589 | 35 | 5 | 1 | 5 | .0076269 |
| 25 | Datsun | 5079 | 24 | 4 | 1 | 5 | .0047253 |
| 26 | Datsun | 8129 | 21 | 4 | 1 | 8 | .0025833 |

Note that **cost** is just a one or two-digit value. The vehicle that achieves the best **mpgptd** is the Chev. for observation 17 which gets 9+ miles per gallon for every thousand dollars in price. The Cad. in observation 14 has the worst **mpgptd**.

Also note that there are two missing values for **mpgptd** because of the missing values in **mpg**.

### Recoding variables in SAS

The variable **rep78** is coded 1 through 5 standing for poor, fair, average, good and excellent. We would like to change **rep78** so that it has only three values, 1 through 3, standing for below average, average, and above average. We will do this by creating a new variable called **repair** and recoding the values of **rep78** into it.

We will also create a new variable called **himpg** that is a dummy coding of **mpg**. All vehicles with better than 20 **mpg** will be coded 1 and those with 20 or less will be coded 0.

SAS does not have a recode command, so we will use a series of **if-then/else** commands in a **data** step to do the job. This **data** step creates a temporary data file called **auto2**.

```
DATA auto2;
  SET auto;

  repair = .;
  IF (rep78=1) or (rep78=2) THEN repair = 1;
  IF (rep78=3) THEN repair = 2;
  IF (rep78=4) or (rep78=5) THEN repair = 3;

  himpg = .;
  IF (mpg <= 20) THEN himpg = 0;
  IF (mpg >  20) THEN himpg = 1;
RUN;
```

Note that we begin by setting **repair** and **himpg** to missing, just in case we make a mistake in the recoding. **Proc freq** will show us how the recoding worked.

```
PROC FREQ DATA=auto2;
  TABLES repair*rep78 repair*himpg / MISSING;
RUN;
```

```
TABLE OF REPAIR BY REP78

REPAIR     REP78

Frequency|
Percent  |
Row Pct  |
Col Pct  |       2|       3|       4|       5|  Total
---------+--------+--------+--------+--------+
       1 |      3 |      0 |      0 |      0 |      3
         |  11.54 |   0.00 |   0.00 |   0.00 |  11.54
         | 100.00 |   0.00 |   0.00 |   0.00 |
         | 100.00 |   0.00 |   0.00 |   0.00 |
---------+--------+--------+--------+--------+
       2 |      0 |     15 |      0 |      0 |     15
         |   0.00 |  57.69 |   0.00 |   0.00 |  57.69
         |   0.00 | 100.00 |   0.00 |   0.00 |
         |   0.00 | 100.00 |   0.00 |   0.00 |
---------+--------+--------+--------+--------+
       3 |      0 |      0 |      6 |      2 |      8
         |   0.00 |   0.00 |  23.08 |   7.69 |  30.77
         |   0.00 |   0.00 |  75.00 |  25.00 |
         |   0.00 |   0.00 | 100.00 | 100.00 |
---------+--------+--------+--------+--------+
Total           3       15        6        2      26
            11.54    57.69    23.08     7.69  100.00
```

```
TABLE OF REPAIR BY HIMPG

REPAIR     HIMPG

Frequency|
Percent  |
Row Pct  |
Col Pct  |       0|       1|  Total
---------+--------+--------+
       1 |      1 |      2 |      3
         |   3.85 |   7.69 |  11.54
         |  33.33 |  66.67 |
         |   7.69 |  15.38 |
---------+--------+--------+
       2 |      9 |      6 |     15
         |  34.62 |  23.08 |  57.69
         |  60.00 |  40.00 |
         |  69.23 |  46.15 |
---------+--------+--------+
       3 |      3 |      5 |      8
         |  11.54 |  19.23 |  30.77
         |  37.50 |  62.50 |
         |  23.08 |  38.46 |
---------+--------+--------+
Total          13       13      26
            50.00    50.00  100.00
```

Uh oh, there's a problem with **himpg**. There are no missing values for **himpg** even though there were two missing values of **mpg**. SAS treats missing values (values coded with a . ) as the smallest number possible (i.e., negative infinity). When we recoded **mpg** we wrote

```
IF (mpg <= 20) THEN himpg = 0;
```

which converted all values of **mpg** that were 20 or less into a value of 0 for **himpg**. Since a missing value is also less than 20, the missing values got recoded to 0 as well. (It is unforeseen mistakes like this that make it so important to check every variable that you recode.) Let's try recoding **himpg**again, being careful to properly treat missing values like this:

```
IF (. < mpg <= 20) THEN himpg = 0;
```

The complete program, with the fixed **if** statement, is shown below.

```
DATA auto2;
  SET auto;

  repair = .;
  IF (rep78=1) or (rep78=2) THEN repair = 1;
  IF (rep78=3) THEN repair = 2;
  IF (rep78=4) or (rep78=5) THEN repair = 3;

  himpg = .;
  IF (.  < mpg <= 20) THEN himpg = 0;
  IF (mpg >  20) THEN himpg = 1;
RUN;
```

Now let's use **proc freq** again to check the recoding.

```
PROC FREQ DATA=auto2;
  TABLES repair*himpg / MISSING;
RUN;
```

```
TABLE OF REPAIR BY HIMPG

REPAIR     HIMPG

Frequency|
Percent  |
Row Pct  |
Col Pct  |       .|       0|       1|  Total
---------+--------+--------+--------+
       1 |      0 |      1 |      2 |      3
         |   0.00 |   3.85 |   7.69 |  11.54
         |   0.00 |  33.33 |  66.67 |
         |   0.00 |   9.09 |  15.38 |
---------+--------+--------+--------+
       2 |      1 |      8 |      6 |     15
         |   3.85 |  30.77 |  23.08 |  57.69
         |   6.67 |  53.33 |  40.00 |
         |  50.00 |  72.73 |  46.15 |
---------+--------+--------+--------+
       3 |      1 |      2 |      5 |      8
         |   3.85 |   7.69 |  19.23 |  30.77
         |  12.50 |  25.00 |  62.50 |
         |  50.00 |  18.18 |  38.46 |
---------+--------+--------+--------+
Total           2       11       13       26
             7.69    42.31    50.00   100.00
```

There, that's better, this time there are two missing values for **himpg**.

## Problems to look out for

Watch out for math errors, such as, division by zero and square root of a negative number.

## Helpful hints and suggestions

- Set values to missing and then recode them.
- Use new variable names when you create or recode variables. Avoid constructions like this, **total = total + sub1 + sub2;**that reuse the variable name **total**.
- Use the **missing** option with **proc freq** to make sure all missing values are accounted for

# USING SAS FUNCTIONS FOR MAKING AND RECODING VARIABLES

## Introduction

A SAS **function** returns a value from a computation or system manipulation that requires zero or more arguments. Most functions use arguments supplied by the user; however, a few obtain their arguments from the operating system. Here is the syntax of a function:

function-name(argument1, argument2)

We will illustrate some functions using the following dataset that includes **name**, **x**, **test1**, **test2**, and **test3.**

```
DATA getdata;
  INPUT name $14. x test1 test2 test3;
DATALINES;
John Smith        4.2 86.5 84.55 81
Samuel Adams      9.0 70.3 82.37 .
Ben Johnson      -6.2 82.1 84.81 87
Chris Adraktas    9.5 94.2 92.64 93
John Brown         .  79.7 79.07 72
;
RUN;
```

The data set **funct1** will create new variables using the **int**, **round** and **mean** numeric functions. What happens to **tave** due to the missing value of **test3**?

```
DATA funct1;
  SET getdata;
  t1int = INT(test1);  t2int = INT(test2);        /* integer part of a number */
  t1rnd = ROUND(test1);t2rnd = ROUND(test2,.1); /* round to nearest whole number */
  tave = MEAN(test1, test2, test3);               /* mean across variables */
RUN;

PROC PRINT DATA=funct1;
  VAR test1 test2 test3 t1int t2int t1rnd t2rnd tave;
RUN;
```

```
OBS  TEST1  TEST2  TEST3  T1INT  T2INT  T1RND  T2RND     TAVE
 1   86.5   84.55   81     86     84     87    84.6   84.0167
 2   70.3   82.37    .     70     82     70    82.4   76.3350
 3   82.1   84.81   87     82     84     82    84.8   84.6367
 4   94.2   92.64   93     94     92     94    92.6   93.2800
 5   79.7   79.07   72     79     79     80    79.1   76.9233
```

Now let's try some more math functions. What happens when there is a missing or negative value of **x**?

```
DATA funct2;
  SET getdata;
  xsqrt = SQRT(x);      /* square root */
  xlog = LOG(x);       /* log base e */
  xexp = EXP(x);       /* e raised to the power */
RUN;

PROC PRINT DATA=funct2;
  VAR x xsqrt xlog xexp;
RUN;
```

```
OBS     X      XSQRT       XLOG        XEXP
 1     4.2    2.04939    1.43508       66.69
 2     9.0    3.00000    2.19722     8103.08
 3    -6.2     .          .              0.00
 4     9.5    3.08221    2.25129    13359.73
 5      .      .          .               .
```

This time we'll try some string functions. In particular, look closely at the **substr** function that is used in **fname** and **lname**.

```
DATA funct3;
  SET getdata;
  c1  = UPCASE(name);      /* convert to upper case */
  c2  = SUBSTR(name,3,8); /* substring */
  len = LENGTH(name);      /* length of string */
  ind = INDEX(name,' ');  /* position in string */
  fname = SUBSTR(name,1,INDEX(name,' '));
  lname = SUBSTR(name,INDEX(name,' '));
RUN;

PROC PRINT DATA=funct3;
  VAR name c1 c2 len ind fname lname;
RUN;
```

```
OBS      NAME             C1              C2        LEN   IND   FNAME    LNAME
 1   John Smith       JOHN SMITH       hn Smith    10     5    John     Smith
 2   Samuel Adams     SAMUEL ADAMS     muel Ada    12     7    Samuel   Adams
 3   Ben Johnson      BEN JOHNSON      n Johnso    11     4    Ben      Johnson
 4   Chris Adraktas   CHRIS ADRAKTAS   ris Adra    14     6    Chris    Adraktas
 5   John Brown       JOHN BROWN       hn Brown    10     5    John     Brown
```

## Random numbers in SAS

Random numbers are more useful than you might imagine. They are used extensively in Monte Carlo studies, as well as in many other situations. We will look at two of SAS's random number functions.

- **UNIFORM(SEED)** - generates values from a random uniform distribution between 0 and 1

- **NORMAL(SEED)** - generates values from a random normal distribution with mean 0 and standard deviation 1

The statements **if x>.5 then coin = 'heads'** and **else coin = ‹tails›** create a random variable called **coins** that has values 'heads' and 'tails'. The data setsr**andom1** and **random2** use a **seed** value of -1. Negative **seed** values will result in different random numbers being generated each time.

```
DATA random1;
    x = UNIFORM(-1);
    y = 50 + 3*NORMAL(-1);
    IF x>.5 THEN coin = 'heads';
      ELSE coin = 'tails';
RUN;

DATA random2;
    x = UNIFORM(-1);
    y = 50 + 3*NORMAL(-1);
    IF x>.5 THEN coin = 'heads';
      ELSE coin = 'tails';
RUN;

PROC PRINT DATA=random1;
  VAR x y coin;
RUN;
PROC PRINT DATA=random2;
  VAR x y coin;
RUN;
```

```
OBS      X          Y        COIN
 1    0.24441    49.7470    heads

OBS      X          Y        COIN
 1    0.16922    49.1155    tails
```

Sometimes we will want to generate the same random numbers each time so that we can debug our programs. To do this we just enter the same positive number as the **seed** value. The data sets **random3** and **random4** illustrate how to generate the same results each time.

```
data random3;
    x = UNIFORM(123456);
    y = 50 + 3*NORMAL(123456);
    IF x>.5 THEN coin = 'heads';
      ELSE coin = 'tails';
RUN;

data random4;
    x = UNIFORM(123456);
    y = 50 + 3*NORMAL(123456);
    IF x>.5 THEN coin = 'heads';
      ELSE coin = 'tails';
RUN;

PROC PRINT DATA=random3;
  VAR x y coin;
RUN;
PROC PRINT DATA=random4;
  VAR x y coin;
RUN;
```

```
OBS      X          Y        COIN
 1    0.73902    48.7832    heads

OBS      X          Y        COIN
 1    0.73902    48.7832    heads
```

Now let's generate 100 random coin tosses and compute a frequency table of the results.

```
DATA random5;
  DO i=1 to 100;
    x = UNIFORM(123456);
    IF x>.5 THEN coin = 'heads';
      ELSE coin = 'tails';
    OUTPUT;
  END;
RUN;

PROC FREQ DATA=random5;
  table coin;
RUN;
```

```
                                   Cumulative   Cumulative
COIN     Frequency     Percent     Frequency      Percent
----------------------------------------------------------
heads          48        48.0            48         48.0
tails          52        52.0           100        100.0
```

## Problems to look out for

Watch out for math errors, such as division by zero, square root of a negative number and taking the log of a negative number.

## For more information

For information on functions is SAS consult the SAS Language manual.

## Web notes

You can view the SAS program associated with this module by clicking funct.sas . While viewing the file, you can save it by choosing **File** then **Save As**from the pull-down menu of your web browser. In the **Save As** dialog box, change the file name to funct.sas and then choose the directory where you want to save the file, then click **Save.**

## SUBSETTING DATA IN SAS

### Introduction

This module demonstrates how to select variables using the **keep** and **drop** statements, using keep and drop data step options records, and using the subsetting **if** and **delete** statement(s). Selecting variables: The SAS file structure is similar to a spreadsheet. Data values are stored as variables, which are like fields or columns on a spreadsheet. Sometimes data files contain information that is superfluous to a particular analysis, in which case we might want to change the data file to contain only variables of interest. Programs will run more quickly and occupy less storage space if files contain only necessary variables. The following program builds a SAS file called **auto**. (For information about creating SAS files from raw data, see the SAS Learning Module on Inputting Data into SAS .)

```
DATA auto ;
  LENGTH make $ 20 ;
  INPUT make $ 1-17 price mpg rep78 hdroom trunk weight length turn
        displ gratio foreign ;
CARDS;
AMC Concord        4099 22 3 2.5 11 2930 186 40 121 3.58 0
AMC Pacer          4749 17 3 3.0 11 3350 173 40 258 2.53 0
AMC Spirit         3799 22 . 3.0 12 2640 168 35 121 3.08 0
Audi 5000          9690 17 5 3.0 15 2830 189 37 131 3.20 1
Audi Fox           6295 23 3 2.5 11 2070 174 36  97 3.70 1
BMW 320i           9735 25 4 2.5 12 2650 177 34 121 3.64 1
Buick Century      4816 20 3 4.5 16 3250 196 40 196 2.93 0
Buick Electra      7827 15 4 4.0 20 4080 222 43 350 2.41 0
Buick LeSabre      5788 18 3 4.0 21 3670 218 43 231 2.73 0
Buick Opel         4453 26 . 3.0 10 2230 170 34 304 2.87 0
Buick Regal        5189 20 3 2.0 16 3280 200 42 196 2.93 0
Buick Riviera     10372 16 3 3.5 17 3880 207 43 231 2.93 0
Buick Skylark      4082 19 3 3.5 13 3400 200 42 231 3.08 0
Cad. Deville      11385 14 3 4.0 20 4330 221 44 425 2.28 0
Cad. Eldorado     14500 14 2 3.5 16 3900 204 43 350 2.19 0
Cad. Seville      15906 21 3 3.0 13 4290 204 45 350 2.24 0
Chev. Chevette     3299 29 3 2.5  9 2110 163 34 231 2.93 0
Chev. Impala       5705 16 4 4.0 20 3690 212 43 250 2.56 0
Chev. Malibu       4504 22 3 3.5 17 3180 193 31 200 2.73 0
Chev. Monte Carlo  5104 22 2 2.0 16 3220 200 41 200 2.73 0
Chev. Monza        3667 24 2 2.0  7 2750 179 40 151 2.73 0
Chev. Nova         3955 19 3 3.5 13 3430 197 43 250 2.56 0
Datsun 200         6229 23 4 1.5  6 2370 170 35 119 3.89 1
Datsun 210         4589 35 5 2.0  8 2020 165 32  85 3.70 1
Datsun 510         5079 24 4 2.5  8 2280 170 34 119 3.54 1
Datsun 810         8129 21 4 2.5  8 2750 184 38 146 3.55 1
Dodge Colt         3984 30 5 2.0  8 2120 163 35  98 3.54 0
Dodge Diplomat     4010 18 2 4.0 17 3600 206 46 318 2.47 0
Dodge Magnum       5886 16 2 4.0 17 3600 206 46 318 2.47 0
Dodge St. Regis    6342 17 2 4.5 21 3740 220 46 225 2.94 0
Fiat Strada        4296 21 3 2.5 16 2130 161 36 105 3.37 1
Ford Fiesta        4389 28 4 1.5  9 1800 147 33  98 3.15 0
Ford Mustang       4187 21 3 2.0 10 2650 179 43 140 3.08 0
Honda Accord       5799 25 5 3.0 10 2240 172 36 107 3.05 1
Honda Civic        4499 28 4 2.5  5 1760 149 34  91 3.30 1
Linc. Continental 11497 12 3 3.5 22 4840 233 51 400 2.47 0
Linc. Mark V      13594 12 3 2.5 18 4720 230 48 400 2.47 0
Linc. Versailles  13466 14 3 3.5 15 3830 201 41 302 2.47 0
Mazda GLC          3995 30 4 3.5 11 1980 154 33  86 3.73 1
Merc. Bobcat       3829 22 4 3.0  9 2580 169 39 140 2.73 0
Merc. Cougar       5379 14 4 3.5 16 4060 221 48 302 2.75 0
Merc. Marquis      6165 15 3 3.5 23 3720 212 44 302 2.26 0
Merc. Monarch      4516 18 3 3.0 15 3370 198 41 250 2.43 0
Merc. XR-7         6303 14 4 3.0 16 4130 217 45 302 2.75 0
Merc. Zephyr       3291 20 3 3.5 17 2830 195 43 140 3.08 0
Olds 98            8814 21 4 4.0 20 4060 220 43 350 2.41 0
Olds Cutl Supr     5172 19 3 2.0 16 3310 198 42 231 2.93 0
Olds Cutlass       4733 19 3 4.5 16 3300 198 42 231 2.93 0
Olds Delta 88      4890 18 4 4.0 20 3690 218 42 231 2.73 0
Olds Omega         4181 19 3 4.5 14 3370 200 43 231 3.08 0
Olds Starfire      4195 24 1 2.0 10 2730 180 40 151 2.73 0
Olds Toronado     10371 16 3 3.5 17 4030 206 43 350 2.41 0
Peugeot 604       12990 14 . 3.5 14 3420 192 38 163 3.58 1
Plym. Arrow        4647 28 3 2.0 11 3260 170 37 156 3.05 0
Plym. Champ        4425 34 5 2.5 11 1800 157 37  86 2.97 0
Plym. Horizon      4482 25 3 4.0 17 2200 165 36 105 3.37 0
Plym. Sapporo      6486 26 . 1.5  8 2520 182 38 119 3.54 0
Plym. Volare       4060 18 2 5.0 16 3330 201 44 225 3.23 0
Pont. Catalina     5798 18 4 4.0 20 3700 214 42 231 2.73 0
Pont. Firebird     4934 18 1 1.5  7 3470 198 42 231 3.08 0
Pont. Grand Prix   5222 19 3 2.0 16 3210 201 45 231 2.93 0
Pont. Le Mans      4723 19 3 3.5 17 3200 199 40 231 2.93 0
Pont. Phoenix      4424 19 . 3.5 13 3420 203 43 231 3.08 0
Pont. Sunbird      4172 24 2 2.0  7 2690 179 41 151 2.73 0
Renault Le Car     3895 26 3 3.0 10 1830 142 34  79 3.72 1
Subaru             3798 35 5 2.5 11 2050 164 36  97 3.81 1
Toyota Celica      5899 18 5 2.5 14 2410 174 36 134 3.06 1
Toyota Corolla     3748 31 5 3.0  9 2200 165 35  97 3.21 1
Toyota Corona      5719 18 5 2.0 11 2670 175 36 134 3.05 1
Volvo 260         11995 17 5 2.5 14 3170 193 37 163 2.98 1
VW Dasher          7140 23 4 2.5 12 2160 172 36  97 3.74 1
VW Diesel          5397 41 5 3.0 15 2040 155 35  90 3.78 1
VW Rabbit          4697 25 4 3.0 15 1930 155 35  89 3.78 1
VW Scirocco        6850 25 4 2.0 16 1990 156 36  97 3.78 1
;
RUN;

PROC CONTENTS DATA=auto;
RUN;
```

The **proc contents** provides information about the file.

```
CONTENTS PROCEDURE

Data Set Name: WORK.AUTO          Observations:          74
Member Type:   DATA               Variables:             12

-----Alphabetic List of Variables and Attributes-----

 #    Variable    Type    Len    Pos
-----------------------------------
10    DISPL       Num       8     84
12    FOREIGN     Num       8    100
11    GRATIO      Num       8     92
 5    HDROOM      Num       8     44
 8    LENGTH      Num       8     68
 1    MAKE        Char     20      0
 3    MPG         Num       8     28
 2    PRICE       Num       8     20
 4    REP78       Num       8     36
 6    TRUNK       Num       8     52
 9    TURN        Num       8     76
 7    WEIGHT      Num       8     60
```

### Subsetting variables

For example, if we wanted to examine the relationship between **mpg** and **price** for various **make**s, but had no interest in the automobile's dimensions, we could create a smaller file, by keeping only these three variables.

```
DATA auto2;
   SET auto;
   KEEP make mpg price;
RUN;
```

To verify the contents of the new file, run the **proc contents** command again.

```
PROC CONTENTS DATA=AUTO2;
RUN;

CONTENTS PROCEDURE
Data Set Name: WORK.AUTO2       Observations:         74
Member Type:   DATA             Variables:            3
-----Alphabetic List of Variables and Attributes-----

#    Variable     Type     Len     Pos
-----------------------------------
1    MAKE         Char     20      0
3    MPG          Num       8      28
2    PRICE        Num       8      20
```

Note that the number of observations, or records, remains unchanged. This program makes a smaller version of **auto** called **auto2** that just has the three variables **make mpg** and **price**. The new file, named **auto2,** is identical to **auto** except that it contains only the variables listed in the **keep** statement. To compare the contents of the two files, run **proc contents** on each.

```
PROC CONTENTS DATA = auto;
RUN;
PROC CONTENTS DATA = auto2;
RUN;
```

The output is shown below.

```
CONTENTS PROCEDURE
Data Set Name: WORK.AUTO   Observations:         74
Member Type:   DATA        Variables:            12

-----Alphabetic List of Variables and Attributes-----

 #    Variable     Type     Len     Pos
------------------------------------
10    DISPL        Num       8      84
12    FOREIGN      Num       8     100
11    GRATIO       Num       8      92
 5    HDROOM       Num       8      44
 8    LENGTH       Num       8      68
 1    MAKE         Char     20       0
 3    MPG          Num       8      28
 2    PRICE        Num       8      20
 4    REP78        Num       8      36
 6    TRUNK        Num       8      52
 9    TURN         Num       8      76
 7    WEIGHT       Num       8      60

CONTENTS PROCEDURE
Data Set Name: WORK.AUTO2     Observations:         74
Member Type:   DATA           Variables:            3

-----Alphabetic List of Variables and Attributes-----

#    Variable     Type     Len     Pos
-----------------------------------
1    MAKE         Char     20      0
3    MPG          Num       8      28
2    PRICE        Num       8      20
```

Conversely, we can obtain the same results by using the **drop** statement.

```
DATA auto3;
   SET auto;
   DROP rep78 hdroom trunk weight length turn displ gratio foreign;
RUN;
```

The **keep** statement names variables to include, while the **drop** statement names variables to exclude.

```
PROC CONTENTS DATA = auto3;
RUN;

CONTENTS PROCEDURE
Data Set Name: WORK.AUTO3       Observations: 74
Member Type:   DATA             Variables:     3

-----Alphabetic List of Variables and Attributes-----

#    Variable     Type     Len     Pos
-----------------------------------
1    MAKE         Char     20      0
3    MPG          Num       8      28
2    PRICE        Num       8      20
```

Notice that the number of observations in all the examples above remain constant. The **keep** and **drop** statements control the selection of variables only.

## Subsetting observations

The above illustrates the use of **keep** and **drop** statements and data step options to select variables.

The subsetting **if** is typically used to control the selection of records in the file. Records, or observations in SAS, correspond to rows in a spreadsheet application.

The **auto** file contains a variable **rep78** with data values from 1 to 5, and missing, which we ascertain from running the following program.

```
PROC FREQ DATA = auto ;
  TABLES rep78 / MISSING ;
RUN ;

                                   Cumulative    Cumulative
REP78    Frequency     Percent     Frequency      Percent
-------------------------------------------------------
  .           5          6.8            5           6.8
  1           2          2.7            7           9.5
  2           8         10.8           15          20.3
  3          30         40.5           45          60.8
  4          18         24.3           63          85.1
  5          11         14.9           74         100.0
```

Note that this program includes the **/ missing** option on the **tables** statement. Without it, SAS will print only frequencies for non-missing values.

If we are only interested in cars with data for **rep78** is not missing, we may eliminate records with missing data from the file by using a subsetting **if.**

```
DATA auto2;
   SET auto;
   IF rep78 ^= . ;
RUN;
```

This program creates a new file **auto2** which will be identical to **auto**, except that it will include only observations where **rep78** has a value other than missing. **proc freq** verifies the change.

```
PROC FREQ DATA=auto2;
  TABLES rep78 / MISSING ;
RUN;

                                    Cumulative  Cumulative
REP78     Frequency    Percent     Frequency     Percent
--------------------------------------------------------
   1           2         2.9            2         2.9
   2           8        11.6           10        14.5
   3          30        43.5           40        58.0
   4          18        26.1           58        84.1
   5          11        15.9           69       100.0
```

The subsetting **if** specifies which observations to keep, i.e., only cars with data for **rep78**. Alternately, we may use the **delete** statement to specify which observations to eliminate from the file. The following program keeps in the output file only cars with repair ratings of 3 or less.

```
DATA auto2;
  SET auto;
  IF rep78 > 3 THEN DELETE ;
RUN;
```

Let's check the results using **proc freq**.

```
PROC FREQ DATA = auto2;
  TABLES rep78 / MISSING;
RUN;

                                    Cumulative  Cumulative
REP78   Frequency    Percent     Frequency     Percent
--------------------------------------------------------
   .         5         11.1            5         11.1
   1         2          4.4            7         15.6
   2         8         17.8           15         33.3
   3        30         66.7           45        100.0
```

Using the subsetting **if** statement as follows yields the same result.

```
DATA auto2;
  SET auto;
IF (rep78 <= 3);
```

The results from **proc freq** confirm this.

```
PROC FREQ DATA = auto2;
  TABLES rep78 / MISSING;
RUN;

                                    Cumulative  Cumulative
REP78   Frequency    Percent     Frequency     Percent
--------------------------------------------------------
   .         5         11.1            5         11.1
   1         2          4.4            7         15.6
   2         8         17.8           15         33.3
   3        30         66.7           45        100.0
```

Note that missing values are included, since missing values are smaller than any other value. To delete missing values, change the program as follows.

```
DATA auto2;
  SET auto;
  IF (rep78 <= 3) AND (rep78 ^= .);
run;
```

**Proc freq** confirms that missing values have been deleted.

```
PROC FREQ DATA = auto2;
  TABLES rep78 / MISSING ;
RUN;

REP78    Frequency    Percent    Frequency    Percent
----------------------------------------------------
  1           2         5.0           2          5.0
  2           8        20.0          10         25.0
  3          30        75.0          40        100.0
```

## Problems to look out for

- When you create a subset of your original data, sometimes you may drop variables or cases that you did not intend to drop. If you find variables or cases are gone that should not be gone, double check your subsetting commands.

**For more information**

- For information on making SAS data files from raw data see Inputting data into SAS.
- For information about making permanent SAS data files, see Reading and writing SAS system files
- For more advanced issues in subsetting, data transformations and data manipulation see Data transformations and manipulation in SAS in the SAS Library-Web page resources

# LABELING IN SAS

## Introduction

This module illustrates how to create and use labels in SAS. There are two main items that can be labeled, variables and values. Once created these labels will appear in the output of statistical procedures and reports that you may produce from SAS. They are also displayed by some of the SAS/GRAPH procedures. The program below reads the data and creates a temporary data file called **auto**. The labeling shown in this module are all applied to this data file called**auto**.

```
DATA auto ;
  INPUT make $  mpg rep78 weight foreign ;
CARDS;
AMC     22 3 2930 0
AMC     17 3 3350 0
AMC     22 . 2640 0
Audi    17 5 2830 1
Audi    23 3 2070 1
BMW     25 4 2650 1
Buick   20 3 3250 0
Buick   15 4 4080 0
Buick   18 3 3670 0
Buick   26 . 2230 0
Buick   20 3 3280 0
Buick   16 3 3880 0
Buick   19 3 3400 0
Cad.    14 3 4330 0
Cad.    14 2 3900 0
Cad.    21 3 4290 0
Chev.   29 3 2110 0
Chev.   16 4 3690 0
Chev.   22 3 3180 0
Chev.   22 2 3220 0
Chev.   24 2 2750 0
Chev.   19 3 3430 0
Datsun  23 4 2370 1
Datsun  35 5 2020 1
Datsun  24 4 2280 1
Datsun  21 4 2750 1
;
RUN;
PROC CONTENTS DATA=auto;
RUN;
```

The output of the **proc contents** is shown below. You can see in this portion of the output of the **proc contents** that there are no labels attached to the variables in this file.

```
-----Alphabetic List of Variables and Attributes-----

#    Variable    Type    Len    Pos
-----------------------------------
5    FOREIGN     Num       8     32
1    MAKE        Char      8      0
2    MPG         Num       8      8
3    REP78       Num       8     16
4    WEIGHT      Num       8     24
```

## Creating variable labels

We use the **label** statement in the **data** step to assign labels to the variables. You could also assign labels to variables in **proc** steps, but then the labels only exist for that step. When labels are assigned in the **data** step they are available for all procedures that use that data set.

The following program assigns variable labels to **rep78**, **mpg** and **foreign**.

```
DATA  auto2;
   SET auto;
   LABEL  rep78  ="1978 Repair Record"
          mpg    ="Miles Per Gallon"
          foreign="Where Car Was Made";
RUN;

PROC CONTENTS DATA=auto2;
RUN;
```

Looking at the output produced by the **proc contents** step shows that the labels were indeed assigned. The relevant part of this output follows.

```
-----Alphabetic List of Variables and Attributes-----

#    Variable    Type    Len    Pos    Label
---------------------------------------------------------
5    FOREIGN     Num       8     32    Where Car Was Made
1    MAKE        Char      8      0
2    MPG         Num       8      8    Miles Per Gallon
3    REP78       Num       8     16    1978 Repair Record
4    WEIGHT      Num       8     24
```

These labels will also appear on the output of other procedures giving a fuller description of the variables involved. This is demonstrated in the **proc means**below.

```
PROC MEANS DATA=auto2;
RUN;
```

Looking at the output produced by the **proc means** shows that the labels were indeed assigned. Look at the column titled **Label**. The relevant part of this output follows.

```
Variable  Label                N        Mean  Std Dev     Minimum
------------------------------------------------------------------
MPG       Miles Per Gallon    26 20.9230769   4.7575042      14
REP78     1978 Repair Record  24  3.2916667   0.8064504       2
WEIGHT                        26    3099.23 695.0794089    2020
FOREIGN   Where Car Was Made  26  0.2692308   0.4523443       0
------------------------------------------------------------------
```

## Creating and using value labels

Labeling values is a two step process. First, you must create the label formats with **proc format** using a **value** statement. Next, you attach the label format to the variable with a **format** statement. This **format** statement can be used in either **proc** or **data** steps. An example of the **proc format** step for creating the value formats, **forgnf** and **$makef** follows.

```
PROC FORMAT;
  VALUE  forgnf 0="domestic"
                1="foreign" ;
  VALUE  $makef "AMC"     ="American Motors"
                "Buick"   ="Buick (GM)"
                "Cad."    ="Cadillac (GM)"
                "Chev."   ="Chevrolet (GM)"
                "Datsun"  ="Datsun (Nissan)";
RUN;
```

You may include any number of value statements to create label formats as needed. Since **make** is a variable that contains character values, when you define the formats for it you have to precede the format name with a **$** so the format name becomes **$makef**. Additionally, for character variables the values of the variables must be enclosed in quotes.

Now that the formats **forgnf** and **$makef** have been created, they must be linked to the variables, **foreign** and **make**. This is accomplished by including a**format** statement in either a **proc** or a **data** step. In the program below the **format** statement is used in a **proc freq**.

```
PROC FREQ DATA=auto2;
   FORMAT  foreign forgnf.
           make    $makef.;
   TABLES foreign make;
RUN;
```

Notice that the formats **forgnf.** and **$makef.** are each followed by a period in the **format** statement. This is the way that SAS tells the difference between the name of a format and the name of a variable in a **format** statement.

The output of the frequencies procedure for **foreign** displays the newly defined labels instead of the values of the variable.

```
                      Where Car Was Made

                                         Cumulative  Cumulative
FOREIGN    Frequency    Percent           Frequency     Percent
----------------------------------------------------------------
domestic          19       73.1                  19        73.1
foreign            7       26.9                  26       100.0
```

The output of the frequencies procedure for **make** displays the newly defined labels instead of the values of the variable. Values for which formats haven't been defined (**Audi** and **BMW**) appear in the table without modification.

```
MAKE               Frequency   Percent   Frequency    Percent
--------------------------------------------------------------
American Motors            3      11.5           3       11.5
Audi                       2       7.7           5       19.2
BMW                        1       3.8           6       23.1
Buick (GM)                 7      26.9          13       50.0
Cadillac (GM)              3      11.5          16       61.5
Chevrolet (GM)             6      23.1          22       84.6
Datsun (Nissan)            4      15.4          26      100.0
```

If you link formats to variables in a **data** step where a permanent file is created, then every time you use that file SAS expects to find the formats. Thus you will have to supply the **proc format** code in each program that uses the file. Since this can make each of your programs much longer than you might like, I would like to provide a tip for accomplishing this task without repeating the code for the **proc format** in every program. Assuming that a small program containing only the **proc format** is stored in a file called **fmats.sas** in a directory on your **C:** drive called **myfiles**, the following statement will bring that code into your current program:

```
%INCLUDE 'C:\myfiles\fmats.sas';
```

This should save time and make maintenance of your programs easier. The remainder of your program would follow this statement.

## Problems to look out for

- Common errors in dealing with value labels are; 1) leaving off the period at the end of the format in a **format** statement, and 2) leaving off the dollar sign before a character format.
- If you leave out the **proc format** code in a program using a permanent file where formats are defined SAS will require the formats be available for use. In this case you can either follow the instructions for including code (**%include**) above, or copy the **proc format** code into your current program. You can also include the **nofmterr** option to allow the program to run with out errors.
- Another common error is to reference the format with a **format** statement before defining the format with **proc format** code. Simply move your **proc format** code to the beginning of the program to fix this problem.

# USING PROC SORT AND BY STATEMENTS

## Introduction

This module will examine the use of **proc sort** and use of the **by** statement with SAS procedures. The program below creates a data file called **auto** that we will use in our examples. Note that this file has a duplicate record for the BMW.

```
DATA auto ;
  INPUT make $  mpg rep78 weight foreign ;
CARDS ;
AMC     22 3 2930 0
AMC     17 3 3350 0
AMC     22 . 2640 0
Audi    17 5 2830 1
Audi    23 3 2070 1
BMW     25 4 2650 1
BMW     25 4 2650 1
Buick   20 3 3250 0
Buick   15 4 4080 0
Buick   18 3 3670 0
Buick   26 . 2230 0
Buick   20 3 3280 0
Buick   16 3 3880 0
Buick   19 3 3400 0
Cad.    14 3 4330 0
Cad.    14 2 3900 0
Cad.    21 3 4290 0
Chev.   29 3 2110 0
Chev.   16 4 3690 0
Chev.   22 3 3180 0
Chev.   22 2 3220 0
Chev.   24 2 2750 0
Chev.   19 3 3430 0
Datsun  23 4 2370 1
Datsun  35 5 2020 1
Datsun  24 4 2280 1
Datsun  21 4 2750 1
;
RUN ;

PROC PRINT DATA=auto ;
RUN ;
```

The output from the program is shown below. The **proc print** shows that the data file has been successfully created.

| OBS | MAKE | MPG | REP78 | WEIGHT | FOREIGN |
|---|---|---|---|---|---|
| 1 | AMC | 22 | 3 | 2930 | 0 |
| 2 | AMC | 17 | 3 | 3350 | 0 |
| 3 | AMC | 22 | . | 2640 | 0 |
| 4 | Audi | 17 | 5 | 2830 | 1 |
| 5 | Audi | 23 | 3 | 2070 | 1 |
| 6 | BMW | 25 | 4 | 2650 | 1 |
| 7 | BMW | 25 | 4 | 2650 | 1 |
| 8 | Buick | 20 | 3 | 3250 | 0 |
| 9 | Buick | 15 | 4 | 4080 | 0 |
| 10 | Buick | 18 | 3 | 3670 | 0 |
| 11 | Buick | 26 | . | 2230 | 0 |
| 12 | Buick | 20 | 3 | 3280 | 0 |
| 13 | Buick | 16 | 3 | 3880 | 0 |
| 14 | Buick | 19 | 3 | 3400 | 0 |
| 15 | Cad. | 14 | 3 | 4330 | 0 |
| 16 | Cad. | 14 | 2 | 3900 | 0 |
| 17 | Cad. | 21 | 3 | 4290 | 0 |
| 18 | Chev. | 29 | 3 | 2110 | 0 |
| 19 | Chev. | 16 | 4 | 3690 | 0 |
| 20 | Chev. | 22 | 3 | 3180 | 0 |
| 21 | Chev. | 22 | 2 | 3220 | 0 |
| 22 | Chev. | 24 | 2 | 2750 | 0 |
| 23 | Chev. | 19 | 3 | 3430 | 0 |
| 24 | Datsun | 23 | 4 | 2370 | 1 |
| 25 | Datsun | 35 | 5 | 2020 | 1 |
| 26 | Datsun | 24 | 4 | 2280 | 1 |
| 27 | Datsun | 21 | 4 | 2750 | 1 |

## Sorting data with proc sort

We can use **proc sort** to sort this data file. The program below sorts the **auto** data file on the variable **foreign** (1=foreign car, 0=domestic car) and saves the sorted file as **auto2**. The original file remains unchanged since we used **out=auto2** to specify that the sorted data should be placed in **auto2**.

```
PROC SORT DATA=auto OUT=auto2 ;
  BY foreign ;
RUN ;

PROC PRINT DATA=auto2 ;
RUN ;
```

| OBS | MAKE | MPG | REP78 | WEIGHT | FOREIGN |
|---|---|---|---|---|---|
| 1 | AMC | 22 | 3 | 2930 | 0 |
| 2 | AMC | 17 | 3 | 3350 | 0 |
| 3 | AMC | 22 | . | 2640 | 0 |
| 4 | Buick | 20 | 3 | 3250 | 0 |
| 5 | Buick | 15 | 4 | 4080 | 0 |
| 6 | Buick | 18 | 3 | 3670 | 0 |
| 7 | Buick | 26 | . | 2230 | 0 |
| 8 | Buick | 20 | 3 | 3280 | 0 |
| 9 | Buick | 16 | 3 | 3880 | 0 |
| 10 | Buick | 19 | 3 | 3400 | 0 |
| 11 | Cad. | 14 | 3 | 4330 | 0 |
| 12 | Cad. | 14 | 2 | 3900 | 0 |
| 13 | Cad. | 21 | 3 | 4290 | 0 |
| 14 | Chev. | 29 | 3 | 2110 | 0 |
| 15 | Chev. | 16 | 4 | 3690 | 0 |
| 16 | Chev. | 22 | 3 | 3180 | 0 |
| 17 | Chev. | 22 | 2 | 3220 | 0 |
| 18 | Chev. | 24 | 2 | 2750 | 0 |
| 19 | Chev. | 19 | 3 | 3430 | 0 |
| 20 | Audi | 17 | 5 | 2830 | 1 |
| 21 | Audi | 23 | 3 | 2070 | 1 |
| 22 | BMW | 25 | 4 | 2650 | 1 |
| 23 | BMW | 25 | 4 | 2650 | 1 |
| 24 | Datsun | 23 | 4 | 2370 | 1 |
| 25 | Datsun | 35 | 5 | 2020 | 1 |
| 26 | Datsun | 24 | 4 | 2280 | 1 |
| 27 | Datsun | 21 | 4 | 2750 | 1 |

From the **proc print** below, you can see that **auto2** is indeed sorted on **foreign**. The observations where **foreign** is 0 precede all of the observations where**foreign** is 1. Note that the order of the observations within each group remain unchanged, (i.e., the observations where **foreign** is 0 remain in the same order).

Suppose you wanted the data sorted, but with the foreign cars (**foreign**=1) first and the domestic cars (**foreign**=0) second. The example below shows the use of the **descending** keyword to tell SAS that you want to sort by **foreign**, but you want the sort order reversed (i.e., largest to smallest).

```
PROC SORT DATA=auto OUT=auto3 ;
  BY DESCENDING foreign ;
RUN ;

PROC PRINT DATA=auto3 ;
RUN ;
```

You can see in the **proc print** below that the data are now ordered by **foreign**, but highest to lowest.

| OBS | MAKE | MPG | REP78 | WEIGHT | FOREIGN |
|---|---|---|---|---|---|
| 1 | Audi | 17 | 5 | 2830 | 1 |
| 2 | Audi | 23 | 3 | 2070 | 1 |
| 3 | BMW | 25 | 4 | 2650 | 1 |
| 4 | BMW | 25 | 4 | 2650 | 1 |
| 5 | Datsun | 23 | 4 | 2370 | 1 |
| 6 | Datsun | 35 | 5 | 2020 | 1 |
| 7 | Datsun | 24 | 4 | 2280 | 1 |
| 8 | Datsun | 21 | 4 | 2750 | 1 |
| 9 | AMC | 22 | 3 | 2930 | 0 |
| 10 | AMC | 17 | 3 | 3350 | 0 |
| 11 | AMC | 22 | . | 2640 | 0 |
| 12 | Buick | 20 | 3 | 3250 | 0 |
| 13 | Buick | 15 | 4 | 4080 | 0 |
| 14 | Buick | 18 | 3 | 3670 | 0 |
| 15 | Buick | 26 | . | 2230 | 0 |
| 16 | Buick | 20 | 3 | 3280 | 0 |
| 17 | Buick | 16 | 3 | 3880 | 0 |
| 18 | Buick | 19 | 3 | 3400 | 0 |
| 19 | Cad. | 14 | 3 | 4330 | 0 |
| 20 | Cad. | 14 | 2 | 3900 | 0 |
| 21 | Cad. | 21 | 3 | 4290 | 0 |
| 22 | Chev. | 29 | 3 | 2110 | 0 |
| 23 | Chev. | 16 | 4 | 3690 | 0 |
| 24 | Chev. | 22 | 3 | 3180 | 0 |
| 25 | Chev. | 22 | 2 | 3220 | 0 |
| 26 | Chev. | 24 | 2 | 2750 | 0 |
| 27 | Chev. | 19 | 3 | 3430 | 0 |

It is also possible to sort on more than one variable at a time. Perhaps you would like the data sorted on **foreign** (this time we will go back to the normal sort order for **foreign**) and then sorted by **rep78** within each level of **foreign**. The example below shows how this can be done.

```
PROC SORT DATA=auto OUT=auto4 ;
  BY foreign rep78 ;
RUN ;

PROC PRINT DATA=auto4 ;
RUN ;
```

You can see in the **proc print** below that the data are now ordered by **foreign**, domestic cars (**foreign**=0) followed by foreign (**foreign**=1) cars. Within the domestic cars, the data are sorted by **rep78** and within foreign cars the data are also sorted by **rep78**.

| OBS | MAKE | MPG | REP78 | WEIGHT | FOREIGN |
|---|---|---|---|---|---|
| 1 | AMC | 22 | . | 2640 | 0 |
| 2 | Buick | 26 | . | 2230 | 0 |
| 3 | Cad. | 14 | 2 | 3900 | 0 |
| 4 | Chev. | 22 | 2 | 3220 | 0 |
| 5 | Chev. | 24 | 2 | 2750 | 0 |
| 6 | AMC | 22 | 3 | 2930 | 0 |
| 7 | AMC | 17 | 3 | 3350 | 0 |
| 8 | Buick | 20 | 3 | 3250 | 0 |
| 9 | Buick | 18 | 3 | 3670 | 0 |
| 10 | Buick | 20 | 3 | 3280 | 0 |
| 11 | Buick | 16 | 3 | 3880 | 0 |
| 12 | Buick | 19 | 3 | 3400 | 0 |
| 13 | Cad. | 14 | 3 | 4330 | 0 |
| 14 | Cad. | 21 | 3 | 4290 | 0 |
| 15 | Chev. | 29 | 3 | 2110 | 0 |
| 16 | Chev. | 22 | 3 | 3180 | 0 |
| 17 | Chev. | 19 | 3 | 3430 | 0 |
| 18 | Buick | 15 | 4 | 4080 | 0 |
| 19 | Chev. | 16 | 4 | 3690 | 0 |
| 20 | Audi | 23 | 3 | 2070 | 1 |
| 21 | BMW | 25 | 4 | 2650 | 1 |
| 22 | BMW | 25 | 4 | 2650 | 1 |
| 23 | Datsun | 23 | 4 | 2370 | 1 |
| 24 | Datsun | 24 | 4 | 2280 | 1 |
| 25 | Datsun | 21 | 4 | 2750 | 1 |
| 26 | Audi | 17 | 5 | 2830 | 1 |
| 27 | Datsun | 35 | 5 | 2020 | 1 |

In the output above, note how the missing values of **rep78** were treated. Since a missing value is treated as the lowest value possible (e.g., negative infinity), the missing values come before all other values of **rep78**.

## Removing duplicates with proc sort

At the beginning of this page, we noted that there was a duplicate observation in **auto**, that there were two identical records for BMW. We can use **proc sort** to remove the duplicate observations from our data file using the **noduplicates** option, **as long as the duplicate observations are next to each other**. The example below sorts the data by **foreign** and removes the duplicates at the same time. Note that it did not matter what variable we chose for sorting the data. As you see in the output below, the extra observation for BMW was deleted.

| Obs | make | mpg | rep78 | weight | foreign |
|---|---|---|---|---|---|
| 1 | AMC | 22 | 3 | 2930 | 0 |
| 2 | AMC | 17 | 3 | 3350 | 0 |
| 3 | AMC | 22 | . | 2640 | 0 |
| 4 | Buick | 20 | 3 | 3250 | 0 |
| 5 | Buick | 15 | 4 | 4080 | 0 |
| 6 | Buick | 18 | 3 | 3670 | 0 |
| 7 | Buick | 26 | . | 2230 | 0 |
| 8 | Buick | 20 | 3 | 3280 | 0 |
| 9 | Buick | 16 | 3 | 3880 | 0 |
| 10 | Buick | 19 | 3 | 3400 | 0 |
| 11 | Cad. | 14 | 3 | 4330 | 0 |
| 12 | Cad. | 14 | 2 | 3900 | 0 |
| 13 | Cad. | 21 | 3 | 4290 | 0 |
| 14 | Chev. | 29 | 3 | 2110 | 0 |
| 15 | Chev. | 16 | 4 | 3690 | 0 |
| 16 | Chev. | 22 | 3 | 3180 | 0 |
| 17 | Chev. | 22 | 2 | 3220 | 0 |
| 18 | Chev. | 24 | 2 | 2750 | 0 |
| 19 | Chev. | 19 | 3 | 3430 | 0 |
| 20 | Audi | 17 | 5 | 2830 | 1 |
| 21 | Audi | 23 | 3 | 2070 | 1 |
| **22** | **BMW** | **25** | **4** | **2650** | **1** |
| 23 | Datsun | 23 | 4 | 2370 | 1 |
| 24 | Datsun | 35 | 5 | 2020 | 1 |
| 25 | Datsun | 24 | 4 | 2280 | 1 |
| 26 | Datsun | 21 | 4 | 2750 | 1 |

When you use the **noduplicates** option, the SAS Log displays a note telling you how many duplicates were removed. As you see below, SAS informs us that 1 duplicate observation was deleted.

```
PROC SORT DATA=auto OUT=auto5 NODUPLICATES ;
  BY foreign ;
RUN ;

NOTE: 1 duplicate observations were deleted.
NOTE: The data set WORK.AUTO3 has 26 observations and 5 variables.
```

It is common for duplicate observations to be next to each other in the same file, but if the duplicate observations are not next to each other, there is another strategy you can use to remove the duplicates. You can sort the data file by all of the variables (which can be indicated with the special keyword**_ALL_**), which would force the duplicate observations to be next to each other. This is illustrated below.

```
PROC SORT DATA=auto OUT=auto6 NODUPLICATES ;
  BY _all_ ;
RUN ;
```

## Obtaining separate analyses with sorted data

Sometimes you would like to obtain results separately for different groups. For example, you might want to get the mean **mpg** and **weight** separately for**foreign** and **domestic** cars. As you see below, it is possible to use **proc means** with the **class** statement to get these results.

```
PROC MEANS DATA=auto ;
  CLASS foreign ;
  VAR mpg weight ;
RUN ;
```

However, what if you wanted to obtain the correlation of **weight** and **mpg** separately for foreign and domestic cars? **Proc corr** does not support a **class**statement like **proc means** does, but you can use the **by** statement as in the example below.

```
PROC SORT DATA=auto OUT=auto6 ;
  BY foreign ;
RUN ;

PROC CORR DATA=auto6 ;
  BY foreign ;
  VAR weight mpg ;
RUN ;
```

As you see in the output below, using the **by** statement resulted in getting a **proc corr** for the domestic cars and a **proc corr** for the foreign cars. In general, using the **by** statement requests that the **proc** be performed for every level of the **by** variable (in this case, for every level of **foreign**).

```
FOREIGN=0

Correlation Analysis
   2 'VAR' Variables:  WEIGHT   MPG

                                      Simple Statistics

Variable   N          Mean       Std Dev           Sum       Minimum       Maximum
WEIGHT    19   3347.894737    627.176911         63610   2110.000000   4330.000000
MPG       19     19.789474      4.035660    376.000000     14.000000     29.000000

Pearson Correlation Coefficients / Prob > |R| under Ho: Rho=0 / N = 19

                WEIGHT          MPG
WEIGHT         1.00000     -0.86236
                0.0          0.0001

MPG           -0.86236      1.00000
               0.0001        0.0

FOREIGN=1

Correlation Analysis

   2 'VAR' Variables:  WEIGHT   MPG
                                      Simple Statistics

Variable   N          Mean       Std Dev           Sum       Minimum       Maximum
WEIGHT     8   2452.500000    311.436763         19620   2020.000000   2830.000000
MPG        8     24.125000      5.111262    193.000000     17.000000     35.000000

Pearson Correlation Coefficients / Prob > |R| under Ho: Rho=0 / N = 8

                WEIGHT          MPG
WEIGHT         1.00000     -0.66702
                0.0          0.0708

MPG           -0.66702      1.00000
               0.0708        0.0
```

Here are other examples of where you might use a **by** statement with the **auto** data file. (Note that some of these analyses are not very practical because of the small size of the **auto** data file, so please imagine that we would be analyzing a larger version of the **auto** data file.)

- You might use a **by** statement with **proc univariate** to request univariate statistics for **mpg** separately for foreign and domestic cars so you can seen if **mpg** is normally distributed for foreign cars and normally distributed for domestic cars. This also allows you to generate **side by side box and whisker** plots allowing you to compare the distributions of **mpg** for the separate groups.

- You might use a **by** statement with **proc reg** if you would like to do separate regression analyses for foreign and domestic cars.

- You might use a **by** statement with **proc means** even though it has the **class** statement. If you wanted the means displayed on separate pages, then using the **by** statement would give you the kind of output you desire.

**Problems to look out for**

- If you use a **BY** statement in a procedure, make sure the data has been sorted first. For example, if you use **by foreign** then be sure that you have first sorted the file **by foreign**.

- If you want to delete duplicate observations **and** the duplicate observations are not next to each other, be sure to sort the data on all of the variables (i.e., using **by _ALL_;** ) so the **noduplicates** option will work properly and indeed remove duplicate observations.

**For more information**

For more information about **proc sort** see the chapter on **PROC SORT** in the SAS Procedures Guide.

## MAKING AND USING PERMANENT SAS DATA FILES (VERSION 8)

Making and using permanent SAS data files (version 8)

This will illustrate how to make and use SAS data files in version 8. If you have used SAS version 6.xx, you will notice it is much easier to create and use permanent SAS data files in SAS version 8.

Consider this simple example. This shows how you can make a SAS version 8 file the traditional way using a **libname** statement. The file **salary** will be stored in the directory **c:\dissertation**.

```
libname diss 'c:\dissertation\';

data diss.salary;
  input sal1996-sal2000 ;
  cards;
10000 10500 11000 12000 12700
14000 16500 18000 22000 29000
;
run;
```

Below we use **proc print** and **proc contents** to look at the file that we have created.

```
proc print data=diss.salary;
run;

proc contents data=diss.salary;
run;
```

We can see the data from the **proc print** and the **proc contents** shows us the data file that has been created, called **c:\dissertation\salary.sas7bdat**.

```
Obs    sal1996    sal1997    sal1998    sal1999    sal2000
 1      10000      10500      11000      12000      12700
 2      14000      16500      18000      22000      29000

The CONTENTS Procedure

Data Set Name: DISS.SALARY                                 Observations:         2
Member Type:   DATA                                        Variables:            5
Engine:        V8                                          Indexes:              0
Created:       16:53 Thursday, November 16, 2000           Observation Length:   40
Last Modified: 16:53 Thursday, November 16, 2000           Deleted Observations: 0
Protection:                                                Compressed:           NO
Data Set Type:                                             Sorted:               NO
Label:
         -----Engine/Host Dependent Information-----
<output edited to save space>
File Name:                    c:\dissertation\salary.sas7bdat
Release Created:              8.0101M0
Host Created:                 WIN_NT

-----Alphabetic List of Variables and Attributes-----

#    Variable    Type    Len    Pos
-----------------------------------
1    sal1996     Num       8      0
2    sal1997     Num       8      8
3    sal1998     Num       8     16
4    sal1999     Num       8     24
5    sal2000     Num       8     32
```

Below we make a file similar to the one above, but we will illustrate some of the new features in SAS version 8. First, we did not need to use a **libname**statement. We were able to specify the name of the data file by directly specifying the path name of the file (i.e., **c:\dissertation\salarylong**). Also note that the names of the variables are over 8 characters long. They can be up to 32 characters long. This step creates a data file named**c:\dissertation\salarylong.sas7bdat** .

```
data 'c:\dissertation\salarylong';
  input Salary1996-Salary2000 ;
cards;
10000 10500 11000 12000 12700
14000 16500 18000 22000 29000
;
run;
```

Below we can do a **proc print** and **proc contents** on this data file.

```
proc print data='c:\dissertation\salarylong';
run;
proc contents data='c:\dissertation\salarylong';
run;
```

Note the names of the variables in the **proc print** and **proc contents** below SAS shows the variable name as **Salary1996**showing that we used an uppercase **S**. When you first create a variable, SAS will remember the case of each of the letters and show the variable names using the case you originally used. However, you do **not** need to always refer to the variable as**Salary1996**, you can refer to it as **SALARY1996** or as **salary1996** or however you like, as long as the variable is spelled properly. But this can help make your variable names more readable for outputs.

```
Obs    Salary1996    Salary1997    Salary1998    Salary1999    Salary2000
 1        10000         10500         11000         12000         12700
 2        14000         16500         18000         22000         29000

The CONTENTS Procedure
Data Set Name: c:\dissertation\salarylong                    Observations:          2
Member Type:   DATA                                          Variables:             5
Engine:        V8                                            Indexes:               0
Created:       16:53 Thursday, November 16, 2000             Observation Length:    40
Last Modified: 16:53 Thursday, November 16, 2000             Deleted Observations:  0
Protection:                                                  Compressed:            NO
Data Set Type:                                               Sorted:                NO
Label:
         -----Engine/Host Dependent Information-----
<output edited to save space>
File Name:                 c:\dissertation\salarylong.sas7bdat
Release Created:           8.0101M0
Host Created:              WIN_NT

-----Alphabetic List of Variables and Attributes-----

#    Variable      Type    Len    Pos
-------------------------------------
1    Salary1996    Num       8      0
2    Salary1997    Num       8      8
3    Salary1998    Num       8     16
4    Salary1999    Num       8     24
5    Salary2000    Num       8     32
```

When you read and write SAS version 8 files, you can choose whether you wish to use the **libname** statement as we showed in our first example, or if you prefer to write out the name of the file as we showed in our second example. Either will work with SAS version 8 data files. If you are unsure of whether a SAS data file is a version 8 data file, you can look at the extension of the file. If it ends with **.sas7bdat** then it is a version 8 data file that can be used on the PC or on UNIX. However, if the extension is **.sd2** it is a Windows SAS 6.12 file, or if the extension is **.ssd01** it is a Unix SAS 6.12 file.

## MATCH MERGING DATA FILES IN SAS

### Introduction

When you have two data files, you can combine them by merging them side by side, matching up observations based on an identifier. For example, below we have a data file containing information on dads and we have a file containing information on family income called **faminc**. We would like to match merge the files together so we have the dads observation on the same line with the **faminc** observation based on the key variable **famid**.

```
dads

famid name inc
2     Art  22000
1     Bill 30000
3     Paul 25000

faminc

famid faminc96 faminc97 faminc98
3     75000    76000    77000
1     40000    40500    41000
2     45000    45400    45800
```

After match merging the files, they would look like this.

```
famid name    inc faminc96 faminc97 faminc98
  1   Bill  30000    40000    40500    41000
  2   Art   22000    45000    45400    45800
  3   Paul  25000    75000    76000    77000
```

### One-to-one merge

There are three steps to match merge the **dads** file with the **faminc** file (this is called a **one-to-one** merge because there is a one to one correspondence between the **dads** and **faminc** records). These three steps are illustrated in the SAS program **merge1.sas** below.

1. Use **proc sort** to sort **dads** on **famid** and save that file (we will call it **dads2**)

2. Use **proc sort** to sort **faminc** on **famid** and save that file (we will call it **faminc2**)

3. merge the **dads2** and **faminc2** files based on **famid**

These three steps are illustrated in the program below.

```
* We first created the dads and faminc data files below ;

DATA dads;
  INPUT famid name $ inc ;
CARDS;
2 Art  22000
1 Bill 30000
3 Paul 25000
;
RUN;

DATA faminc;
  INPUT famid faminc96 faminc97 faminc98 ;
CARDS;
3 75000 76000 77000
1 40000 40500 41000
2 45000 45400 45800

* 1. Sort the dads file by "famid" & save sorted file as dads2 ;

PROC SORT DATA=dads OUT=dads2;
  BY famid;
RUN;

* 2. Sort faminc by "famid" & save sorted file as faminc2 ;

PROC SORT DATA=faminc OUT=faminc2;
  BY famid;
RUN;

* 3. Merge dads2 and faminc2 by famid in a data step ;

DATA dadfam ;
  MERGE dads2 faminc2;
  BY famid;
RUN;

* Let's do a proc print and look at the results. ;

PROC PRINT DATA=dadfam;
RUN;
```

The output of the program is shown below.

| OBS | FAMID | NAME | INC | FAMINC96 | FAMINC97 | FAMINC98 |
|---|---|---|---|---|---|---|
| 1 | 1 | Bill | 30000 | 40000 | 40500 | 41000 |
| 2 | 2 | Art | 22000 | 45000 | 45400 | 45800 |
| 3 | 3 | Paul | 25000 | 75000 | 76000 | 77000 |

The output from shows that the match merge worked properly. The **dad** and **faminc** are merged side by side. The next example considers a **one-to-many**merge where one observation in one file may have multiple matching records in another file. We will see that kind of merge is really no different from the**one-to-one** merge we saw here.

## One-to-many merge

Imagine that we had a file with dads like we saw in the previous example, and we had a file with kids where a dad could have more than one kid. Matching up the "dads" with the "kids" is called a "one-to-many" merge since you are matching one dad observation to possibly many kids records. The dads and kids records are shown below.

dads

| famid | name | inc |
|---|---|---|
| 2 | Art | 22000 |
| 1 | Bill | 30000 |
| 3 | Paul | 25000 |

kids

| famid | kidname | birth | age | wt | sex |
|---|---|---|---|---|---|
| 1 | Beth | 1 | 9 | 60 | f |
| 1 | Bob | 2 | 6 | 40 | m |
| 1 | Barb | 3 | 3 | 20 | f |
| 2 | Andy | 1 | 8 | 80 | m |
| 2 | Al | 2 | 6 | 50 | m |
| 2 | Ann | 3 | 2 | 20 | f |
| 3 | Pete | 1 | 6 | 60 | m |
| 3 | Pam | 2 | 4 | 40 | f |
| 3 | Phil | 3 | 2 | 20 | m |

After matching the **dads** with the **kids** you get a file that looks like the one below. **Bill** is matched up with his kids **Beth, Bob** and **Barb**; **Art** is matched up with **Andy Al,** and **Ann**; and **Paul** is matched up with **Pete, Pam** and **Phil**.

dadkid

| FAMID | NAME | INC | KIDNAME | BIRTH | AGE | WT | SEX |
|---|---|---|---|---|---|---|---|
| 1 | Bill | 30000 | Beth | 1 | 9 | 60 | f |
| 1 | Bill | 30000 | Bob | 2 | 6 | 40 | m |
| 1 | Bill | 30000 | Barb | 3 | 3 | 20 | f |
| 2 | Art | 22000 | Andy | 1 | 8 | 80 | m |
| 2 | Art | 22000 | Al | 2 | 6 | 50 | m |
| 2 | Art | 22000 | Ann | 3 | 2 | 20 | f |
| 3 | Paul | 25000 | Pete | 1 | 6 | 60 | m |
| 3 | Paul | 25000 | Pam | 2 | 4 | 40 | f |
| 3 | Paul | 25000 | Phil | 3 | 2 | 20 | m |

Just like the "one-to-one" merge, we follow the same three steps for a "one-to-many" merge. These three steps are illustrated in the SAS program**merge2.sas** below.

1. Use **proc sort** to sort **dads** on **famid** and save that file (we will call it **dads2**)
2. Use **proc sort** to sort **kids** on **famid** and save that file (we will call it **kids2**)
3. merge the **dads2** and **kids2** files based on **famid**

The program below illustrates these steps.

```
* first we make the "dads" data file ;

DATA dads;
  INPUT famid name $ inc ;
CARDS;
2 Art  22000
1 Bill   30000
3 Paul  25000
;
RUN;

* Next we make the "kids" data file ;

DATA kids;
  INPUT famid kidname $ birth age wt sex $ ;
CARDS;
1 Beth 1 9 60 f
1 Bob  2 6 40 m
1 Barb 3 3 20 f
2 Andy 1 8 80 m
2 Al   2 6 50 m
2 Ann  3 2 20 f
3 Pete 1 6 60 m
3 Pam  2 4 40 f
3 Phil 3 2 20 m
;
RUN;
```

```
* 1. sort "dads" on famid and save the sorted file as "dads2" ;

PROC SORT DATA=dads OUT=dads2;
  BY famid;
RUN;

* 2. sort "kids" on famid and save the sorted file as "kids2" ;

PROC SORT DATA=kids OUT=kids2;
  BY famid;
RUN;

* 3. merge "dads2" and "kids2" based on famid, creating "dadkid" ;

DATA dadkid;
  MERGE dads2 kids2;
  BY famid;
RUN;

* Let's do a PROC PRINT of "dadkid" to see if the merge worked ;

PROC PRINT DATA=dadkid;
RUN;
```

The output of the program is shown below.

```
OBS FAMID NAME   INC   KIDNAME BIRTH AGE WT SEX

 1    1   Bill  30000  Beth      1    9  60  f
 2    1   Bill  30000  Bob       2    6  40  m
 3    1   Bill  30000  Barb      3    3  20  f
 4    2   Art   22000  Andy      1    8  80  m
 5    2   Art   22000  Al        2    6  50  m
 6    2   Art   22000  Ann       3    2  20  f
 7    3   Paul  25000  Pete      1    6  60  m
 8    3   Paul  25000  Pam       2    4  40  f
 9    3   Paul  25000  Phil      3    2  20  m
```

The output shows just what we hoped to see, the dads merged along side of their kids. You might have wondered what would have happened if the **merge**statement had reversed the order of the files, had we changed step 3 to look like below.

```
* 3. merge "dads2" and "kids2" based on famid, creating "dadkid" ;

DATA dadkid;
  MERGE kids2 dads2;
  BY famid;
RUN;

* Let's do a PROC PRINT of "dadkid" see what happens ;

PROC PRINT DATA=dadkid;
RUN;
```

The output with the modified step 3 is shown below.

```
OBS FAMID KIDNAME BIRTH AGE WT SEX NAME  INC

 1    1    Beth     1    9  60  f  Bill 30000
 2    1    Bob      2    6  40  m  Bill 30000
 3    1    Barb     3    3  20  f  Bill 30000
 4    2    Andy     1    8  80  m  Art  22000
 5    2    Al       2    6  50  m  Art  22000
 6    2    Ann      3    2  20  f  Art  22000
 7    3    Pete     1    6  60  m  Paul 25000
 8    3    Pam      2    4  40  f  Paul 25000
 9    3    Phil     3    2  20  m  Paul 25000
```

This output shows what happened when we switched the order of **kids2** and **dads2** in the **merge** statement. The merge results are basically the same, except that the order of the variables is modified -- the kids variables are on the left and the dads variables are at the right. Other than that, the results are the same.

## Problems to look out for

These examples cover situations where there are no complications. We show some examples of complications that can arise and how you can solve them below.

### *Mismatching records in one-to-one merge*

The two data files have may have records that do not match. Below we illustrate this by including an extra dad (**Karl** in **famid**4) that does not have a corresponding family, and there are two extra families (5 and 6) in the family file that do not have a corresponding dad.

```
DATA dads;
 INPUT famid name $ inc;
DATALINES;
2 Art  22000
1 Bill 30000
3 Paul 25000
4 Karl 95000
;
RUN;

DATA faminc;
 INPUT famid faminc96 faminc97 faminc98;
DATALINES;
3 75000 76000 77000
1 40000 40500 41000
2 45000 45400 45800
5 55000 65000 70000
6 22000 24000 28000
;
RUN;

PROC SORT DATA=dads;
 BY famid;
RUN;

PROC SORT DATA=faminc;
 BY famid;
RUN;

DATA merge121;
  MERGE dads(IN=fromdadx) faminc(IN=fromfamx);
  BY famid;
  fromdad = fromdadx;
  fromfam = fromfamx;
RUN;
```

As you see above, we use the **in** option to create a 0/1 variable **fromdadx** that indicates whether the resulting file contains a record with data from the **dads** file. Likewise, we use **IN** option to create a 0/1 variable **fromfamx** that indicates if the observation came from the **faminc** file. The **fromdadx** and **fromfamx** variables are temporary, so we make copies of them in**fromdad** and **fromfam** so we have copies of these variables that stay with the file. We can then use **proc print** and **proc freq** to identify the mismatching records.

```
PROC PRINT DATA=merge121;
RUN;
PROC FREQ DATA=merge121;
TABLES fromdad*fromfam;
RUN;
```

The output below illustrates that there were mismatching records. For **famid** 4, the value of **fromdad** is 1 and **fromfam** is 0, as we would expect since there was data from **dads** for **famid** 4, but no data from **faminc**. Also, as we expect, this record has valid data for the variables from the **dads** file (**name** and **inc**) and missing data for the variables from **faminc** (**faminc96 faminc97** and **faminc98**). We see the reverse pattern for **famid**'s5 and 6.

| OBS | FAMID | NAME | INC | FAMINC96 | FAMINC97 | FAMINC98 | FROMDAD | FROMFAM |
|---|---|---|---|---|---|---|---|---|
| 1 | 1 | Bill | 30000 | 40000 | 40500 | 41000 | 1 | 1 |
| 2 | 2 | Art | 22000 | 45000 | 45400 | 45800 | 1 | 1 |
| 3 | 3 | Paul | 25000 | 75000 | 76000 | 77000 | 1 | 1 |
| 4 | 4 | Karl | 95000 | . | . | . | 1 | 0 |
| 5 | 5 | | . | 55000 | 65000 | 70000 | 0 | 1 |
| 6 | 6 | | . | 22000 | 24000 | 28000 | 0 | 1 |

A closer look at the **fromdad** and **fromfam** variables reveals that there are three records that have matching data: one that has data from the **dads** only, and two records that have data from the **faminc** file only. The crosstab table below confirms this.

```
TABLE OF FROMDAD BY FROMFAM

FROMDAD     FROMFAM

Frequency|
Percent  |
Row Pct  |
Col Pct  |       0|       1|  Total
---------+--------+--------+
       0 |      0 |      2 |      2
         |   0.00 |  33.33 |  33.33
         |   0.00 | 100.00 |
         |   0.00 |  40.00 |
---------+--------+--------+
       1 |      1 |      3 |      4
         |  16.67 |  50.00 |  66.67
         |  25.00 |  75.00 |
         | 100.00 |  60.00 |
---------+--------+--------+
Total           1        5        6
            16.67    83.33   100.00
```

You may want to use this strategy to check the matching of the two files. If there are unexpected mismatched records, then you should investigate to understand the cause of the mismatched records.

Use the **where** statement in a **proc print** to eliminate some of the non-matching records.

***Variables with the same name, but different information***

Below we have the files with the information about the dads and family, but look more closely at the names of the variables. In the **dads** file, there is a variable called **inc98**, and in the family file there are variables **inc96, inc97** and **inc98.** Let's attempt to merge these files and see what happens.

```
DATA dads;
 INPUT famid name $ inc98;
DATALINES;
2 Art  22000
1 Bill 30000
3 Paul 25000
;
RUN;

DATA faminc;
 INPUT famid inc96 inc97 inc98;
DATALINES;
3 75000 76000 77000
1 40000 40500 41000
2 45000 45400 45800
;
RUN;

PROC SORT DATA=dads;
 BY famid;
RUN;

PROC SORT DATA=faminc;
 BY famid;
RUN;

DATA merge121;
 MERGE faminc dads;
 BY famid;
RUN;

PROC PRINT DATA=merge121;
RUN;
```

The results are shown below. As you see, the variable **inc98** has the data from the **dads** file, the file that appears last on the**merge** statement. When you merge files that have the same variable, SAS will use the values from the file that appears last on the **merge** statement.

| OBS | FAMID | INC96 | INC97 | INC98 | NAME |
|---|---|---|---|---|---|
| 1 | 1 | 40000 | 40500 | 30000 | Bill |
| 2 | 2 | 45000 | 45400 | 22000 | Art |
| 3 | 3 | 75000 | 76000 | 25000 | Paul |

There are a couple of ways you can solve this problem.

**Solution #1**. The most obvious solution is to choose variable names in the original files that will not conflict with each other. However, you may have files where the names have already been chosen.

**Solution #2.** You can rename the variables in a **data step** using the **rename** option (which renames the variables before doing the merging). This allows you to select variable names that do not conflict with each other, as illustrated below.

```
DATA merge121;
MERGE faminc(RENAME=(inc96=faminc96 inc97=faminc97 inc98=faminc98))
dads(RENAME=(inc98=dadinc98));
BY famid;
RUN;
PROC PRINT DATA=merge121;
RUN;
```

As you can see below, the variables were renamed as specified.

```
OBS   FAMID   FAMINC96   FAMINC97   FAMINC98   NAME   DADINC98

 1      1      40000      40500      41000     Bill    30000
 2      2      45000      45400      45800     Art     22000
 3      3      75000      76000      77000     Paul    25000
```

# CONCATENATING DATA FILES IN SAS

## Introduction

When you have two data files, you may want to combine them by stacking them one on top of the other (referred to as **concatenating** files). Below we have a file called **dads** and a file containing **moms**.

```
dads

famid name inc
2     Art  22000
1     Bill 30000
3     Paul 25000

moms

famid name inc
1     Bess 15000
3     Pat  50000
2     Amy  18000
```

Below we have stacked (concatenated) these files creating a file we called **momdad**. These examples will show how to concatenate files in SAS.

```
momdad

famid name inc
2     Art  22000
1     Bill 30000
3     Paul 25000
1     Bess 15000
3     Pat  50000
2     Amy  18000
```

## Concatenating the moms and dads

The SAS program below creates a SAS data file called **dads** and a file called **moms**. It then combines them (concatenates them) creating a file called**dadmom**.

```
* Here is a file with information about dads with their family id name and income ;

DATA dads;
  INPUT famid name $ inc ;
CARDS;
2 Art  22000
1 Bill 30000
3 Paul 25000
;
RUN;

* Here is a file with information about moms with their family id name and income ;

DATA moms;
  INPUT famid name $ inc ;
CARDS;
1 Bess 15000
3 Pat  50000
2 Amy  18000
;
RUN;

* We can combine these files by stacking them one on top the other ;
* by setting them both together in the same data step as shown below ;

DATA dadmom;
  SET dads moms;
RUN;

 * Let's use PROC PRINT to look at the result ;

PROC PRINT DATA=dadmom;
RUN;
```

The output of this program is shown below.

| OBS | FAMID | NAME | INC |
|---|---|---|---|
| 1 | 2 | Art | 22000 |
| 2 | 1 | Bill | 30000 |
| 3 | 3 | Paul | 25000 |
| 4 | 1 | Bess | 15000 |
| 5 | 3 | Pat | 50000 |
| 6 | 2 | Amy | 18000 |

The output from this program shows that the files were combined properly. The **dads** and **moms** are stacked together in one file. But, there is a little problem. We can't tell the dads from the moms. Let's try doing this again but in such a way that we can tell which observations are the moms and which are the dads.

### Concatenating the moms and dads, a better example

In order to tell the dads from the moms, let's create a variable called **momdad** in the **dads** and **moms** data files that will contain **dad** for the **dads** data file and **mom** for the **moms** data file. When we combine the two files together the **momdad** variable will tell us who the moms and dads are.

```
DATA dads;
  INPUT famid name $ inc ;
  momdad = "dad";
CARDS;
2 Art  22000
1 Bill   30000
3 Paul  25000
;
RUN;

DATA moms;
  INPUT famid name $ inc ;
  momdad = "mom";
CARDS;
1 Bess  15000
3 Pat    50000
2 Amy  18000
;
RUN;

DATA dadmom;
  SET dads moms;
RUN;

* Now when we do the proc print you can see the dads from the moms ;

PROC PRINT DATA=dadmom;
RUN;
```

The output of this program is shown below.

| OBS | FAMID | NAME | INC | MOMDAD |
|---|---|---|---|---|
| 1 | 2 | Art | 22000 | dad |
| 2 | 1 | Bill | 30000 | dad |
| 3 | 3 | Paul | 25000 | dad |
| 4 | 1 | Bess | 15000 | mom |
| 5 | 3 | Pat | 50000 | mom |
| 6 | 2 | Amy | 18000 | mom |

Here we get a more desirable result, because we can tell the dads from the moms by looking at the variable **momdad**. This required some thinking ahead because we had to put **momdad** in both the **dads** data file and the **moms** data file before we merged the data files.

### Problems to look out for

These above examples cover situations where there are no complications. However, look out for the following problems.

***The two data files have different variable names for the same thing***

For example, income is called **dadinc** and in the dads file and called **mominc** in the moms file, as shown below.

```
DATA dads;
 INPUT famid name $  dadinc ;
DATALINES;
2 Art   22000
1 Bill 30000
3 Paul 25000
;
RUN;

DATA moms;
 INPUT famid name $  mominc ;
DATALINES;
1 Bess 15000
3 Pat   50000
2 Amy   18000
;
RUN;

DATA momdad;
 SET dads(IN=dad) moms(IN=mom);
 IF dad=1 THEN momdad="dad";
 IF mom=1 THEN momdad="mom";
run;

PROC PRINT DATA=momdad;
RUN;
```

You can see the problem illustrated below.

| OBS | FAMID | NAME | DADINC | MOMINC | DAD | MOM | MOMDAD |
|---|---|---|---|---|---|---|---|
| 1 | 2 | Art | 22000 | . | 1 | 0 | dad |
| 2 | 1 | Bill | 30000 | . | 1 | 0 | dad |
| 3 | 3 | Paul | 25000 | . | 1 | 0 | dad |
| 4 | 1 | Bess | . | 15000 | 0 | 1 | mom |
| 5 | 3 | Pat | . | 50000 | 0 | 1 | mom |
| 6 | 2 | Amy | . | 18000 | 0 | 1 | mom |

**Solution #1.** The most obvious solution is to choose appropriate variable names for the original files (i.e., name the variable-**inc** in both the moms and dads file). This solution is not always possible since you might be concatenating files that you did not originally create. To save space, we omit illustrating this solution.

**Solution #2.** If solution #1 is not possible, then this problem can be addressed using an **if** statement in a **data step**.

```
DATA momdad;
  SET dads(IN=dad) moms(IN=mom);
  IF dad=1 THEN
  DO;
    momdad="dad";
    inc=dadinc;
  END;
  IF mom=1 THEN
  DO;
    momdad="mom";
    inc=mominc;
  END;
RUN;

PROC PRINT DATA=momdad;
RUN;
```

The results are shown below, where **inc** now has the income for both the moms and dads.

| OBS | FAMID | NAME | DADINC | MOMINC | DAD | MOM | MOMDAD | INC |
|---|---|---|---|---|---|---|---|---|
| 1 | 2 | Art | 22000 | . | 1 | 0 | dad | 22000 |
| 2 | 1 | Bill | 30000 | . | 1 | 0 | dad | 30000 |
| 3 | 3 | Paul | 25000 | . | 1 | 0 | dad | 25000 |
| 4 | 1 | Bess | . | 15000 | 0 | 1 | mom | 15000 |
| 5 | 3 | Pat | . | 50000 | 0 | 1 | mom | 50000 |
| 6 | 2 | Amy | . | 18000 | 0 | 1 | mom | 18000 |

**Solution 3.** Another way you can fix this is by using the **rename** option on the **set** statement of a **data step** to rename the variables just before the files are combined.

```
DATA momdad;
  SET dads(RENAME=(dadinc=inc)) moms(RENAME=(mominc=inc));
RUN;

PROC PRINT DATA=momdad;
RUN;
```

The output for **Solution 3** is below.

| OBS | FAMID | NAME | INC |
|---|---|---|---|
| 1 | 2 | Art | 22000 |
| 2 | 1 | Bill | 30000 |
| 3 | 3 | Paul | 25000 |
| 4 | 1 | Bess | 15000 |
| 5 | 3 | Pat | 50000 |
| 6 | 2 | Amy | 18000 |

## *The two data files have different lengths for variables of the same name*

In all of the examples above, the variable name was input with the format $ indicating name is an alphabetic (string) variable with a default length of 8. What would happen if **name** in the dads file was input using **$3.** and **name** in the moms file was input using **$4.** ? This is illustrated below.

```
DATA dads;
  INPUT famid name $3. inc;
DATALINES;
 2 Art  22000
 1 Bob  30000
 3 Tom  25000
 RUN;

DATA moms;
  INPUT famid name $4. inc;
DATALINES;
 1 Bess 15000
 3 Rory 50000
 2 Jane 18000
 RUN;

DATA momdad;
  SET dads moms;
RUN;
PROC PRINT DATA=momdad;
RUN;
```

The output is below.

| OBS | FAMID | NAME | INC |
|---|---|---|---|
| 1 | 2 | Art | 22000 |
| 2 | 1 | Bob | 30000 |
| 3 | 3 | Tom | 25000 |
| 4 | 1 | Bes | 15000 |
| 5 | 3 | Ror | 50000 |
| 6 | 2 | Jan | 18000 |

Note that the names for the **moms** are truncated to be length 3. This is because the length for names in the **dads** file is 3. To fix this, use the **length** statement in the **data step** that merges the two files.

```
DATA momdad;
  LENGTH name $ 4;
  SET dads moms;
RUN;
PROC PRINT DATA=momdad;
RUN;
```

The output is below.

| OBS | NAME | FAMID | INC |
|---|---|---|---|
| 1 | Art | 2 | 22000 |
| 2 | Bob | 1 | 30000 |
| 3 | Tom | 3 | 25000 |
| 4 | Bess | 1 | 15000 |
| 5 | Rory | 3 | 50000 |
| 6 | Jane | 2 | 18000 |

### *The two data files have variables with the same name but different codes*

This problem is similar to the problem above, except that it has an additional wrinkle, illustrated below. In the **dads** file there is a variable called **fulltime** that is coded 1 if the dad is working full time, 0 if he is not. The **moms** file also has a variable called**fulltime** that is coded **Y** is she is working full time, and **N** if she is not. Not only are these variables of different types (numeric and character), but they are coded differently as well.

```
DATA dads;
 INPUT famid name $ inc fulltime;
DATALINES;
2 Art  22000 0
1 Bill 30000 1
3 Paul 25000 1
;
RUN;

DATA moms;
 INPUT famid name $ inc fulltime $1.;
DATALINES;
1 Bess 15000 N
3 Pat  50000 Y
2 Amy  18000 N
;
RUN;
```

**Solution #1.** Code the variables in the two files in the same way. For example, code **fulltime** using 0/1 for both files with 1 indicating working fulltime. This is the simplest solution if you are creating the files yourself. We will omit illustrating this solution to save space.

**Solution #2.** You may not have created the original raw data files, so solution #1 may not be possible for you. In that case, you can create a new variable in each file that has the same coding and will be compatible when you merge the files. Below we illustrate this strategy.

For the **dads** file, we make a variable called **full** that is the same as **fulltime**, and save the file as **dads2**, dropping **fulltime**. For the moms, we create **full**by recoding **fulltime**, and save the file as **moms2**, also dropping **fulltime**. The files **dads2** and **moms2** both have the variable **full** coded the same way (0/1 where 1=works full time) so we can combine those files together.

```
DATA dads2;
 SET dads;
 full=fulltime;
 DROP fulltime;
RUN;

DATA moms2;
 SET moms;
 IF fulltime="Y" THEN full=1;
 IF fulltime="N" THEN full=0;
 DROP fulltime;
RUN;

DATA momdad;
  SET dads2 moms2;
RUN;

PROC PRINT DATA=momdad;
RUN;
```

The results are shown below.

| OBS | FAMID | NAME | INC | FULL |
|---|---|---|---|---|
| 1 | 2 | Art | 22000 | 0 |
| 2 | 1 | Bill | 30000 | 1 |
| 3 | 3 | Paul | 25000 | 1 |
| 4 | 1 | Bess | 15000 | 0 |
| 5 | 3 | Pat | 50000 | 1 |
| 6 | 2 | Amy | 18000 | 0 |

## WORKING ACROSS VARIABLES

### Introduction

This module illustrates (1) how to compute variables manually in a **data step** and (2) how to work across variables using the **array** statement in a **data step**.

Consider the sample program below, which reads in family income data for twelve months.

```
DATA faminc;
   INPUT famid faminc1-faminc12 ;
CARDS;
1 3281 3413 3114 2500 2700 3500 3114 3319 3514 1282 2434 2818
2 4042 3084 3108 3150 3800 3100 1531 2914 3819 4124 4274 4471
3 6015 6123 6113 6100 6100 6200 6186 6132 3123 4231 6039 6215
;
RUN;

PROC PRINT DATA=faminc;
RUN;
```

The output is shown below

| OBS | FAMID | FAMINC1 | FAMINC2 | FAMINC3 | FAMINC4 | FAMINC5 | FAMINC6 | FAMINC7 | FAMINC8 | FAMINC9 | FAMINC10 | FAMINC11 | FAMINC12 |
|---|---|---|---|---|---|---|---|---|---|---|---|---|---|
| 1 | 1 | 3281 | 3413 | 3114 | 2500 | 2700 | 3500 | 3114 | 3319 | 3514 | 1282 | 2434 | 2818 |
| 2 | 2 | 4042 | 3084 | 3108 | 3150 | 3800 | 3100 | 1531 | 2914 | 3819 | 4124 | 4274 | 4471 |
| 3 | 3 | 6015 | 6123 | 6113 | 6100 | 6100 | 6200 | 6186 | 6132 | 3123 | 4231 | 6039 | 6215 |

## Computing variables (manually)

Computing variables in a **data step** can be accomplished a number of ways in SAS. For example, if one wanted to compute the amount of tax (10%) paid for each month, the simplest way to do this is to compute 12 variables (**taxinc1-taxinc12**) by multiplying each of the (**faminc1-faminc12**) by .10 as illustrated below. As you see, this requires entering a command computing the tax for each month of data (for months 1 to 12).

```
DATA fAMINCla;
   SET faminc;
     taxinc1 = faminc1 * .10 ;
     taxinc2 = faminc2 * .10 ;
     taxinc3 = faminc3 * .10 ;
     taxinc4 = faminc4 * .10 ;
     taxinc5 = faminc5 * .10 ;
     taxinc6 = faminc6 * .10 ;
     taxinc7 = faminc7 * .10 ;
     taxinc8 = faminc8 * .10 ;
     taxinc9 = faminc9 * .10 ;
     taxinc10= faminc10 * .10 ;
     taxinc11= faminc11 * .10 ;
     taxinc12= faminc12 * .10 ;
RUN;

PROC PRINT DATA=faminc1a;
RUN;
```

The output is shown below.

| OBS | FAMID | FAMINC1 | FAMINC2 | FAMINC3 | FAMINC4 | FAMINC5 | FAMINC6 | FAMINC7 | FAMINC8 | FAMINC9 | FAMINC10 | FAMINC11 | FAMINC12 | TAXINC1 |
|---|---|---|---|---|---|---|---|---|---|---|---|---|---|---|
| 1 | 1 | 3281 | 3413 | 3114 | 2500 | 2700 | 3500 | 3114 | 3319 | 3514 | 1282 | 2434 | 2818 | 328.1 |
| 2 | 2 | 4042 | 3084 | 3108 | 3150 | 3800 | 3100 | 1531 | 2914 | 3819 | 4124 | 4274 | 4471 | 404.2 |
| 3 | 3 | 6015 | 6123 | 6113 | 6100 | 6100 | 6200 | 6186 | 6132 | 3123 | 4231 | 6039 | 6215 | 601.5 |

| OBS | TAXINC2 | TAXINC3 | TAXINC4 | TAXINC5 | TAXINC6 | TAXINC7 | TAXINC8 | TAXINC9 | TAXINC10 | TAXINC11 | TAXINC12 |
|---|---|---|---|---|---|---|---|---|---|---|---|
| 1 | 341.3 | 311.4 | 250 | 270 | 350 | 311.4 | 331.9 | 351.4 | 128.2 | 243.4 | 281.8 |
| 2 | 308.4 | 310.8 | 315 | 380 | 310 | 153.1 | 291.4 | 381.9 | 412.4 | 427.4 | 447.1 |
| 3 | 612.3 | 611.3 | 610 | 610 | 620 | 618.6 | 613.2 | 312.3 | 423.1 | 603.9 | 621.5 |

## Computing variables (using the array statement)

Another way to compute 12 variables representing the amount of tax paid (10%) for each month is to use the **array** statement. In the example below, two "arrays" are declared: **Afaminc** and **Ataxinc**. The elements of **Afaminc** are the variables **faminc1-faminc12** and the elements of **Ataxinc** are the variables **taxinc1-taxinc12**. You can refer to the variables **faminc1-faminc12** by referring to the elements of the array **Afaminc**. For example, **Afaminc(3)**refers to **faminc3**.

Note that the array **Afaminc** is defined using the existing variables **faminc1-faminc12** from the dataset **faminc**, whereas the values of the array **Ataxinc(taxinc1-taxinc12)** are created by multiplying **Afaminc** (**faminc1-faminc12**) by .10 in the **do** loop shown below.

```
DATA faminc1b;
   SET faminc ;

   ARRAY Afaminc(12) faminc1-faminc12 ;
   ARRAY Ataxinc(12) taxinc1-taxinc12 ;

   DO month = 1 TO 12;
     Ataxinc(month) = Afaminc(month) * .10 ;
   END;
RUN;

PROC PRINT DATA=faminc1b;
   VAR faminc1-faminc12 taxinc1-taxinc12;
RUN;
```

The output is shown below:

| Obs | faminc1 | faminc2 | faminc3 | faminc4 | faminc5 | faminc6 | faminc7 | faminc8 | faminc9 | faminc10 | faminc11 | faminc12 | taxinc1 |
|---|---|---|---|---|---|---|---|---|---|---|---|---|---|
| 1 | 3281 | 3413 | 3114 | 2500 | 2700 | 3500 | 3114 | 3319 | 3514 | 1282 | 2434 | 2818 | 328.1 |
| 2 | 4042 | 3084 | 3108 | 3150 | 3800 | 3100 | 1531 | 2914 | 3819 | 4124 | 4274 | 4471 | 404.2 |
| 3 | 6015 | 6123 | 6113 | 6100 | 6100 | 6200 | 6186 | 6132 | 3123 | 4231 | 6039 | 6215 | 601.5 |

| Obs | taxinc2 | taxinc3 | taxinc4 | taxinc5 | taxinc6 | taxinc7 | taxinc8 | taxinc9 | taxinc10 | taxinc11 | taxinc12 |
|---|---|---|---|---|---|---|---|---|---|---|---|
| 1 | 341.3 | 311.4 | 250 | 270 | 350 | 311.4 | 331.9 | 351.4 | 128.2 | 243.4 | 281.8 |
| 2 | 308.4 | 310.8 | 315 | 380 | 310 | 153.1 | 291.4 | 381.9 | 412.4 | 427.4 | 447.1 |
| 3 | 612.3 | 611.3 | 610 | 610 | 620 | 618.6 | 613.2 | 312.3 | 423.1 | 603.9 | 621.5 |

In summary, the new variables become new columns of the dataset **faminc1b** and one can compute new variables as transformations of these variables, just like any other variables.

Note that the **array** statement **cannot** loop over observations for any one variable. If your data are in this "long" form and you need to loop over observations, you must reshape the data to "wide" form in order to use the **array** statement. Another option for looping across observations in the "long" form is to read the variable into a vector array using **proc iml** (**I**nteractive **M**atrix **L**anguage), loop over the elements of the vector, and then append the results back to the SAS dataset using **proc append.**

## Collapsing across variables (manually)

Often one needs to sum across variables (also known as collapsing across variables). For example, let's say the quarterly income for each family is desired. In order to get this information, four quarterly variables **incqtr1-incqtr4** need to be computed. Again, this can be achieved manually or by using the **array**statement. Below is an example of how to compute four quarterly income variables **incqtr1-incqtr4** by simply adding together the months that comprise a quarter.

```
DATA faminc2a;
   SET faminc;
    incqtr1 = faminc1+faminc2+faminc3 ;
    incqtr2 = faminc4+faminc5+faminc6 ;
    incqtr3 = faminc7+faminc8+faminc9 ;
    incqtr4 = faminc10+faminc11+faminc12 ;
RUN;

PROC PRINT DATA=faminc2a;
   var faminc1-faminc12 incqtr1-incqtr4;
RUN;
```

The output is shown below.

| OBS | FAMINC1 | FAMINC2 | FAMINC3 | FAMINC4 | FAMINC5 | FAMINC6 | FAMINC7 | FAMINC8 | FAMINC9 | FAMINC10 | FAMINC11 | FAMINC12 | INCQTR1 | INCQTR2 | INCQTR3 | INCQTR4 |
|---|---|---|---|---|---|---|---|---|---|---|---|---|---|---|---|---|
| 1 | 3281 | 3413 | 3114 | 2500 | 2700 | 3500 | 3114 | 3319 | 3514 | 1282 | 2434 | 2818 | 9808 | 8700 | 9947 | 6534 |
| 2 | 4042 | 3084 | 3108 | 3150 | 3800 | 3100 | 1531 | 2914 | 3819 | 4124 | 4274 | 4471 | 10234 | 10050 | 8264 | 12869 |
| 3 | 6015 | 6123 | 6113 | 6100 | 6100 | 6200 | 6186 | 6132 | 3123 | 4231 | 6039 | 6215 | 18251 | 18400 | 15441 | 16485 |

## Collapsing across variables (using the array statement)

This same result as above can be achieved using the **array** statement. The example below illustrates how to compute the quarterly income variables**incqtr1-incqtr4** using the **array** statement in a more elegant fashion.

The array **Aincqtr** has four elements which are computed in the **do** loop as the sum of sets of three months. The trick here is that the quarterly intervals begin with months 1,4,7 and 10 respectively, which can be indexed as (**month3** - 2) where **month3** is the set of numbers {3,6,9,12}during the execution of the **do** loop. Hence, the first element of the array **Aincqtr** is equal to the sum of the first three elements of **Afaminc**, the second element of the array **Aincqtr** is equal to the sum of the next three elements of **Afaminc**, etc., until the **do** loop is finished, as shown below.

```
DATA faminc2b;
   SET faminc ;

   ARRAY Afaminc(12) faminc1-faminc12 ;
   ARRAY Aincqtr(4)  incqtr1-incqtr4 ;

   DO qtr = 1 TO 4 ;
     month3 = 3*qtr;
     Aincqtr(qtr) = Afaminc(month3-2) + Afaminc(month3-1) + Afaminc(month3) ;
   END;
RUN;

PROC PRINT DATA=faminc2b;
   var faminc1-faminc12 incqtr1-incqtr4;
RUN;
```

The output is shown below.

| OBS | FAMINC1 | FAMINC2 | FAMINC3 | FAMINC4 | FAMINC5 | FAMINC6 | FAMINC7 | FAMINC8 | FAMINC9 | FAMINC10 | FAMINC11 | FAMINC12 | INCQTR1 | INCQTR2 | INCQTR3 | INCQTR4 |
|---|---|---|---|---|---|---|---|---|---|---|---|---|---|---|---|---|
| 1 | 3281 | 3413 | 3114 | 2500 | 2700 | 3500 | 3114 | 3319 | 3514 | 1282 | 2434 | 2818 | 9808 | 8700 | 9947 | 6534 |
| 2 | 4042 | 3084 | 3108 | 3150 | 3800 | 3100 | 1531 | 2914 | 3819 | 4124 | 4274 | 4471 | 10234 | 10050 | 8264 | 12869 |
| 3 | 6015 | 6123 | 6113 | 6100 | 6100 | 6200 | 6186 | 6132 | 3123 | 4231 | 6039 | 6215 | 18251 | 18400 | 15441 | 16485 |

## Identifying patterns across variables (using the array statement)

The **array** statement can also be used to identify patterns across variables of a dataset. Let's say, for example, that one needs to know which months had income that was less than half of the income of the previous month. To obtain this information, dummy indicators can be created to indicate in which months this occurred. In the example below, two arrays are defined, **Afaminc** and **Alowinc**, and the elements of **Afaminc** and **Alowinc** are the variables**faminc1-faminc12** and **lowinc2-lowinc12**, respectively, in the SAS dataset **faminc4**.

Note that only 11 dummy indicators are needed for a 12 month period because the interest is in the change from one month to the next. In the **DO** loop, when a month has income that is less than half of the income of the previous month, the dummy indicators **lowinc2-lowinc12** get assigned a "1". When this is not the case, they are assigned a "0".

Lastly, a character variable named **ever** is created (with help from the **array** statement) indicating whether or not there were *any* months where income was less than half of the income of the previous month. This is accomplished by summing up all of the elements of **Alowinc** (which contains 1›s and 0›s). If the sum of the elements of **Alowinc** is greater than zero, than there was *at least one* month where income was less than half of the previous month, and **ever**equals "Y". Otherwise, if there were no months where income was less than half of the previous month, the sum of the elements of **Alowinc** is zero, and**ever** equals "N".

```
DATA faminc4;
   SET faminc ;

   ARRAY Afaminc(12) faminc1-faminc12 ;
   ARRAY Alowinc(2:12) lowinc2-lowinc12 ;

   DO month = 2 to 12 ;
     IF Afaminc(month) < ( Afaminc(month-1) / 2) THEN Alowinc(month) = 1;
       ELSE Alowinc(month) = 0;
   END;

   sum_low=0; /*THIS INITIALIZES sum_low TO ZERO AT THE BEGINNING OF THE LOOP*/;
   DO month = 2 to 12 ;
     sum_low =sum_low + Alowinc(month) ;
   END;

   IF sum_low GT 0 THEN ever='Y';
   IF sum_low EQ 0 THEN ever='N';
RUN;

PROC PRINT DATA=faminc4;
  VAR famid faminc1-faminc12 lowinc2-lowinc12 ever;
RUN;
```

The output is shown below.

```
                                                  F    F    F                   L L L
       F    F    F    F    F    F    F    F    F    A    A    A L L L L L L L L O O O
       A    A    A    A    A    A    A    A    A    M    M    M O O O O O O O O W W W
   F   M    M    M    M    M    M    M    M    M    I    I    I W W W W W W W W I I I
   A   I    I    I    I    I    I    I    I    I    N    N    N I I I I I I I I N N N E
 O M   N    N    N    N    N    N    N    N    N    C    C    C N N N N N N N N C C C V
 B I   C    C    C    C    C    C    C    C    C    1    1    1 C C C C C C C C 1 1 1 E
 S D   1    2    3    4    5    6    7    8    9    0    1    2 2 3 4 5 6 7 8 9 0 1 2 R
 1 1 3281 3413 3114 2500 2700 3500 3114 3319 3514 1282 2434 2818 0 0 0 0 0 0 0 0 1 0 0 Y
 2 2 4042 3084 3108 3150 3800 3100 1531 2914 3819 4124 4274 4471 0 0 0 0 0 1 0 0 0 0 0 Y
 3 3 6015 6123 6113 6100 6100 6200 6186 6132 3123 4231 6039 6215 0 0 0 0 0 0 0 0 0 0 0 N
```

## COLLAPSING ACROSS OBSERVATIONS IN SAS

Here we illustrate how to collapse data across observations using **proc means**. Our example uses a hypothetical data set containing information about kids in three families. These examples show how you can collapse across kids to form family records from the kids records.

### Reading the data file

Here is the SAS program that makes a data file called **kids**. It contains three families (**famid**) each with three kids. It contains the family ID, the name of the kid, the order of birth (1 2 3 for 1st, 2nd, 3rd), and the age, weight and sex of each kid.

```
DATA kids;
  LENGTH kidname $ 4 sex $ 1;
  INPUT famid kidname birth age wt sex ;
CARDS;
1 Beth 1  9  60  f
1 Bob  2  6  40  m
1 Barb 3  3  20  f
2 Andy 1  8  80  m
2 Al   2  6  50  m
2 Ann  3  2  20  f
3 Pete 1  6  60  m
3 Pam  2  4  40  f
3 Phil 3  2  20  m
;
RUN;

PROC PRINT DATA=kids;
RUN;
```

Here is the output of the **proc print**.

| OBS | KIDNAME | SEX | FAMID | BIRTH | AGE | WT |
|---|---|---|---|---|---|---|
| 1 | Beth | f | 1 | 1 | 9 | 60 |
| 2 | Bob | m | 1 | 2 | 6 | 40 |
| 3 | Barb | f | 1 | 3 | 3 | 20 |
| 4 | Andy | m | 2 | 1 | 8 | 80 |
| 5 | Al | m | 2 | 2 | 6 | 50 |
| 6 | Ann | f | 2 | 3 | 2 | 20 |
| 7 | Pete | m | 3 | 1 | 6 | 60 |
| 8 | Pam | f | 3 | 2 | 4 | 40 |
| 9 | Phil | m | 3 | 3 | 2 | 20 |

### Using proc means to collapse data across records

We can use **proc means** to collapse across across families. The example below computes the average age of each child within each family (because of the**class famid;** statement) and then outputs the results into a SAS data file called **fam2**.

```
PROC MEANS DATA=kids ;
  CLASS famid;
  VAR age;
  OUTPUT OUT=fam2 MEAN= ;
RUN;
```

The output of the **proc means** is shown below.

| FAMID | N Obs | N | Mean | Std Dev | Minimum | Maximum |
|---|---|---|---|---|---|---|
| 1 | 3 | 3 | 6.000 | 3.00000 | 3.00000 | 9.0000000 |
| 2 | 3 | 3 | 5.333 | 3.05505 | 2.00000 | 8.0000000 |
| 3 | 3 | 3 | 4.000 | 2.00000 | 2.00000 | 6.0000000 |

And we use **proc print** to have a look at **fam2**.

```
PROC PRINT DATA=fam2;
RUN;
```

And this output shows that the data file **fam2** contains the average of **age** for the kids for each family.

| OBS | FAMID | _TYPE_ | _FREQ_ | AGE |
|---|---|---|---|---|
| 1 | . | 0 | 9 | 5.11111 |
| 2 | 1 | 1 | 3 | 6.00000 |
| 3 | 2 | 1 | 3 | 5.33333 |
| 4 | 3 | 1 | 3 | 4.00000 |

However, there is one extra record (the one shown below). This is the overall mean (notice that the **_FREQ_** for it is 9, and there are a total of nine kids). We really don't want this record.

| OBS | FAMID | _TYPE_ | _FREQ_ | AGE |
|---|---|---|---|---|
| 1 | . | 0 | 9 | 5.11111 |

We can suppress the creation of the record with the overall mean with the **nway** option on the **proc means** statement. In general, when you use **proc means** with the **class** statement and make an **output** data file, you usually will want to use the **nway** option as shown below.

```
PROC MEANS DATA=kids NWAY ;
  CLASS famid;
  VAR age;
  OUTPUT OUT=fam3 MEAN= ;
RUN;
```

[we omit the proc means output]

```
PROC PRINT DATA=fam3;
RUN;
```

Now, the **fam3** data file had just has three records with the average age for each family.

| OBS | FAMID | _TYPE_ | _FREQ_ | AGE |
|---|---|---|---|---|
| 1 | 1 | 1 | 3 | 6.00000 |
| 2 | 2 | 1 | 3 | 5.33333 |
| 3 | 3 | 1 | 3 | 4.00000 |

### Explicitly naming the collapsed variables

The following **proc means** example does the exact same thing as the prior example, except that the average of **age** is explicitly named, calling it **avgage**.

```
PROC MEANS DATA=kids NWAY ;
  CLASS famid;
  VAR age;
  OUTPUT OUT=fam4 MEAN=avgage ;
RUN;
```

[we omit the proc means output]

```
PROC PRINT DATA=fam4;
RUN;
```

The output is the same as before, except that the average of **age** is called **avgage**.

| OBS | FAMID | _TYPE_ | _FREQ_ | AVGAGE |
|---|---|---|---|---|
| 1 | 1 | 1 | 3 | 6.00000 |
| 2 | 2 | 1 | 3 | 5.33333 |
| 3 | 3 | 1 | 3 | 4.00000 |

The rest of the examples will explicitly name the collapsed variables (e.g., use **mean=avgage** instead of just **mean=** ). In general, it is better to explicitly name the variables to avoid confusion between the original variable and the collapsed variable.

### Getting means of more than one variable

We can request averages for more than one variable. Here we get the average for **age** and for **wt** all in the same command.

```
PROC MEANS DATA=kids NWAY ;
  CLASS famid;
  VAR age wt;
  OUTPUT OUT=fam5 MEAN=avgage avgwt;
RUN;
```

```
FAMID  N Obs  Variable  N   Mean       Std Dev      Minimum
-------------------------------------------------------------
    1      3  AGE       3   6.0000     3.0000000    3.0000000
              WT        3  40.0000    20.0000000   20.0000000
    2      3  AGE       3   5.3333     3.0550505    2.0000000
              WT        3  50.0000    30.0000000   20.0000000
    3      3  AGE       3   4.0000     2.0000000    2.0000000
              WT        3  40.0000    20.0000000   20.0000000
-------------------------------------------------------------
[to save space, we omit the output with the maximum of age and wt]
```

```
PROC PRINT DATA=fam5;
RUN;
```

As you see in the output below, **avgage** is the average age and **avgwt** is the average weight of the kids in each family.

| OBS | FAMID | _TYPE_ | _FREQ_ | AVGAGE | AVGWT |
|---|---|---|---|---|---|
| 1 | 1 | 1 | 3 | 6.00000 | 40 |
| 2 | 2 | 1 | 3 | 5.33333 | 50 |
| 3 | 3 | 1 | 3 | 4.00000 | 40 |

## Requesting multiple statistics at once

We can request multiple statistics at once. The command below gets the mean, standard deviation and age (**mean std** and **N**) for **age** and **wt** within each family.

```
PROC MEANS DATA=kids NWAY;
  CLASS famid;
  VAR age wt;
  OUTPUT OUT=fam6 MEAN=avgage avgwt STD=stdage stdwt N=nage nwt ;
RUN;
```

The results below shows the output of the **proc means**.

```
FAMID  N Obs  Variable  N        Mean      Std Dev      Minimum
----------------------------------------------------------------
    1      3  AGE       3    6.0000000   3.0000000    3.0000000
              WT        3   40.0000000  20.0000000   20.0000000
    2      3  AGE       3    5.3333333   3.0550505    2.0000000
              WT        3   50.0000000  30.0000000   20.0000000
    3      3  AGE       3    4.0000000   2.0000000    2.0000000
              WT        3   40.0000000  20.0000000   20.0000000
----------------------------------------------------------------
[to save space, we omit the output with the maximum of age and wt]
```

```
PROC PRINT DATA=fam6;
RUN;
```

The results below correspond to the **proc means** above. You can see that the average **age** and **wt** by family are in **avgage** and **avgwt**. Likewise **stdage**and **stdwt** contain the standard deviation of **age** and **wt** for each family, and **nage** and **nwt** have the valid number of observations for **age** and **wt** for each family.

| OBS | FAMID | _TYPE_ | _FREQ_ | AVGAGE | AVGWT | STDAGE | STDWT | NAGE | NWT |
|---|---|---|---|---|---|---|---|---|---|
| 1 | 1 | 1 | 3 | 6.00000 | 40 | 3.00000 | 20 | 3 | 3 |
| 2 | 2 | 1 | 3 | 5.33333 | 50 | 3.05505 | 30 | 3 | 3 |
| 3 | 3 | 1 | 3 | 4.00000 | 40 | 2.00000 | 20 | 3 | 3 |

## Suppressing proc means output

In our example, we have just three families. For your data, you might have dozens, hundreds, or thousands of families (or whatever grouping you are using). The output of the **proc means** can get very long, so you may want to suppress the output. You can do that with the **noprint** option as shown below.

```
DATA kids2 ;
  SET kids;

  If sex = "m" THEN boy = 1; ELSE boy = 0 ;
  If sex = "f" THEN girl= 1; ELSE girl= 0 ;
RUN;
```

The output from the **proc means** is not printed due to the **noprint** option.

## Counting the number of boys and girls in the family

Suppose you wanted a count of the number of boys and girls in the family. We can do that with one extra step. We will make a dummy variable that is 1 if a boy (0 if not), and a dummy variable that is 1 if a girl (and 0 if not). The sum of the **boy** dummy variable within a family is the number of boys in the family and the sum of the **girl** dummy variable within a family is the number of girls in the family.

First, we use a data step to make the **boy** and **girl** dummy variable.

```
DATA kids2 ;
  SET kids;

  If sex = "m" THEN boy = 1; ELSE boy = 0 ;
  If sex = "f" THEN girl= 1; ELSE girl= 0 ;
RUN;
```

We use **proc print** to look at the **boy** and **girl** variables to double check them.

```
PROC PRINT DATA=kids2;
  VAR sex boy girl ;
RUN;
```

| OBS | SEX | BOY | GIRL |
|---|---|---|---|
| 1 | f | 0 | 1 |
| 2 | m | 1 | 0 |
| 3 | f | 0 | 1 |
| 4 | m | 1 | 0 |
| 5 | m | 1 | 0 |
| 6 | f | 0 | 1 |
| 7 | m | 1 | 0 |
| 8 | f | 0 | 1 |
| 9 | m | 1 | 0 |

We use **proc means** to sum up the **boy** and **girl** dummy variables for each family and to create a data file called **fam8** that contains the sum of **boy** in**boys** and the sum of **girl** in **girls**. We use the **noprint** option to suppress the output of the **proc means**.

```
PROC MEANS DATA=kids2 NWAY NOPRINT ;
  CLASS famid;
  VAR boy girl ;
  OUTPUT OUT=fam8 SUM=boys girls ;
RUN;
```

We do a **proc print** to look at the output data file.

```
PROC PRINT DATA=fam8;
RUN;
```

As we expect, the **proc print** shows that **boys** contains the count of boys in each family and **girls** contains the count of girls in each family.

| OBS | FAMID | _TYPE_ | _FREQ_ | BOYS | GIRLS |
|---|---|---|---|---|---|
| 1 | 1 | 1 | 3 | 1 | 2 |
| 2 | 2 | 1 | 3 | 2 | 1 |
| 3 | 3 | 1 | 3 | 2 | 1 |

## Merging the collapsed data back with the original data

Sometimes you want to merge the collapsed data back with the original data. Let's use an example creating **avgage** and **avgwt** for each family, then merge those results back with the original kids data.

First, let›s collapse the data across families to make **avgage** and **avgwt** just as we have done before.

```
PROC MEANS DATA=kids NWAY NOPRINT ;
  CLASS famid;
  VAR age wt;
  OUTPUT OUT=fam9 MEAN=avgage avgwt;
RUN;
```

Second, we sort **kids** and sort **fam9** both on **famid**, preparing for merging them together.

```
PROC SORT DATA=kids OUT=skids ;
  BY famid ;
RUN;

PROC SORT DATA=fam9 OUT=sfam9 ;
  BY famid ;
RUN;
```

Third, we merge the sorted files together (**skids** and **sfam9) by famid.** We can drop **_type_** and **_freq_** since they are not needed, but we don't have to drop them.

```
DATA kidsmrg ;
  MERGE skids sfam9 ;
  BY famid ;
  DROP _type_ _freq_ ;
RUN;
```

We can print out the results, showing that the variables **avgage** and **avgwt** are now merged back with the original kids so each kid has the associated average age and weight for their family.

```
PROC PRINT DATA=kidsmrg;
RUN;
```

| OBS | KIDNAME | SEX | FAMID | BIRTH | AGE | WT | AVGAGE | AVGWT |
|---|---|---|---|---|---|---|---|---|
| 1 | Beth | f | 1 | 1 | 9 | 60 | 6.00000 | 40 |
| 2 | Bob | m | 1 | 2 | 6 | 40 | 6.00000 | 40 |
| 3 | Barb | f | 1 | 3 | 3 | 20 | 6.00000 | 40 |
| 4 | Andy | m | 2 | 1 | 8 | 80 | 5.33333 | 50 |
| 5 | Al | m | 2 | 2 | 6 | 50 | 5.33333 | 50 |
| 6 | Ann | f | 2 | 3 | 2 | 20 | 5.33333 | 50 |
| 7 | Pete | m | 3 | 1 | 6 | 60 | 4.00000 | 40 |
| 8 | Pam | f | 3 | 2 | 4 | 40 | 4.00000 | 40 |
| 9 | Phil | m | 3 | 3 | 2 | 20 | 4.00000 | 40 |

## Problems to look out for

- You may end up with records that you were not

expecting if you forget to use the **nway** option.

- If you collapse across records, and then remerge back with the original data, be sure that you explicitly name the variables when you collapse them. If you don›t, the variables from the collapsed data will have the same names as the original data, and they will clash when you remerge the data.

## COLLAPSING ACROSS OBSERVATIONS, INTERMEDIATE

### Introduction

This module will illustrate how to collapse across variables. First, let's read in a sample dataset named **kids** which includes the variables **famid** (family id) and **wt** (kids weight in pounds).

```
DATA kids;
  LENGTH kidname $ 4 sex $ 1;
  INPUT famid kidname birth age wt sex ;
CARDS;
1 Beth 1  9  60  f
1 Bob  2  6  40  m
1 Barb 3  3  20  f
2 Andy 1  8  80  m
2 Al   2  6  50  m
2 Ann  3  2  20  f
3 Pete 1  6  60  m
3 Pam  2  4  40  f
3 Phil 3  2  20  m
4 Sam  1 11 100  m
4 Stu  2  8  90  m
;
RUN;

PROC PRINT DATA=kids;
RUN;
```

The output is shown below.

OBS KIDNAME SEX FAMID BIRTH AGE WT

| OBS | KIDNAME | SEX | FAMID | BIRTH | AGE | WT |
|---|---|---|---|---|---|---|
| 1 | Beth | f | 1 | 1 | 9 | 60 |
| 2 | Bob | m | 1 | 2 | 6 | 40 |
| 3 | Barb | f | 1 | 3 | 3 | 20 |
| 4 | Andy | m | 2 | 1 | 8 | 80 |
| 5 | Al | m | 2 | 2 | 6 | 50 |
| 6 | Ann | f | 2 | 3 | 2 | 20 |
| 7 | Pete | m | 3 | 1 | 6 | 60 |
| 8 | Pam | f | 3 | 2 | 4 | 40 |
| 9 | Phil | m | 3 | 3 | 2 | 20 |
| 10 | Sam | m | 4 | 1 | 11 | 100 |
| 11 | Stu | m | 4 | 2 | 8 | 90 |

### Collapsing and computing average weights using proc means

Next, by using **proc means**, one can create a variable that represents the sum of ALL the weights of each person within a family, a variable that represents the average weight of each person within a family, and a variable that counts the number of people within a family. This can be seen in the example below, where three new variables, **sumwt**, **meanwt** and **cnt**, are created **by famid**, and then written to the new dataset **fam1**.

```
PROC MEANS DATA=kids NWAY ;
  CLASS famid ;
  VAR wt ;
  OUTPUT OUT=fam1 SUM=sumwt MEAN=meanwt N=cnt ;
RUN;

PROC PRINT DATA=fam1;
  VAR famid sumwt meanwt cnt;
RUN;
```

The output is shown below.

Analysis Variable : WT

| FAMID | N Obs | N | Mean | Std Dev | Minimum | Maximum |
|---|---|---|---|---|---|---|
| 1 | 3 | 3 | 40.0000000 | 20.0000000 | 20.0000000 | 60.0000000 |
| 2 | 3 | 3 | 50.0000000 | 30.0000000 | 20.0000000 | 80.0000000 |
| 3 | 3 | 3 | 40.0000000 | 20.0000000 | 20.0000000 | 60.0000000 |
| 4 | 2 | 2 | 95.0000000 | 7.0710678 | 90.0000000 | 100.0000000 |

| OBS | FAMID | SUMWT | MEANWT | CNT |
|---|---|---|---|---|
| 1 | 1 | 120 | 40 | 3 |
| 2 | 2 | 150 | 50 | 3 |
| 3 | 3 | 120 | 40 | 3 |
| 4 | 4 | 190 | 95 | 2 |

### Collapsing and computing average weights manually (collapsing across observations)

Of course, collapsing can always be done manually within a **data step**. This, however, requires a bit more complex SAS programming. To create sum, mean, and N (sample size) variables that summarize values within a group (e.g., families), one can count over observations within a group by using a retained variable and a counter. In the example below, retained counter variables are created that count across observations within families until the last record within a family is encountered. (This is possible because a retained variable allows the value for the last observation to be available for use when accessing the current observation.) Then, the retained variable from the last observation within each family is written to the new SAS dataset **fam2**. At the final step, only the variables **famid**, **sumwt**, **meanwt**, and **cnt** are kept in the dataset **fam2**. Note that the variable **meanwt** does NOT need to be retained. This is because at each step, it is simply a function of the retained variables **sumwt** and **cnt**.

```
PROC SORT DATA=kids OUT=sortkids ;
  BY famid ;
RUN ;

DATA fam2 ;
 SET sortkids ;

  BY famid ;

  RETAIN sumwt cnt;

  IF first.famid THEN
   DO;
     sumwt = 0;
     cnt   = 0;
   END;

  sumwt = sumwt + wt ;
  cnt = cnt + 1;

  meanwt=sumwt/cnt;

  /* this outputs a record ONLY when at the last obs in a family*/ ;

  IF last.famid THEN OUTPUT;

  KEEP famid sumwt meanwt cnt ;

RUN;

PROC PRINT DATA=fam2 ;
RUN;
```

The output is shown below.

| OBS | FAMID | SUMWT | CNT | MEANWT |
|---|---|---|---|---|
| 1 | 1 | 120 | 3 | 40 |
| 2 | 2 | 150 | 3 | 50 |
| 3 | 3 | 120 | 3 | 40 |
| 4 | 4 | 190 | 2 | 95 |

## Computing sums, counts and other summary information

The above example illustrated how one can compute sums, means, and counts within groups using the **retain** statement within a data step. Other variables, such as dummy or flag variables, can also be computed using the **retain** statement. For example, say a study is interested in **(1)** the number of boys in each family, **(2)** whether or not there is a girl in the family and **(3)** if any of the children in each family are over 85 pounds in weight. All of this information can be collected and stored using the **retain** statement. The example below works similarly to the example above; however, this example additionally creates a variable **numboys**, which counts the number of boys in each family, and the flag variables **hasgirl** and **over85**, which take on the values of '1' or '0', depending on whether or not there is a girl in the family, or if a family has a child over 85 pounds, respectively.

```
PROC SORT DATA=kids OUT=sortkids ;
  BY famid ;
RUN ;

DATA fam3 ;
  SET sortkids ;
  BY famid ;
  RETAIN sumwt cnt numboys hasgirl over85 ;
  IF first.famid THEN
  DO;
    sumwt  = 0;  /* sum of weights for family */ ;
    cnt    = 0;  /* count of kids in family */;
    numboys= 0;  /* number of boys in family */;
    hasgirl= 0;  /* 1 if family has girl, 0 if no girl */;
    over85 = 0;  /* 1 if family has child with wt over 85, 0 if not */;
  END;

  sumwt = sumwt + wt ;
  cnt = cnt + 1;
  IF (sex = 'm') THEN numboys = numboys + 1 ;
  IF (sex = 'f') THEN hasgirl = 1 ;
  IF (wt > 85) THEN over85 =  1 ;

   /* this outputs a record ONLY when at the last obs in a family */;

  IF last.famid THEN
   DO;
    meanwt = sumwt / cnt ; /* do any final computations before outputting record */;
    OUTPUT;
   END;

  KEEP famid sumwt cnt numboys hasgirl over85 meanwt ;

RUN;

PROC PRINT DATA=fam3 ;
RUN;
```

The output is shown below.

| OBS | FAMID | SUMWT | CNT | NUMBOYS | HASGIRL | OVER85 | MEANWT |
|---|---|---|---|---|---|---|---|
| 1 | 1 | 120 | 3 | 1 | 1 | 0 | 40 |
| 2 | 2 | 150 | 3 | 2 | 1 | 0 | 50 |
| 3 | 3 | 120 | 3 | 2 | 1 | 0 | 40 |
| 4 | 4 | 190 | 2 | 2 | 0 | 1 | 95 |

## HOW TO RESHAPE DATA WIDE TO LONG USING PROC TRANSPOSE

### Transposing one group of variables

For a data set in wide format such as the one below, we can reshape it into long format using **proc transpose**. From the first output of **proc print**, we see that the data now is in long format except that we don't have a numeric variable indicating year; instead; we have a character variable that has information on year in it. So we have to do a data step to extract the information on year. The second output of **proc print** shows that our data step after the **proc transpose** has successfully created a numeric variable **year** and has rename the variable COL1 to **faminc**.

```
data wide1;
  input famid faminc96 faminc97 faminc98 ;
cards;
1 40000 40500 41000
2 45000 45400 45800
3 75000 76000 77000
;
run;

proc transpose data=wide1 out=long1;
   by famid;
run;

proc print data=long1;
run;
```

| Obs | famid | _NAME_ | COL1 |
|---|---|---|---|
| 1 | 1 | faminc96 | 40000 |
| 2 | 1 | faminc97 | 40500 |
| 3 | 1 | faminc98 | 41000 |
| 4 | 2 | faminc96 | 45000 |
| 5 | 2 | faminc97 | 45400 |
| 6 | 2 | faminc98 | 45800 |
| 7 | 3 | faminc96 | 75000 |
| 8 | 3 | faminc97 | 76000 |
| 9 | 3 | faminc98 | 77000 |

```
data long1;
  set long1 (rename=(col1=faminc));
  year=input(substr(_name_, 7), 5.);
  drop _name_;
run;

proc print data=long1;
run;
```

| Obs | famid | faminc | year |
|---|---|---|---|
| 1 | 1 | 40000 | 96 |
| 2 | 1 | 40500 | 97 |
| 3 | 1 | 41000 | 98 |
| 4 | 2 | 45000 | 96 |
| 5 | 2 | 45400 | 97 |
| 6 | 2 | 45800 | 98 |
| 7 | 3 | 75000 | 96 |
| 8 | 3 | 76000 | 97 |
| 9 | 3 | 77000 | 98 |

### Transposing two groups of variables

In the following data set we have two groups of variables that need to be transposed. The first group is family income across years and the second group is the spending across year. A simple approach here is to transpose one group of variables at a time and then merge them back together. In the data step where we merge the transposed data sets, we also create a numeric variable year based on the SAS automatic variable _ **NAME_** from the second transposed data set.

```
data wide2 ;
  input famid faminc96 faminc97 faminc98 spend96 spend97 spend98 ;
cards ;
1 40000 40500 41000 38000 39000 40000
2 45000 45400 45800 42000 43000 44000
3 75000 76000 77000 70000 71000 72000
;
run ;

proc transpose data=wide2 out=longf prefix=faminc ;
  by famid;
var faminc96-faminc98;
run;

proc transpose data=wide2 out=longs prefix=spend ;
  by famid;
var spend96-spend98;
run;

data long2;
  merge longf (rename=(faminc1=faminc) drop=_name_) longs (rename=(spend1=spend));
  by famid;
  year=input(substr(_name_, 6), 5.);
  drop _name_;
run;

proc print data=long2;
run;
```

| Obs | famid | faminc | spend | year |
|---|---|---|---|---|
| 1 | 1 | 40000 | 38000 | 96 |
| 2 | 1 | 40500 | 39000 | 97 |
| 3 | 1 | 41000 | 40000 | 98 |
| 4 | 2 | 45000 | 42000 | 96 |
| 5 | 2 | 45400 | 43000 | 97 |
| 6 | 2 | 45800 | 44000 | 98 |
| 7 | 3 | 75000 | 70000 | 96 |
| 8 | 3 | 76000 | 71000 | 97 |
| 9 | 3 | 77000 | 72000 | 98 |

### A more realistic example

```
data wide3;
  input id inc90 inc91 inc92 inc93 inc94 inc95
cards;
1  66483 69146 74643 79783 81710 86143
2  17510 17947 19484 20979 21268 22998
3  57947 62964 68717 70957 75198 75722
4  64831 71060 71918 72514 73100 74379
5  18904 19949 21335 22237 23829 23913
6  32057 34770 35834 37387 40899 42372
7  60551 64869 67983 70498 71253 75177
8  16553 18189 18349 19815 21739 22980
9  32611 33465 35961 36416 37183 40627
10 61379 66002 67936 70513 74405 76009
11 24065 24229 25709 26121 26617 28142
12 32975 36185 37601 41336 43399 43670
13 69548 71341 72455 76552 80538 85330
14 50274 53349 55900 59375 61216 63911
15 72011 73334 76248 77724 78638 80582
16 18911 20046 21343 21630 22330 23081
17 68841 75410 80806 81327 81571 86499
18 28099 30716 32986 36097 39124 39866
19 17302 18778 18872 19884 20665 21855
20 16291 16674 16770 17182 17979 18917
21 43244 46545 47633 50744 54734 59075
22 56393 59120 60801 61404 63111 69278
23 47347 49571 50101 51345 56463 56927
24 16076 17217 17296 17900 18171 18366
25 65906 69679 76131 77676 81980 85426
26 58586 61188 66542 69267 71063 74549
27 61674 66584 69185 75193 78647 81898
28 31673 31883 32774 34485 36929 39751
29 63412 67593 69911 73092 80105 81840
30 27684 28439 30861 31406 32960 35530
31 71873 76449 80848 88691 94149 97431
32 62177 63812 64235 65703 69985 71136
33 37684 38258 39208 39489 39745 41236
34 64013 66398 71877 75610 76395 79644
35 16011 16847 17746 19123 19183 19996
36 49215 52195 52343 56365 58752 59354
37 15774 16643 17605 18781 18996 19685
38 29106 31693 31852 34505 35806 36179
39 25147 26923 28785 30987 34036 34106
40 71978 79144 80453 86580 95164 96155
41 46166 47579 49455 53849 56630 57473
42 55810 59443 65291 66065 69009 74365
43 49642 50603 53917 54858 58470 59767
44 21348 22361 23412 24038 24774 25828
45 44361 48720 51356 54927 56670 58800
46 56509 60517 61532 65077 69594 73089
47 39097 40293 43237 44809 48782 53091
48 18685 19405 20165 20316 22197 23557
49 73103 76243 76778 82734 86279 86784
50 48129 49267 53799 58768 63011 66461
;
run ;

proc transpose data=wide3 out=long3;
  by id;
run;

data long3;
  set long3 (rename=(col1=inc));
  year=input(substr(_name_, 4), 5.);
  drop _name_;
run;

proc print data=long3 (obs=20);
run;
```

| Obs | id | inc | year |
|---|---|---|---|
| 1 | 1 | 66483 | 90 |
| 2 | 1 | 69146 | 91 |
| 3 | 1 | 74643 | 92 |
| 4 | 1 | 79783 | 93 |
| 5 | 1 | 81710 | 94 |
| 6 | 1 | 86143 | 95 |
| 7 | 2 | 17510 | 90 |
| 8 | 2 | 17947 | 91 |
| 9 | 2 | 19484 | 92 |
| 10 | 2 | 20979 | 93 |
| 11 | 2 | 21268 | 94 |
| 12 | 2 | 22998 | 95 |
| 13 | 3 | 57947 | 90 |
| 14 | 3 | 62964 | 91 |
| 15 | 3 | 68717 | 92 |
| 16 | 3 | 70957 | 93 |
| 17 | 3 | 75198 | 94 |
| 18 | 3 | 75722 | 95 |
| 19 | 4 | 64831 | 90 |
| 20 | 4 | 71060 | 91 |

## Reshape wide to long with a character variable

In the following data set we have three groups of variables that needs to be transposed. One of the groups is the indicator of debt across years. The approach is the same with either numeric variables or character variables. Since there are three groups of variables, we need to use **proc transpose** three times, one for each group. Then we merge them back together. In the data step where we merge the transposed data files together, we also create a numeric variable for year and rename each of the variables properly. The variable **year** is created based on the SAS automatic variable **_NAME_** from the last transposed data set.

```
data wide4;
  input famid faminc96 faminc97 faminc98 spend96 spend97
  spend98 debt96 $ debt97 $ debt98 $ ;
cards;
1 40000 40500 41000 38000 39000 40000 yes yes no
2 45000 45400 45800 42000 43000 44000 yes no  no
3 75000 76000 77000 70000 71000 72000 no  no  no
;
run ;

proc transpose data=wide4 out=longf prefix=faminc;
by famid;
var faminc96-faminc98;
run;

proc transpose data=wide4 out=longs prefix=spend;
by famid;
var spend96-spend98;
run;

proc transpose data=wide4 out=longd prefix=debt;
by famid;
var debt96-debt98;
run;

data long4;
      merge longf (rename=(faminc1=faminc) drop=_name_)
            longs (rename=(spend1=spend) drop=_name_)
            longd (rename=(debt1=debt));
      by famid;
      year=input(substr(_name_, 5), 5.);
   drop _name_;
run;

proc print data=long4;
run;
```

```
Obs   famid   faminc   spend   debt   year

 1      1     40000    38000   yes     96
 2      1     40500    39000   yes     97
 3      1     41000    40000   no      98
 4      2     45000    42000   yes     96
 5      2     45400    43000   no      97
 6      2     45800    44000   no      98
 7      3     75000    70000   no      96
 8      3     76000    71000   no      97
 9      3     77000    72000   no      98
```

The following examples will illustrate how to reshape data from wide to long using the data step.

## Example 1: A simple example

We will begin with a small data set with only one variable to be reshaped.

```
DATA wide;
  input famid faminc96 faminc97 faminc98 ;
CARDS;
1 40000 40500 41000
2 45000 45400 45800
3 75000 76000 77000
;
RUN;
```

The technique we will use to reshape this data set works well if you have only a few variables to be reshaped. We will create a new variable called **year**, which will be set equal to each year for which we have data. After setting the variable **year** equal to a year in our data set, we will set the value of another new variable, **faminc**, equal to the value of the **faminc** variable (**faminc96**, **faminc97** or **faminc98)** for that year. Next, we will use the **output** statement to have SAS output the results to the data set. Note that if you do not include an **output** statement after creating the variables for that year, that year will not be included in the new data set. Finally, we will use the **drop** statement to drop **faminc96**, **faminc97** and **faminc98** from our data set once we have finished reshaping it.

```
DATA long1 ;
  SET wide ;

  year = 96 ;
  faminc = faminc96 ;
  OUTPUT ;

  year = 97 ;
  faminc = faminc97 ;
  OUTPUT ;

  year = 98 ;
  faminc = faminc98 ;
  OUTPUT ;

  DROP faminc96-faminc98 ;
RUN;
```

Let's look at the data to ensure that the reshaping worked as we expected. We will run a **proc print** on the **long1** data file to visually inspect it, and then we will run a **proc means** on both the original data file, **wide**, and the new data file, **long1**, to compare the descriptive statistics.

```
PROC PRINT DATA=long1;
RUN;

Obs   famid   year   faminc

 1      1      96    40000
 2      1      97    40500
 3      1      98    41000
 4      2      96    45000
 5      2      97    45400
 6      2      98    45800
 7      3      96    75000
 8      3      97    76000
 9      3      98    77000
```

The above output looks like we expect: we have nine observations, the **famid** is the same for each of the three years for each family, and the year variable ranges from 96 to 99. Now let's run a **proc means** on both the old and the new data sets.

```
PROC MEANS DATA=wide fw=8 ;
  VAR faminc96-faminc98 ;
RUN;

The MEANS Procedure

Variable    N      Mean      Std Dev     Minimum     Maximum
-------------------------------------------------------------
faminc96    3    53333.3     18929.7     40000.0     75000.0
faminc97    3    53966.7     19238.1     40500.0     76000.0
faminc98    3    54600.0     19546.9     41000.0     77000.0
-------------------------------------------------------------

PROC MEANS DATA=long1 fw=8 ;
  CLASS year;
  VAR faminc;
RUN;

The MEANS Procedure
                    Analysis Variable : faminc

              N
    year    Obs    N      Mean     Std Dev     Minimum     Maximum
-------------------------------------------------------------------
      96      3    3   53333.3     18929.7     40000.0     75000.0

      97      3    3   53966.7     19238.1     40500.0     76000.0

      98      3    3   54600.0     19546.9     41000.0     77000.0
-------------------------------------------------------------------
```

To ensure that the reshaping was successful, we need to compare the output of the **proc means** for both the old and the new data sets. All of the descriptive statistics for **faminc96** in the first output should be the same as those for **year** 96 in the second output. For example, we see that there are three observations for **faminc96**, the mean is 53333.3, the standard deviation is 18929.7, the minimum is 40000.0 and the maximum is 75000.0. These are the exact values that we see in second output for **year** 96. Likewise, we compare the row in the first output for **faminc97** with the corresponding row in the second output and see that they are exactly the same. This is also the case for the third variable, **faminc98**. While this is not absolute proof that the reshaping was successful, we can be pretty certain that it was.

## Example 2: Reshaping one variable using an array

A second method of reshaping variables in a data step is to use an **array** statement. This method is useful if you have more than a few variables to reshape. We will begin with an example using only one variable, and then move on to an example with two variables to be reshaped.

As in the last example, we want to reshape the variables **faminc96**, **faminc97** and **faminc98** into two long variables, **year** and **faminc**. We will first show you the code used to accomplish this and then explain each piece of the code below.

```
DATA longla;
  SET wide;

  ARRAY afaminc(96:98) faminc96 - faminc98 ;

  DO year = 96 to 98 ;
    faminc = afaminc(year);
    OUTPUT;
  END;

  DROP faminc96 - faminc98 ;
RUN;
```

Regarding the **array** statement (**ARRAY afaminc(96:98) faminc96 - faminc98 ;**), the name of the array is **afaminc** (many researchers will simply add an "a" (for array) to the new variable name to create the name of the array to make it easy to know what variable the array is working on). The numbers in parentheses **(96:98)** indicate the first and last numbers of the series to be reshaped. Finally, the actual variable names are listed. You can use a dash to indicate the inclusion of consecutive numbers.

On the first line of the do-loop ( **DO year = 96 to 98 ;** ), you put the name of the new variable that will contain the suffix for the old variables. On the second line of the do-loop, we set our new variable (**faminc**) equal to the value of the array for the given year ( **afaminc(year)** ), i.e., when year is **96** then**afaminc(96)** refers to **faminc96**.

We then use the **output** statement to force SAS to output the results before starting the loop over again. If this is omitted, only the record for the last observation in each group will be output and you will have only three records in the new data set instead of nine.

Finally, we use the **drop** statement to drop the variables from the wide data file that have been reshaped and are no longer needed.

Below we run **proc print** on the new data file and **proc means** on both the old and the new data sets to ensure that the reshaping went as expected.

```
PROC PRINT DATA=longla ;
RUN ;

Obs    famid    year    faminc

 1       1       96      40000
 2       1       97      40500
 3       1       98      41000
 4       2       96      45000
 5       2       97      45400
 6       2       98      45800
 7       3       96      75000
 8       3       97      76000
 9       3       98      77000

PROC MEANS DATA=wide fw = 8 ;
  VAR faminc96-faminc98 ;
RUN ;

The MEANS Procedure

Variable     N        Mean     Std Dev     Minimum     Maximum
--------------------------------------------------------------
faminc96     3     53333.3     18929.7     40000.0     75000.0
faminc97     3     53966.7     19238.1     40500.0     76000.0
faminc98     3     54600.0     19546.9     41000.0     77000.0
--------------------------------------------------------------

PROC MEANS DATA=longla fw=8 ;
  CLASS year ;
  VAR faminc ;
RUN ;

The MEANS Procedure
                    Analysis Variable : faminc

              N
    year    Obs    N        Mean     Std Dev     Minimum     Maximum
--------------------------------------------------------------------
      96      3    3     53333.3     18929.7     40000.0     75000.0

      97      3    3     53966.7     19238.1     40500.0     76000.0

      98      3    3     54600.0     19546.9     41000.0     77000.0
--------------------------------------------------------------------
```

The output from the **proc print** of the new data set looks as we expect: there are three observations per family and the variable **year** ranges from 96 to 99. We also compare the output of the **proc means** for the old and the new data sets. We compare the descriptive statistics for each variable to ensure that they did not change during the course of the reshaping. We see that they have not, which is a good indication that the reshaping was successful.

## Example 3: Reshaping two variables using an array

This example is very similar to the last one except that now we will reshape two variables in the same data step. There are three places where this program has been modified from the version shown in the example above. They are denoted with a comment to the right of the statement in the program. Please note that you can reshape as many variables as you want in a single data step. To reshape additional variables, you would add an **array** statement, another line within the do-loop and drop the reshaped variables for each set of variables to be reshaped.

```
data wide2 ;
  input famid faminc96 faminc97 faminc98 spend96 spend97 spend98 ;
cards ;
1 40000 40500 41000 38000 39000 40000
2 45000 45400 45800 42000 43000 44000
3 75000 76000 77000 70000 71000 72000
;
RUN ;

DATA long2 ;
  SET wide2 ;

  ARRAY afaminc(96:98) faminc96-faminc98 ;
  ARRAY aspend(96:98) spend96-spend98 ;          * added statement ;

  DO year = 96 to 98 ;
    faminc = afaminc(year) ;
    spend  = aspend(year) ;                      * added statement ;
    OUTPUT ;
  END ;

  DROP faminc96-faminc98 spend96-spend98 ;       * added variables ;

RUN ;
```

As before, we check to ensure that the reshaping went as expected.

```
PROC PRINT DATA=long2 ;
RUN ;
```

| Obs | famid | year | faminc | spend |
|---|---|---|---|---|
| 1 | 1 | 96 | 40000 | 38000 |
| 2 | 1 | 97 | 40500 | 39000 |
| 3 | 1 | 98 | 41000 | 40000 |
| 4 | 2 | 96 | 45000 | 42000 |
| 5 | 2 | 97 | 45400 | 43000 |
| 6 | 2 | 98 | 45800 | 44000 |
| 7 | 3 | 96 | 75000 | 70000 |
| 8 | 3 | 97 | 76000 | 71000 |
| 9 | 3 | 98 | 77000 | 72000 |

```
PROC MEANS DATA=long2 fw=8 ;
  CLASS year ;
  VAR faminc spend ;
RUN ;
```

The MEANS Procedure

| year | N Obs | Variable | N | Mean | Std Dev | Minimum | Maximum |
|---|---|---|---|---|---|---|---|
| 96 | 3 | faminc | 3 | 53333.3 | 18929.7 | 40000.0 | 75000.0 |
| | | spend | 3 | 50000.0 | 17435.6 | 38000.0 | 70000.0 |
| 97 | 3 | faminc | 3 | 53966.7 | 19238.1 | 40500.0 | 76000.0 |
| | | spend | 3 | 51000.0 | 17435.6 | 39000.0 | 71000.0 |
| 98 | 3 | faminc | 3 | 54600.0 | 19546.9 | 41000.0 | 77000.0 |
| | | spend | 3 | 52000.0 | 17435.6 | 40000.0 | 72000.0 |

```
PROC MEANS DATA=wide2 fw=8 ;
  VAR faminc96-faminc98 spend96-spend98 ;
RUN ;
```

The MEANS Procedure

| Variable | N | Mean | Std Dev | Minimum | Maximum |
|---|---|---|---|---|---|
| faminc96 | 3 | 53333.3 | 18929.7 | 40000.0 | 75000.0 |
| faminc97 | 3 | 53966.7 | 19238.1 | 40500.0 | 76000.0 |
| faminc98 | 3 | 54600.0 | 19546.9 | 41000.0 | 77000.0 |
| spend96 | 3 | 50000.0 | 17435.6 | 38000.0 | 70000.0 |
| spend97 | 3 | 51000.0 | 17435.6 | 39000.0 | 71000.0 |
| spend98 | 3 | 52000.0 | 17435.6 | 40000.0 | 72000.0 |

## Example 4: A more realistic example

This example is much like example 2 in that only one variable (**income**) is being reshaped. However, this example is somewhat more realistic in that there are more years of income and more cases. You will note that the structure of the SAS code is identical to example 2; only the variable names are changed.

```
data wide3;
  input id inc90 inc91 inc92 inc93 inc94 inc95 ;
cards;
1  66483 69146 74643 79783 81710 86143
2  17510 17947 19484 20979 21268 22998
3  57947 62964 68717 70957 75198 75722
4  64831 71060 71918 72514 73100 74379
5  18904 19949 21335 22237 23829 23913
6  32057 34770 35834 37387 40899 42372
7  60551 64869 67983 70498 71253 75177
8  16553 18189 18349 19815 21739 22980
9  32611 33465 35961 36416 37183 40627
10 61379 66002 67936 70513 74405 76009
11 24065 24229 25709 26121 26617 28142
12 32975 36185 37601 41336 43399 43670
13 69548 71341 72455 76552 80538 85330
14 50274 53349 55900 59375 61216 63911
15 72011 73334 76248 77724 78638 80582
16 18911 20046 21343 21630 22330 23081
17 68841 75410 80806 81327 81571 86499
18 28099 30716 32986 36097 39124 39866
19 17302 18778 18872 19884 20665 21855
20 16291 16674 16770 17182 17979 18917
21 43244 46545 47633 50744 54734 59075
22 56393 59120 60801 61404 63111 69278
23 47347 49571 50101 51345 56463 56927
24 16076 17217 17296 17900 18171 18366
25 65906 69679 76131 77676 81980 85426
26 58586 61188 66542 69267 71063 74549
27 61674 66584 69185 75193 78647 81898
28 31673 31883 32774 34485 36929 39751
29 63412 67593 69911 73092 80105 81840
30 27684 28439 30861 31406 32960 35530
31 71873 76449 80848 88691 94149 97431
32 62177 63812 64235 65703 69985 71136
33 37684 38258 39208 39489 39745 41236
34 64013 66398 71877 75610 76395 79644
35 16011 16847 17746 19123 19183 19996
36 49215 52195 52343 56365 58752 59354
37 15774 16643 17605 18781 18996 19685
38 29106 31693 31852 34505 35806 36179
39 25147 26923 28785 30987 34036 34106
40 71978 79144 80453 86580 95164 96155

41 46166 47579 49455 53849 56630 57473
42 55810 59443 65291 66065 69009 74365
43 49642 50603 53917 54858 58470 59767
44 21348 22361 23412 24038 24774 25828
45 44361 48720 51356 54927 56670 58800
46 56509 60517 61532 65077 69594 73089
47 39097 40293 43237 44809 48782 53091
48 18685 19405 20165 20316 22197 23557
49 73103 76243 76778 82734 86279 86784
50 48129 49267 53799 58768 63011 66461
;
RUN ;

DATA long3 ;
  SET wide3 ;

  ARRAY ainc(90:95) inc90 - inc95 ;

  DO year = 90 to 95 ;
    inc = ainc(year) ;
    OUTPUT ;
  END ;

  DROP inc90 - inc95 ;
RUN ;
```

Let's start our checking of the reshaping by looking at **proc prints** of the first five observations of both the old and the new data files. Remember that to see the data for the first five observations in the wide data set, you will need the first 30 observation in the long data set (five observations times six variables = 30). Next, we will look at the results of the **proc means** for both data sets.

```
PROC PRINT DATA=wide3(obs = 5) ;
RUN ;
```

| Obs | id | inc90 | inc91 | inc92 | inc93 | inc94 | inc95 |
|---|---|---|---|---|---|---|---|
| 1 | 1 | 66483 | 69146 | 74643 | 79783 | 81710 | 86143 |
| 2 | 2 | 17510 | 17947 | 19484 | 20979 | 21268 | 22998 |
| 3 | 3 | 57947 | 62964 | 68717 | 70957 | 75198 | 75722 |
| 4 | 4 | 64831 | 71060 | 71918 | 72514 | 73100 | 74379 |
| 5 | 5 | 18904 | 19949 | 21335 | 22237 | 23829 | 23913 |

```
PROC PRINT DATA=long3(obs = 30) ;
RUN ;
```

| Obs | id | year | inc |
|---|---|---|---|
| 1 | 1 | 90 | 66483 |
| 2 | 1 | 91 | 69146 |
| 3 | 1 | 92 | 74643 |
| 4 | 1 | 93 | 79783 |
| 5 | 1 | 94 | 81710 |
| 6 | 1 | 95 | 86143 |
| 7 | 2 | 90 | 17510 |
| 8 | 2 | 91 | 17947 |
| 9 | 2 | 92 | 19484 |
| 10 | 2 | 93 | 20979 |
| 11 | 2 | 94 | 21268 |
| 12 | 2 | 95 | 22998 |
| 13 | 3 | 90 | 57947 |
| 14 | 3 | 91 | 62964 |
| 15 | 3 | 92 | 68717 |
| 16 | 3 | 93 | 70957 |
| 17 | 3 | 94 | 75198 |
| 18 | 3 | 95 | 75722 |
| 19 | 4 | 90 | 64831 |
| 20 | 4 | 91 | 71060 |
| 21 | 4 | 92 | 71918 |
| 22 | 4 | 93 | 72514 |
| 23 | 4 | 94 | 73100 |
| 24 | 4 | 95 | 74379 |
| 25 | 5 | 90 | 18904 |
| 26 | 5 | 91 | 19949 |
| 27 | 5 | 92 | 21335 |
| 28 | 5 | 93 | 22237 |
| 29 | 5 | 94 | 23829 |
| 30 | 5 | 95 | 23913 |

```
PROC MEANS DATA = wide3 fw=8 ;
  VAR inc90-inc95 ;
RUN;
```

The MEANS Procedure

| Variable | N | Mean | Std Dev | Minimum | Maximum |
|---|---|---|---|---|---|
| inc90 | 50 | 43899.3 | 19523.4 | 15774.0 | 73103.0 |
| inc91 | 50 | 46380.7 | 20749.4 | 16643.0 | 79144.0 |
| inc92 | 50 | 48519.6 | 21720.1 | 16770.0 | 80848.0 |
| inc93 | 50 | 50842.3 | 22780.1 | 17182.0 | 88691.0 |
| inc94 | 50 | 53289.0 | 23824.0 | 17979.0 | 95164.0 |
| inc95 | 50 | 55379.0 | 24592.8 | 18366.0 | 97431.0 |

```
PROC MEANS DATA = long3 fw=8  ;
  CLASS year ;
  VAR inc ;
RUN;
```

```
The MEANS Procedure
                     Analysis Variable : inc

          N
  year   Obs     N       Mean    Std Dev    Minimum    Maximum
----------------------------------------------------------------
    90    50    50    43899.3    19523.4    15774.0    73103.0

    91    50    50    46380.7    20749.4    16643.0    79144.0

    92    50    50    48519.6    21720.1    16770.0    80848.0

    93    50    50    50842.3    22780.1    17182.0    88691.0

    94    50    50    53289.0    23824.0    17979.0    95164.0

    95    50    50    55379.0    24592.8    18366.0    97431.0
----------------------------------------------------------------
```

## Example 5: Reshaping with a string variable

This example is very similar to example 3, except we will add a string (i.e., character) variable that also needs to be reshaped. In this example we will reshape three variables, **faminc**, **spend** and **debt**. Note that in this data set, **debt** is a string variable. Fortunately, reshaping string variables is as easy reshaping numeric variables. Note that the reshaped variables that are based on the string variable will be string variables in the new data set, so you cannot include them in the **proc means** to check if the variables were reshaped correctly. However, we can do a **proc freq** to check the reshaping of the string variables. Also, we have included a **length** statement after the **set** statement to set the length of our new string variable **debt**. If we did not include this statement, SAS would assign the length of the variable to be the same as the first value encountered. In this example, the first value is "yes", which happens to be the longest string in this variable. However, if "no" was the first value SAS encountered, then the length of **debt** would be set to 2, and instead of seeing "yes", we would see "ye".

```
DATA wide4;
  INPUT famid faminc96 faminc97 faminc98 spend96 spend97
  spend98 debt96 $ debt97 $ debt98 $ ;
cards;
1 40000 40500 41000 38000 39000 40000 yes yes no
2 45000 45400 45800 42000 43000 44000 yes no  no
3 75000 76000 77000 70000 71000 72000 no  no  no
;
RUN ;

DATA long4 ;
  SET wide4 ;
  LENGTH debt $ 3;

  ARRAY afaminc(96:98) faminc96-faminc98 ;
  ARRAY aspend(96:98) spend96-spend98 ;
  ARRAY adebt(96:98) debt96-debt98 ;

  DO year = 96 to 98 ;
    faminc = afaminc(year) ;
    spend = aspend(year) ;
    debt = adebt(year) ;
    OUTPUT ;
  END;

  DROP faminc96-faminc98 spend96-spend98 debt96-debt98 ;

RUN;

PROC PRINT DATA=long4 ;
RUN ;
```

```
Obs   famid   year   faminc   spend   debt

 1      1      96    40000    38000    yes
 2      1      97    40500    39000    yes
 3      1      98    41000    40000    no
 4      2      96    45000    42000    yes
 5      2      97    45400    43000    no
 6      2      98    45800    44000    no
 7      3      96    75000    70000    no
 8      3      97    76000    71000    no
 9      3      98    77000    72000    no
```

```
PROC MEANS DATA=wide4;
  VAR faminc96-faminc98 spend96-spend98;
RUN;
```

```
The MEANS Procedure

Variable    N           Mean         Std Dev         Minimum         Maximum
-----------------------------------------------------------------------------
faminc96    3       53333.33        18929.69        40000.00        75000.00
faminc97    3       53966.67        19238.07        40500.00        76000.00
faminc98    3       54600.00        19546.87        41000.00        77000.00
spend96     3       50000.00        17435.60        38000.00        70000.00
spend97     3       51000.00        17435.60        39000.00        71000.00
spend98     3       52000.00        17435.60        40000.00        72000.00
-----------------------------------------------------------------------------
```

```
PROC MEANS DATA=long4;
  CLASS year;
  VAR faminc spend debt;
RUN;
```

```
The MEANS Procedure

                 N
        year   Obs   Variable   N          Mean        Std Dev        Minimum
-----------------------------------------------------------------------------
          96     3   faminc     3      53333.33       18929.69       40000.00
                     spend      3      50000.00       17435.60       38000.00

          97     3   faminc     3      53966.67       19238.07       40500.00
                     spend      3      51000.00       17435.60       39000.00

          98     3   faminc     3      54600.00       19546.87       41000.00
                     spend      3      52000.00       17435.60       40000.00
-----------------------------------------------------------------------------

                 N
        year   Obs   Variable        Maximum
--------------------------------------------
          96     3   faminc         75000.00
                     spend          70000.00

          97     3   faminc         76000.00
                     spend          71000.00

          98     3   faminc         77000.00
                     spend          72000.00
--------------------------------------------
```

```
PROC FREQ DATA=wide4;
  TABLE debt96 debt97 debt98;
RUN ;
```

```
The FREQ Procedure

                                          Cumulative    Cumulative
debt96    Frequency     Percent            Frequency       Percent
------------------------------------------------------------------
no               1        33.33                    1         33.33
yes              2        66.67                    3        100.00


                                          Cumulative    Cumulative
debt97    Frequency     Percent            Frequency       Percent
------------------------------------------------------------------
no               2        66.67                    2         66.67
yes              1        33.33                    3        100.00


                                          Cumulative    Cumulative
debt98    Frequency     Percent            Frequency       Percent
------------------------------------------------------------------
no               3       100.00                    3        100.00
```

```
PROC FREQ DATA=long4;
  TABLE year*debt / norow nocol nopercent ;
RUN ;

The FREQ Procedure

Table of year by debt

year      debt

Frequency|no      |yes     |  Total
---------+--------+--------+
      96 |      1 |      2 |      3
---------+--------+--------+
      97 |      2 |      1 |      3
---------+--------+--------+
      98 |      3 |      0 |      3
---------+--------+--------+
Total           6        3        9
```

When comparing the output from the **proc freq** for the old data set with the one for the new data set, we can see that the distribution of **debt** is the same in each of the years for the old data file as in the new data file.

## Example 6: Character suffixes

All of the previous examples have shown how to reshape variables that have had numeric suffixes. However, you can reshape variables that have string (i.e., character) suffixes as well. The only modification to the "template" is in the **array** statement. In our example, we have simply listed the variables. For example, **ARRAY aname(2) named namem ;** contains the elements **named** and **namem**. However, this could be cumbersome if you have many elements in the array. If the elements are positionally consecutive in the data set, you can separate the first and last element with a double dash (--). In SAS, one dash (-) indicates elements that are numerically consecutive, while two dashes (--) indicate elements that are positionally consecutive.

```
DATA wide5;
  INPUT famid named $ incd namem $ incm ;
CARDS;
1.00 Bill 30000.00 Bess 15000.00
2.00 Art 22000.00 Amy 18000.00
3.00 Paul 25000.00 Pat 50000.00
;
RUN;

DATA long5 ;
  SET wide5 ;
  LENGTH name $ 4;

  ARRAY aname(2) named namem ;
  ARRAY ainc(2) incd incm ;

  DO parent = 1 to 2 ;
    name = aname(parent) ;
    inc  = ainc(parent) ;
    OUTPUT ;
  END ;

  DROP named namem incd incm ;

RUN ;

PROC PRINT DATA=long5;
RUN;

Obs    famid    name    parent    inc

 1       1      Bill      1      30000
 2       1      Bess      2      15000
 3       2      Art       1      22000
 4       2      Amy       2      18000
 5       3      Paul      1      25000
 6       3      Pat       2      50000
```

```
PROC MEANS DATA=wide5;
  VAR incd incm;
RUN;

The MEANS Procedure

Variable    N          Mean         Std Dev        Minimum        Maximum
--------------------------------------------------------------------------
incd        3      25666.67         4041.45       22000.00       30000.00
incm        3      27666.67        19399.31       15000.00       50000.00
--------------------------------------------------------------------------
```

```
PROC MEANS DATA=long5;
  VAR inc;
RUN;

The MEANS Procedure
                    Analysis Variable : inc

N          Mean         Std Dev         Minimum         Maximum
------------------------------------------------------------------
6      26666.67        12580.41        15000.00        50000.00
------------------------------------------------------------------
```

```
PROC FREQ DATA=wide5;
  TABLE named namem;
RUN;

The FREQ Procedure
                                         Cumulative    Cumulative
named     Frequency      Percent        Frequency      Percent
-----------------------------------------------------------------
Art              1        33.33                1         33.33
Bill             1        33.33                2         66.67
Paul             1        33.33                3        100.00

                                         Cumulative    Cumulative
namem     Frequency      Percent        Frequency      Percent
-----------------------------------------------------------------
Amy              1        33.33                1         33.33
Bess             1        33.33                2         66.67
Pat              1        33.33                3        100.00
```

```
PROC FREQ DATA=long5;
  TABLE parent name;
RUN;

The FREQ Procedure
                                          Cumulative    Cumulative
parent    Frequency      Percent         Frequency      Percent
------------------------------------------------------------------
     1           3        50.00                 3         50.00
     2           3        50.00                 6        100.00

                                         Cumulative    Cumulative
name     Frequency      Percent         Frequency      Percent
-----------------------------------------------------------------
Amy             1        16.67                 1         16.67
Art             1        16.67                 2         33.33
Bess            1        16.67                 3         50.00
Bill            1        16.67                 4         66.67
Pat             1        16.67                 5         83.33
Paul            1        16.67                 6        100.00
```

# HOW TO RESHAPE DATA LONG TO WIDE USING PROC TRANSPOSE

## Transposing one variable

Sometimes you need to reshape your data which is in a long format (shown below)

```
famid year faminc
 1     96   40000
 1     97   40500
 1     98   41000
 2     96   45000
 2     97   45400
 2     98   45800
 3     96   75000
 3     97   76000
 3     98   77000
```

into a wide format (shown below).

```
famid faminc96 faminc97 faminc98
1      40000    40500    41000
2      45000    45400    45800
3      75000    76000    77000
```

Below is an example of using SAS **proc transpose** to reshape the data from a long to a wide format.

```
data long1 ;
  input famid year faminc ;
cards ;
1 96 40000
1 97 40500
1 98 41000
2 96 45000
2 97 45400
2 98 45800
3 96 75000
3 97 76000
3 98 77000
;
run;

proc transpose data=long1 out=wide1 prefix=faminc;
    by famid ;
    id year;
    var faminc;
run;

proc print data = wide1;
run;
```

| Obs | famid | _NAME_ | faminc96 | faminc97 | faminc98 |
|---|---|---|---|---|---|
| 1 | 1 | faminc | 40000 | 40500 | 41000 |
| 2 | 2 | faminc | 45000 | 45400 | 45800 |
| 3 | 3 | faminc | 75000 | 76000 | 77000 |

Notice that the option **prefix= faminc** specifies a prefix to use in constructing names for transposed variables in the output data set. SAS automatic variable **_NAME_** contains the name of the variable being transposed.

## Transposing two variables

With only a few modifications, the above example can be used to reshape two (or more) variables. The approach here is to use **proc transpose** multiple times as needed. The multiple transposed data files then are merged back.

```
data long2;
  input famid year faminc spend ;
cards;
1 96 40000 38000
1 97 40500 39000
1 98 41000 40000
2 96 45000 42000
2 97 45400 43000
2 98 45800 44000
3 96 75000 70000
3 97 76000 71000
3 98 77000 72000
;
run ;

proc transpose data=long2 out=widef prefix=faminc;
   by famid;
   id year;
   var faminc;
run;

proc transpose data=long2 out=wides prefix=spend;
   by famid;
   id year;
   var spend;
run;

data wide2;
    merge  widef(drop=_name_) wides(drop=_name_);
    by famid;
run;

proc print data=wide2;
run;
```

| Obs | famid | faminc96 | faminc97 | faminc98 | spend96 | spend97 | spend98 |
|---|---|---|---|---|---|---|---|
| 1 | 1 | 40000 | 40500 | 41000 | 38000 | 39000 | 40000 |
| 2 | 2 | 45000 | 45400 | 45800 | 42000 | 43000 | 44000 |
| 3 | 3 | 75000 | 76000 | 77000 | 70000 | 71000 | 72000 |

## Reshaping data with two variables that identify the wide record

Sometimes, there is no variable in the data set that uniquely identifies each observation. Rather, two or more variables are necessary to uniquely identify each observation. In this situation, we have to specify these variables in the **by** statement.

```
data long3;
  INPUT famid birth age ht ;
cards;
1 1 1 2.8
1 1 2 3.4
1 2 1 2.9
1 2 2 3.8
1 3 1 2.2
1 3 2 2.9
2 1 1 2.0
2 1 2 3.2
2 2 1 1.8
2 2 2 2.8
2 3 1 1.9
2 3 2 2.4
3 1 1 2.2
3 1 2 3.3
3 2 1 2.3
3 2 2 3.4
3 3 1 2.1
3 3 2 2.9
;
run;
proc transpose data=long3 out=wide3 prefix=ht;
   by famid birth;
   id age;
   var ht;
run;

proc print data=wide3;
run;
```

| Obs | famid | birth | _NAME_ | ht1 | ht2 |
|---|---|---|---|---|---|
| 1 | 1 | 1 | ht | 2.8 | 3.4 |
| 2 | 1 | 2 | ht | 2.9 | 3.8 |
| 3 | 1 | 3 | ht | 2.2 | 2.9 |
| 4 | 2 | 1 | ht | 2.0 | 3.2 |
| 5 | 2 | 2 | ht | 1.8 | 2.8 |
| 6 | 2 | 3 | ht | 1.9 | 2.4 |
| 7 | 3 | 1 | ht | 2.2 | 3.3 |
| 8 | 3 | 2 | ht | 2.3 | 3.4 |
| 9 | 3 | 3 | ht | 2.1 | 2.9 |

**A more realistic example**

The following example is a more realistic example that uses a data file having 300 records in long format (50 wide records and six time points).

```
data long4;
 input id year inc ;
cards;
 1 90 66483
 1 91 69146
 1 92 74643
 1 93 79783
 1 94 81710
 1 95 86143
 2 90 17510
 2 91 17947
 2 92 19484
 2 93 20979
 2 94 21268
 2 95 22998
 3 90 57947
 3 91 62964
 3 92 68717
 3 93 70957
 3 94 75198
 3 95 75722
 4 90 64831
 4 91 71060
 4 92 71918
 4 93 72514
 4 94 73100
 4 95 74379
 5 90 18904
 5 91 19949
 5 92 21335
 5 93 22237
 5 94 23829
 5 95 23913
 6 90 32057
 6 91 34770
 6 92 35834
 6 93 37387
 6 94 40899
 6 95 42372
 7 90 60551
 7 91 64869
 7 92 67983
 7 93 70498
 7 94 71253
 7 95 75177
 8 90 16553
 8 91 18189
 8 92 18349
 8 93 19815
```

**8 94 21739**

**8 95 22980**

**9 90 32611**

**9 91 33465**

**9 92 35961**

**9 93 36416**

**9 94 37183**

**9 95 40627**

**10 90 61379**

**10 91 66002**

**10 92 67936**

**10 93 70513**

**10 94 74405**

**10 95 76009**

**11 90 24065**

**11 91 24229**

**11 92 25709**

**11 93 26121**

**11 94 26617**

**11 95 28142**

**12 90 32975**

**12 91 36185**

**12 92 37601**

**12 93 41336**

**12 94 43399**

**12 95 43670**

**13 90 69548**

**13 91 71341**

**13 92 72455**

**13 93 76552**

**13 94 80538**

**13 95 85330**

**14 90 50274**

**14 91 53349**

**14 92 55900**

**14 93 59375**

**14 94 61216**

**14 95 63911**

**15 90 72011**

**15 91 73334**

**15 92 76248**

**15 93 77724**

**15 94 78638**

**15 95 80582**

**16 90 18911**

**16 91 20046**

**16 92 21343**

**16 93 21630**

**16 94 22330**

**16 95 23081**

**17 90 68841**

**17 91 75410**

**17 92 80806**

**17 93 81327**

**17 94 81571**

**17 95 86499**

**18 90 28099**

**18 91 30716**

**18 92 32986**

**18 93 36097**

**18 94 39124**

**18 95 39866**

**19 90 17302**

**19 91 18778**

**19 92 18872**

**19 93 19884**

**19 94 20665**

**19 95 21855**

**20 90 16291**

**20 91 16674**

**20 92 16770**

**20 93 17182**

**20 94 17979**

**20 95 18917**

21 90 43244

21 91 46545

21 92 47633

21 93 50744

21 94 54734

21 95 59075

22 90 56393

22 91 59120

22 92 60801

22 93 61404

22 94 63111

22 95 69278

23 90 47347

23 91 49571

23 92 50101

23 93 51345

23 94 56463

23 95 56927

24 90 16076

24 91 17217

24 92 17296

24 93 17900

24 94 18171

24 95 18366

25 90 65906

25 91 69679

25 92 76131

25 93 77676

25 94 81980

25 95 85426

26 90 58586

26 91 61188

26 92 66542

26 93 69267

26 94 71063

26 95 74549

27 90 61674

27 91 66584

27 92 69185

27 93 75193

27 94 78647

27 95 81898

28 90 31673

28 91 31883

28 92 32774

28 93 34485

28 94 36929

28 95 39751

29 90 63412

29 91 67593

29 92 69911

29 93 73092

29 94 80105

29 95 81840

30 90 27684

30 91 28439

30 92 30861

30 93 31406

30 94 32960

30 95 35530

31 90 71873

31 91 76449

31 92 80848

31 93 88691

31 94 94149

31 95 97431

32 90 62177

32 91 63812

32 92 64235

32 93 65703

32 94 69985

32 95 71136

33 90 37684

33 91 38258

**33 92 39208**

**33 93 39489**

**33 94 39745**

**33 95 41236**

**34 90 64013**

**34 91 66398**

**34 92 71877**

**34 93 75610**

**34 94 76395**

**34 95 79644**

**35 90 16011**

**35 91 16847**

**35 92 17746**

**35 93 19123**

**35 94 19183**

**35 95 19996**

**36 90 49215**

**36 91 52195**

**36 92 52343**

**36 93 56365**

**36 94 58752**

**36 95 59354**

**37 90 15774**

**37 91 16643**

**37 92 17605**

**37 93 18781**

**37 94 18996**

**37 95 19685**

**38 90 29106**

**38 91 31693**

**38 92 31852**

**38 93 34505**

**38 94 35806**

**38 95 36179**

**39 90 25147**

**39 91 26923**

**39 92 28785**

**39 93 30987**

**39 94 34036**

**39 95 34106**

**40 90 71978**

**40 91 79144**

**40 92 80453**

**40 93 86580**

**40 94 95164**

**40 95 96155**

**41 90 46166**

**41 91 47579**

**41 92 49455**

**41 93 53849**

**41 94 56630**

**41 95 57473**

**42 90 55810**

**42 91 59443**

**42 92 65291**

**42 93 66065**

**42 94 69009**

**42 95 74365**

**43 90 49642**

**43 91 50603**

**43 92 53917**

**43 93 54858**

**43 94 58470**

**43 95 59767**

**44 90 21348**

**44 91 22361**

**44 92 23412**

**44 93 24038**

**44 94 24774**

**44 95 25828**

**45 90 44361**

**45 91 48720**

**45 92 51356**

**45 93 54927**

```
45 94 56670
45 95 58800
46 90 56509
46 91 60517
46 92 61532
46 93 65077
46 94 69594
46 95 73089
47 90 39097
47 91 40293
47 92 43237
47 93 44809
47 94 48782
47 95 53091
48 90 18685
48 91 19405
48 92 20165
48 93 20316
48 94 22197
48 95 23557
49 90 73103
49 91 76243
49 92 76778
49 93 82734
49 94 86279
49 95 86784
50 90 48129
50 91 49267
50 92 53799
50 93 58768
50 94 63011
50 95 66461
;
run;

proc transpose data=long4 out=wide4 prefix=inc;
  by id;
  id year;
  var inc;
run;

proc print data=wide4 (obs=10);
run;
```

| Obs | id | _NAME_ | inc90 | inc91 | inc92 | inc93 | inc94 | inc95 |
|---|---|---|---|---|---|---|---|---|
| 1 | 1 | inc | 66483 | 69146 | 74643 | 79783 | 81710 | 86143 |
| 2 | 2 | inc | 17510 | 17947 | 19484 | 20979 | 21268 | 22998 |
| 3 | 3 | inc | 57947 | 62964 | 68717 | 70957 | 75198 | 75722 |
| 4 | 4 | inc | 64831 | 71060 | 71918 | 72514 | 73100 | 74379 |
| 5 | 5 | inc | 18904 | 19949 | 21335 | 22237 | 23829 | 23913 |
| 6 | 6 | inc | 32057 | 34770 | 35834 | 37387 | 40899 | 42372 |
| 7 | 7 | inc | 60551 | 64869 | 67983 | 70498 | 71253 | 75177 |
| 8 | 8 | inc | 16553 | 18189 | 18349 | 19815 | 21739 | 22980 |
| 9 | 9 | inc | 32611 | 33465 | 35961 | 36416 | 37183 | 40627 |
| 10 | 10 | inc | 61379 | 66002 | 67936 | 70513 | 74405 | 76009 |

## Reshaping data with numeric and character variables

The following example shows how to reshape multiple variables, some of which are numeric and other that are character (i.e., string) variables. The approach here is the same as in Example 2 that **proc transpose** is used multiple times and the data files are then merged together.

```
data long5;
  length debt $ 3;
  input famid year faminc spend debt $ ;
cards;
1 96 40000 38000 yes
1 97 40500 39000 yes
1 98 41000 40000 no
2 96 45000 42000 yes
2 97 45400 43000 no
2 98 45800 44000 no
3 96 75000 70000 no
3 97 76000 71000 no
3 98 77000 72000 no
;
run;

proc transpose data=long5 out=widef prefix=faminc;
  by famid;
  id year;
  var faminc;
run;

proc transpose data=long5 out=wides prefix=spend;
  by famid;
  id year;
  var spend;
run;

proc transpose data=long5 out=wided prefix=debt;
  by famid;
  id year;
  var debt;
run;

data wide5 ;
  merge widef (drop=_name_) wides (drop =_name_) wided (drop=_name_);
  by famid ;
run;

proc print data=wide5;
run;
```

| Obs | famid | faminc96 | faminc97 | faminc98 | spend96 | spend97 | spend98 | debt96 | debt97 | debt98 |
|---|---|---|---|---|---|---|---|---|---|---|
| 1 | 1 | 40000 | 40500 | 41000 | 38000 | 39000 | 40000 | yes | yes | no |
| 2 | 2 | 45000 | 45400 | 45800 | 42000 | 43000 | 44000 | yes | no | no |
| 3 | 3 | 75000 | 76000 | 77000 | 70000 | 71000 | 72000 | no | no | no |

The following examples will illustrate how to reshape data from long to wide using the data step.

## Example 1: Reshaping one variable

We will begin with a small data set with only one variable to be reshaped. We will use the variables **year** and **faminc** (for family income) to create three new variables: **faminc96**, **faminc97** and **faminc98**. First, let's look at the data set and use **proc print** to display it.

```
DATA long ;
  INPUT famid year faminc ;
CARDS ;
1 96 40000
1 97 40500
1 98 41000
2 96 45000
2 97 45400
2 98 45800
3 96 75000
3 97 76000
3 98 77000
;
RUN ;

PROC PRINT DATA=long ;
RUN ;
```

| Obs | famid | year | faminc |
|---|---|---|---|
| 1 | 1 | 96 | 40000 |
| 2 | 1 | 97 | 40500 |
| 3 | 1 | 98 | 41000 |
| 4 | 2 | 96 | 45000 |
| 5 | 2 | 97 | 45400 |
| 6 | 2 | 98 | 45800 |
| 7 | 3 | 96 | 75000 |
| 8 | 3 | 97 | 76000 |
| 9 | 3 | 98 | 77000 |

Now let's look at the program. The first step in the reshaping process is sorting the data (using **proc sort**) on an identification variable (**famid**) and saving the sorted data set (**longsort**). Next we write a data step to do the actual reshaping. We will explain each of the statements in the data step in order.

```
PROC SORT DATA=long OUT=longsort ;
  BY famid ;
RUN ;

DATA wide1 ;
  SET longsort ;
  BY famid ;

  KEEP famid faminc96 -faminc98 ;
  RETAIN faminc96 - faminc98 ;

  ARRAY afaminc(96:98) faminc96 - faminc98 ;

  IF first.famid THEN
  DO;
    DO i = 96 to 98 ;
      afaminc( i ) = . ;
    END;
  END;

  afaminc( year ) = faminc ;

  IF last.famid THEN OUTPUT ;

RUN;
```

The new data set is named **wide1** on the **data** statement. The old set, **longsort**, upon which the new data set will based, is named on the **set** statement. Please note that you must use the sorted version of the old set in order for the reshaping to work properly. The identification variable (**famid**) is used on the**by** statement. Please note that this must be the same identification variable on which the data were sorted. If the **by** statement is omitted, then the **if-then-do** statements (which occur later in the data step) will not work properly, and SAS will issue an error message.

Next, a **keep** statement is used to keep the desired variables in the new data set. We will keep the identification variable (**famid**) and the three variables we are creating, **faminc96**, **faminc97** and **faminc98**. Any variable that is not listed on the **keep** statement will not be present in the new data set. A **retain**statement is used to tell SAS to retain the current values of the variables listed. If the **retain** statement is omitted, only the values for **faminc98** are placed in the new data set, while all of the data for **faminc96** and **faminc97** will be missing.

An **array** statement is used to define the variables **faminc96**, **faminc97** and **faminc98**. In our example, we have named the array **afaminc**. In parenthesis we have given the first and last value of the array separated by a colon (:). The new variable names are then listed. We can list the first and last new variable names separated by a dash because the names are numerically consecutive. This is especially convenient when there are a large number of variables being defined by the array.

We use an **if-then-do** statement to set the conditions for a do-loop. The **by** statement that we used above not only caused SAS to process the data in the groups defined by the variable (**famid**) given on the **by** statement, it also caused SAS to create two temporary variables: **first.famid** and **last.famid**. Temporary variables are variables that you can use during a data step but do not appear in the new data set. The value of **first.famid** is always zero except when SAS is processing the first row of data for a given value of **famid**, then **first.famid** is one. In other words, **first.famid** is an indicator variable that is one when it is true that SAS is processing the first row of data for a given value of **famid**, and zero when it is not. The variable **last.famid** is created with the same logic, except that it equals one when SAS is processing the last row of data for a given value of **famid** and zero otherwise. You can now see why the data needed to be sorted on **famid** before we began the data step.

In the **do-loop**, we set **i** (you can use any name that you like) equal to the range we used in the **array** statement. We then set the array with **i** as the index variable equal to missing, which in SAS is a dot (.). As SAS processes the data through this loop, the missing values will be replaced with the data. If some of the data are missing, the missing value will not be altered. Please note that you can set the array equal to any value and that value will appear in any place that there is missing data.

After ending the **do-loop** and the **if-then-do** statement, we set the array with **year** as the index variable equal to **faminc**, the variable in the old data set. (Please note that you must have an **end** statement for each **do**.) It is at this point that the data in the variable **faminc** are associated with the new variables.

Finally, we use an **if-then** statement to have SAS output the data to the new data set each time it encounters the last occurrence of each value of **famid**. If this statement is omitted, SAS will output the results of its processing after each cycle of the loop, and we will end up with nine records instead of three. At long last, it is time to look at the new data set with a **proc print** to ensure that the reshaping went as desired, and we can see that it did.

```
PROC PRINT DATA=wide1;
RUN;

Obs    famid    faminc96    faminc97    faminc98

 1       1       40000       40500       41000
 2       2       45000       45400       45800
 3       3       75000       76000       77000
```

## Example 2: Reshaping two variables

This example is very similar to the last example, except that in this example we will be reshaping two variables, **faminc** and **spend**.

```
DATA long2;
  INPUT famid year faminc spend ;
CARDS;
1 96 40000 38000
1 97 40500 39000
1 98 41000 40000
2 96 45000 42000
2 97 45400 43000
2 98 45800 44000
3 96 75000 70000
3 97 76000 71000
3 98 77000 72000
;
RUN ;
```

We will modify the previous data step by adding the new variable to two statements that were present in the previous example and adding three new statements. In reshaping the data from long to wide, we will create six new variables: **faminc96**, **faminc97**, **faminc98**, **spend96**, **spend97** and **spend98**. The six variables are listed on both the **keep** and the **retain** statements. Following the same logic as in the previous example, we include an **array**statement to define the variables **spend96**, **spend97** and **spend98**. We have named the array **aspend**. We have also included this array in the do-loop. The third added statement sets **aspend** with **year** as the index variable equal to **spend**. As before, we run a **proc print** on the new data set to ensure that the reshaping was done correctly.

```
PROC SORT DATA=long2 OUT=longsrt2 ;
  BY famid ;
RUN ;

DATA wide2 ;
  SET longsrt2 ;
  BY famid ;

  KEEP famid faminc96-faminc98 spend96-spend98 ;
  RETAIN faminc96-faminc98 spend96-spend98 ;

  ARRAY afaminc(96:98) faminc96-faminc98 ;
  ARRAY aspend(96:98) spend96-spend98 ;

  IF first.famid THEN
  DO;
    DO i = 96 to 98 ;
      afaminc( i ) = 0 ;
      aspend( i ) = 0 ;
    END;
  END;

  afaminc( year ) = faminc ;
  aspend( year ) = spend ;

  IF last.famid THEN OUTPUT ;

RUN;

PROC PRINT DATA=wide2;
RUN;
```

| Obs | famid | faminc96 | faminc97 | faminc98 | spend96 |
|---|---|---|---|---|---|
| 1 | 1 | 40000 | 40500 | 41000 | 38000 |
| 2 | 2 | 45000 | 45400 | 45800 | 42000 |
| 3 | 3 | 75000 | 76000 | 77000 | 70000 |

Please note that you can reshape as many variables as you want in a single data step. All you need to do is list the variables on both the **keep** and **retain**statements and add an **array** statement, include the array in the do-loop and add a statement setting the array with the proper index variable equal to the desired variable in the old data set.

## Example 3: Two variables that identify the wide record

In this example, we have two variables that, when taken together, identify the wide record. In the data set below, the variables **famid** and **birth** together uniquely identify each wide record. (Please note that the data shown below are in long format, so **famid** and **birth** do not uniquely identify each record.) We will reshape one variable, **ht** (for height) from long to wide format.

```
DATA long3;
  INPUT famid birth age ht ;
CARDS;
1 1 1 2.8
1 1 2 3.4
1 2 1 2.9
1 2 2 3.8
1 3 1 2.2
1 3 2 2.9
2 1 1 2.0
2 1 2 3.2
2 2 1 1.8
2 2 2 2.8
2 3 1 1.9
2 3 2 2.4
3 1 1 2.2
3 1 2 3.3
3 2 1 2.3
3 2 2 3.4
3 3 1 2.1
3 3 2 2.9
;
RUN;
```

You will notice that the program used to reshape these data is very similar to the program used in example 1. Clearly, the variable names are different. The other important difference is that the data are sorted on both **famid** and **birth** in the **proc sort**, and both **famid** and **birth** are given in the **by** statement.

```
PROC SORT DATA=long3 OUT=longsrt3 ;
  BY famid birth ;
RUN ;

DATA wide3 ;
  SET longsrt3 ;
  BY famid birth ;

  KEEP famid ht1-ht2 ;
  RETAIN ht1-ht2 ;

  ARRAY aht(1:2) ht1-ht2 ;

  IF first.birth THEN
  DO;
    DO i = 1 to 2 ;
      aht( i ) = 0 ;
    END;
  END;

  aht( age ) = ht ;

  IF last.birth THEN OUTPUT ;

RUN;
```

We will run a **proc print** on the new data set to ensure that the reshaping went as expected.

```
PROC PRINT DATA=wide3;
RUN;
```

## Example 4: A more realistic example

This example is very much like the first example, except that the variable names are different. In this example, we will reshape the variable **inc** (for income). This is a more realistic example of reshaping data from long to wide in that there are many more records (300, instead of nine) and six time points (instead of three). Despite being a much larger data set, you will notice that the program to reshape it is almost identical to the program used to reshape the tiny data set in example 1.

**data long4;**

```
input id year inc ;
cards;
1 90 66483
1 91 69146
1 92 74643
1 93 79783
1 94 81710
1 95 86143
2 90 17510
2 91 17947
2 92 19484
2 93 20979
2 94 21268
2 95 22998
3 90 57947
3 91 62964
3 92 68717
3 93 70957
3 94 75198
3 95 75722
4 90 64831
4 91 71060
4 92 71918
4 93 72514
4 94 73100
4 95 74379
5 90 18904
5 91 19949
5 92 21335
5 93 22237
5 94 23829
5 95 23913
6 90 32057
6 91 34770
6 92 35834
6 93 37387
6 94 40899
6 95 42372
7 90 60551
7 91 64869
7 92 67983
7 93 70498
7 94 71253
7 95 75177
8 90 16553
8 91 18189
8 92 18349
8 93 19815
8 94 21739
8 95 22980
9 90 32611
9 91 33465
9 92 35961
9 93 36416
9 94 37183
9 95 40627
10 90 61379
10 91 66002
10 92 67936
10 93 70513
10 94 74405
10 95 76009
11 90 24065
11 91 24229
11 92 25709
11 93 26121
11 94 26617
11 95 28142
12 90 32975
12 91 36185
12 92 37601
12 93 41336
12 94 43399
12 95 43670
```

**13 90 69548**

**13 91 71341**

**13 92 72455**

**13 93 76552**

**13 94 80538**

**13 95 85330**

**14 90 50274**

**14 91 53349**

**14 92 55900**

**14 93 59375**

**14 94 61216**

**14 95 63911**

**15 90 72011**

**15 91 73334**

**15 92 76248**

**15 93 77724**

**15 94 78638**

**15 95 80582**

**16 90 18911**

**16 91 20046**

**16 92 21343**

**16 93 21630**

**16 94 22330**

**16 95 23081**

**17 90 68841**

**17 91 75410**

**17 92 80806**

**17 93 81327**

**17 94 81571**

**17 95 86499**

**18 90 28099**

**18 91 30716**

**18 92 32986**

**18 93 36097**

**18 94 39124**

**18 95 39866**

**19 90 17302**

**19 91 18778**

**19 92 18872**

**19 93 19884**

**19 94 20665**

**19 95 21855**

**20 90 16291**

**20 91 16674**

**20 92 16770**

**20 93 17182**

**20 94 17979**

**20 95 18917**

**21 90 43244**

**21 91 46545**

**21 92 47633**

**21 93 50744**

**21 94 54734**

**21 95 59075**

**22 90 56393**

**22 91 59120**

**22 92 60801**

**22 93 61404**

**22 94 63111**

**22 95 69278**

**23 90 47347**

**23 91 49571**

**23 92 50101**

**23 93 51345**

**23 94 56463**

**23 95 56927**

**24 90 16076**

**24 91 17217**

**24 92 17296**

**24 93 17900**

**24 94 18171**

**24 95 18366**

**25 90 65906**

**25 91 69679**

25 92 76131
25 93 77676
25 94 81980
25 95 85426
26 90 58586
26 91 61188
26 92 66542
26 93 69267
26 94 71063
26 95 74549
27 90 61674
27 91 66584
27 92 69185
27 93 75193
27 94 78647
27 95 81898
28 90 31673
28 91 31883
28 92 32774
28 93 34485
28 94 36929
28 95 39751
29 90 63412
29 91 67593
29 92 69911
29 93 73092
29 94 80105
29 95 81840
30 90 27684
30 91 28439
30 92 30861
30 93 31406
30 94 32960
30 95 35530
31 90 71873
31 91 76449
31 92 80848
31 93 88691
31 94 94149
31 95 97431
32 90 62177
32 91 63812
32 92 64235
32 93 65703
32 94 69985
32 95 71136
33 90 37684
33 91 38258
33 92 39208
33 93 39489
33 94 39745
33 95 41236
34 90 64013
34 91 66398
34 92 71877
34 93 75610
34 94 76395
34 95 79644
35 90 16011
35 91 16847
35 92 17746
35 93 19123
35 94 19183
35 95 19996
36 90 49215
36 91 52195
36 92 52343
36 93 56365
36 94 58752
36 95 59354
37 90 15774
37 91 16643
37 92 17605
37 93 18781

**37 94 18996**

**37 95 19685**

**38 90 29106**

**38 91 31693**

**38 92 31852**

**38 93 34505**

**38 94 35806**

**38 95 36179**

**39 90 25147**

**39 91 26923**

**39 92 28785**

**39 93 30987**

**39 94 34036**

**39 95 34106**

**40 90 71978**

**40 91 79144**

**40 92 80453**

**40 93 86580**

**40 94 95164**

**40 95 96155**

**41 90 46166**

**41 91 47579**

**41 92 49455**

**41 93 53849**

**41 94 56630**

**41 95 57473**

**42 90 55810**

**42 91 59443**

**42 92 65291**

**42 93 66065**

**42 94 69009**

**42 95 74365**

**43 90 49642**

**43 91 50603**

**43 92 53917**

**43 93 54858**

**43 94 58470**

**43 95 59767**

**44 90 21348**

**44 91 22361**

**44 92 23412**

**44 93 24038**

**44 94 24774**

**44 95 25828**

**45 90 44361**

**45 91 48720**

**45 92 51356**

**45 93 54927**

**45 94 56670**

**45 95 58800**

**46 90 56509**

**46 91 60517**

**46 92 61532**

**46 93 65077**

**46 94 69594**

**46 95 73089**

**47 90 39097**

**47 91 40293**

**47 92 43237**

**47 93 44809**

**47 94 48782**

**47 95 53091**

**48 90 18685**

**48 91 19405**

**48 92 20165**

**48 93 20316**

**48 94 22197**

**48 95 23557**

**49 90 73103**

**49 91 76243**

**49 92 76778**

**49 93 82734**

**49 94 86279**

**49 95 86784**

**50 90 48129**

**50 91 49267**

**50 92 53799**

**50 93 58768**

**50 94 63011**

**50 95 66461**

```
;
run;

PROC SORT DATA=long4 OUT=longsrt4 ;
  BY id ;
RUN ;

DATA wide4 ;
  SET longsrt4 ;
  BY id ;

  KEEP id inc90-inc95 ;
  RETAIN inc90-inc95 ;

  ARRAY ainc(90:95) inc90-inc95 ;

  IF first.id THEN
  DO;
    DO i = 90 to 95 ;
      ainc( i ) = 0 ;
    END;
  END;

  ainc( year ) = inc ;

  IF last.id THEN OUTPUT ;

RUN;
```

Because of the size of the data set, we will limit the **proc print** to the first five observations in the new data set to save space. Please note that the first five observations in the wide data set consist of the first 25 observations in the long data set. We will also run a **proc means** both data sets as well as our usual **proc print** to ensure that the reshaping was successful.

```
PROC PRINT DATA=wide4(obs=5) ;
RUN;
```

| Obs | id | inc90 | inc91 | inc92 | inc93 | inc94 | inc95 |
|---|---|---|---|---|---|---|---|
| 1 | 1 | 66483 | 69146 | 74643 | 79783 | 81710 | 86143 |
| 2 | 2 | 17510 | 17947 | 19484 | 20979 | 21268 | 22998 |
| 3 | 3 | 57947 | 62964 | 68717 | 70957 | 75198 | 75722 |
| 4 | 4 | 64831 | 71060 | 71918 | 72514 | 73100 | 74379 |
| 5 | 5 | 18904 | 19949 | 21335 | 22237 | 23829 | 23913 |

```
PROC PRINT DATA=long4(obs=25) ;
RUN;
```

| Obs | id | year | inc |
|---|---|---|---|
| 1 | 1 | 90 | 66483 |
| 2 | 1 | 91 | 69146 |
| 3 | 1 | 92 | 74643 |
| 4 | 1 | 93 | 79783 |
| 5 | 1 | 94 | 81710 |
| 6 | 1 | 95 | 86143 |
| 7 | 2 | 90 | 17510 |
| 8 | 2 | 91 | 17947 |
| 9 | 2 | 92 | 19484 |
| 10 | 2 | 93 | 20979 |
| 11 | 2 | 94 | 21268 |
| 12 | 2 | 95 | 22998 |
| 13 | 3 | 90 | 57947 |
| 14 | 3 | 91 | 62964 |
| 15 | 3 | 92 | 68717 |
| 16 | 3 | 93 | 70957 |
| 17 | 3 | 94 | 75198 |
| 18 | 3 | 95 | 75722 |
| 19 | 4 | 90 | 64831 |
| 20 | 4 | 91 | 71060 |
| 21 | 4 | 92 | 71918 |
| 22 | 4 | 93 | 72514 |
| 23 | 4 | 94 | 73100 |
| 24 | 4 | 95 | 74379 |
| 25 | 5 | 90 | 18904 |

```
PROC MEANS DATA=wide4 ;
  VAR inc90-inc95 ;
RUN;
```

The MEANS Procedure

| Variable | N | Mean | Std Dev | Minimum | Maximum |
|---|---|---|---|---|---|
| inc90 | 50 | 43899.32 | 19523.39 | 15774.00 | 73103.00 |
| inc91 | 50 | 46380.70 | 20749.43 | 16643.00 | 79144.00 |
| inc92 | 50 | 48519.58 | 21720.12 | 16770.00 | 80848.00 |
| inc93 | 50 | 50842.28 | 22780.12 | 17182.00 | 88691.00 |
| inc94 | 50 | 53289.02 | 23824.01 | 17979.00 | 95164.00 |
| inc95 | 50 | 55379.00 | 24592.83 | 18366.00 | 97431.00 |

```
PROC MEANS DATA=long4 ;
  CLASS year ;
  VAR inc ;
RUN;
```

The MEANS Procedure

Analysis Variable : inc

| year | N Obs | N | Mean | Std Dev | Minimum | Maximum |
|---|---|---|---|---|---|---|
| 90 | 50 | 50 | 43899.32 | 19523.39 | 15774.00 | 73103.00 |
| 91 | 50 | 50 | 46380.70 | 20749.43 | 16643.00 | 79144.00 |
| 92 | 50 | 50 | 48519.58 | 21720.12 | 16770.00 | 80848.00 |
| 93 | 50 | 50 | 50842.28 | 22780.12 | 17182.00 | 88691.00 |
| 94 | 50 | 50 | 53289.02 | 23824.01 | 17979.00 | 95164.00 |
| 95 | 50 | 50 | 55379.00 | 24592.83 | 18366.00 | 97431.00 |

## Example 5: Reshaping with string (character) variables

This example is similar to example 2 except that we have a third variable to reshape, and this new variable, **debt**, is a string (i.e., character) variable. There are only two minor differences between adding a numeric variable to our "template" program and adding a string variable. The first is in the **array** statement for the string variable. Before listing the names of the variables to be created, you need to include a dollar sign ($) to tell SAS to create a string variable and the number of variable to be created. In our example, we are creating three variables. The second difference is that when setting the string variable equal to missing in the do-loop, you use open-quote close-quote to indicate a null string instead of setting it equal to a dot. A dot is a missing value only for a numeric variable; a null string is a missing value for a string variable.

```
data long5;
  length debt $ 3;
  input famid year faminc spend debt $ ;
cards;
1 96 40000 38000 yes
1 97 40500 39000 yes
1 98 41000 40000 no
2 96 45000 42000 yes
2 97 45400 43000 no
2 98 45800 44000 no
3 96 75000 70000 no
3 97 76000 71000 no
3 98 77000 72000 no
;
run;

PROC SORT DATA=long5 OUT=long5srt ;
  BY famid ;
RUN;

DATA wide5 ;
  SET long5srt ;
  BY famid ;

  KEEP famid faminc96-faminc98 spend96-spend98 debt96-debt98 ;
  RETAIN faminc96-faminc98 spend96-spend98 debt96-debt98 ;

  ARRAY afaminc(96:98) faminc96-faminc98 ;
  ARRAY aspend(96:98) spend96-spend98 ;
  ARRAY adebt(96:98) $ 3 debt96-debt98 ;

  IF first.famid THEN
  DO;
    DO i = 96 to 98 ;
      afaminc( i ) = 0 ;
      aspend( i ) = 0 ;
      adebt( i ) = " " ;
    END;
  END;

  afaminc( year ) = faminc ;
  aspend( year ) = spend ;
  adebt( year ) = debt ;

  IF last.famid THEN OUTPUT ;

RUN;
```

We will run a **proc print** on the new data set to ensure that the reshaping was successful.

```
PROC PRINT DATA=wide5 ;
RUN;
```

| Obs | famid | faminc96 | faminc97 | faminc98 | spend96 | spend97 | spend98 | debt96 | debt97 | debt98 |
|---|---|---|---|---|---|---|---|---|---|---|
| 1 | 1 | 40000 | 40500 | 41000 | 38000 | 39000 | 40000 | yes | yes | no |
| 2 | 2 | 45000 | 45400 | 45800 | 42000 | 43000 | 44000 | yes | no | no |
| 3 | 3 | 75000 | 76000 | 77000 | 70000 | 71000 | 72000 | no | no | no |

# SECTION III: PRACTICAL BUSINESS ANALYTICS USING SAS

CHAPTER 3

# FROM BIG DATA TO MEANINGFUL INFORMATION WITH SAS® HIGH-PERFORMANCE ANALYTICS

Silvia Bolohan, and Sebastian Ciobanu

**Keywords:** Big data, data visualization, high-performance analytics, grid computing, inmemory analytics, in database computing, Hadoop

## INTRODUCTION

Big Data At first glance, the term seems rather vague, referring to something that is large and full of information. That description does indeed fit the bill, yet it provides no information on what Big Data really is. Big Data is often described as extremely large data sets that have grown beyond the ability to manage and analyze them with traditional data processing tools. Searching the Web for clues reveals an almost universal definition, shared by the majority of those promoting the ideology of Big Data, that can be condensed into something like this: Big Data defines a situation in which data sets have grown to such enormous sizes that conventional information technologies can no longer effectively handle either the size of the data set or the scale and growth of the data set. In other words, the data set has grown so large that it is difficult to manage and even harder to garner value out of it. The primary difficulties are the acquisition, storage, searching, sharing, analytics, and visualization of data.

There is much more to be said about what Big Data actually is. The concept has evolved to include not only the size of the data set but also the processes involved in leveraging the data. Big Data has even become synonymous with other business concepts, such as business intelligence, analytics, and data mining.

**Citation:** Silvia bolohan, and Sebastian Ciobanu, From Big Data to Meaningful Information with SAS® High-Performance Analytics, http://www.dbjournal.ro/archive/13/13_3.pdf.

Paradoxically, Big Data is not that new. Although massive data sets have been created in just the last two years, Big Data has its roots in the scientific and medical communities, where the complex analysis of massive amounts of data has been done for drug development, physics modeling, and other forms of research, all of which involve large data sets. Yet it is these very roots of the concept that have changed what Big Data has come to be.

Big data is defined less by volume – which is a constantly moving target – than by the ever-increasing variety, complexity, velocity and variability of the data. “When you’re talking about unstructured data, the concept of data variety can become more significant than volume,” said Pope. “Organizations must be able to fold unstructured data into quantitative analysis and decision making. Yet text, video and other unstructured media require different architecture and technologies for analysis. “Legacy data infrastructures are really not designed to effectively handle big data, and that’s why new technologies are coming online to help deal with that. With big data technologies, information users can now examine and analyze more complex problems than ever before. The ability to quickly analyze big data can redefine so many important business functions, such as risk calculation, prize optimization, customer experience and social learning. It’s hard to imagine any forward-looking company that is not considering its big data strategy, regardless of actual data volume.” Some organizations will have to rethink their data management strategies when they face hundreds of gigabytes of data for the first time; others might be OK until they reach tens or hundreds of terabytes. But whenever an organization reaches the critical mass defined as big data for them, change is inevitable.

## BIG DATA TECHNOLOGIES

Accelerated processing with huge data sets is made possible by four primary technologies:

- High-performance computing makes it possible to analyze all available data, for cases where analyzing just a subset or samples would not yield as accurate a result. High-performance computing enables you do things you never thought about before because the data was just way too big.
- In-database analytics, an element of high-performance computing, moves relevant data management, analytics and reporting tasks to where the data resides. This approach improves speed, reduces data movement and promotes better data governance.
- In-memory analytics can solve complex problems and provide answers more rapidly than traditional diskbased processing because data can be quickly pulled into memory.
- The Hadoop framework stores and processes large volumes of data on grids of low-cost commodity hardware.

A number of recent technology advancements enable organizations to make the most of big data and big data analytics:

Cheap, abundant storage.

- Faster processors.
- Affordable open source, distributed big data platforms, such as Hadoop.
- Parallel processing, clustering, MPP, virtualization, large grid environments, high connectivity and high throughputs.
- Cloud computing and other flexible resource allocation arrangements.

The goal of all organizations with access to large data collections should be to harness the most relevant data and use it for better decision making.

"The concept of high-performance analytics is about using these high-performance computing techniques specifically with analytics in mind," said Pope. "It's a bit of a nuance, but it refers to applying advanced analytics as a core piece of the infrastructure."[1]

### What Should You Capture, and What Should You Keep?

Technology enables you to capture every bit and byte, but should you? No. Not all of the data in the big data ocean will be relevant or useful. Organizations must have the means to separate the wheat from the chaff and focus on what counts, instead of boiling the proverbial ocean.

"Organizations shouldn't try to analyze the world just to answer one question," said Pope. "They need to first isolate the relevant data, then further refine the analysis, and be able to iterate large amounts of complex data. These requirements are not mere technical problems; they are central to creating useful knowledge that supports effective decisions." [1]

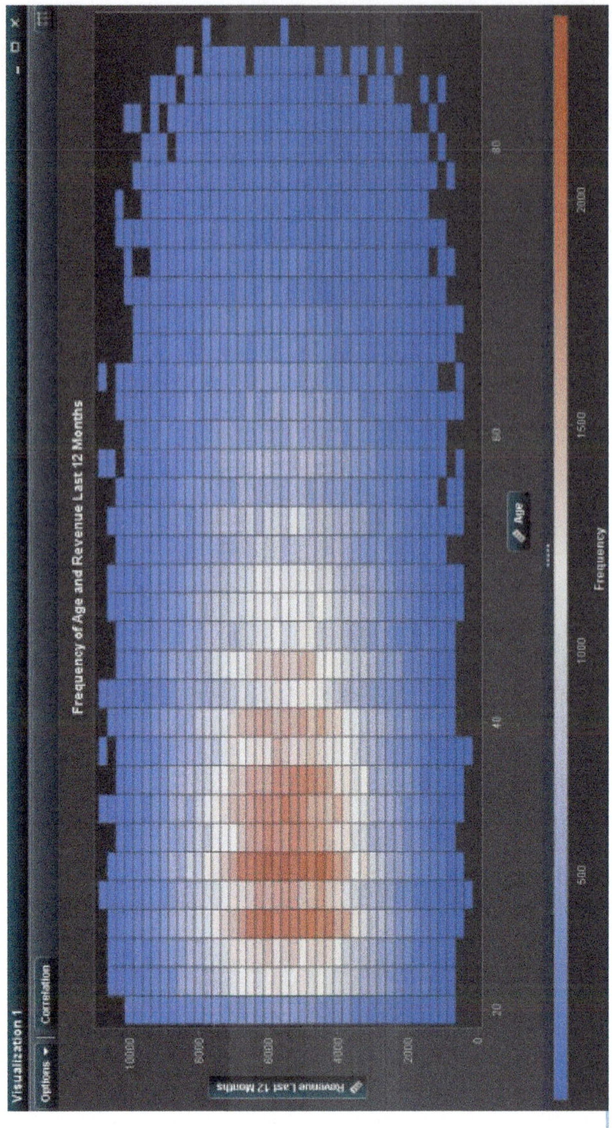


**Figure 1**: Data Visualization: Correlation between Age & Revenue (in last 12 months)

### Smart Filters Identify What to Store

With smart content extraction, the organization captures and stores only what is suspected of being relevant for further processing, and filters out unnecessary documents during the initial retrieval. The goal is to reduce data noise and store only what is needed to answer business questions. "Smart filters help identify the relevant data, so you don't spend time searching large data stores simply because you don't know what subsection of data could contain value," said Pope. Smart filters can apply natural language processing (NLP) and advanced linguistic techniques to identify and extract only the text that is initially believed to be relevant to the business question at hand.

Pope provided an example of smart content extraction for a SAS customer that monitors scientific information sources across disciplines and media outlets to identify potential risks to food production, creating notifications and reports for advance notice to government and production agencies.

"This organization assesses more than 15 million unique

texts looking for relationships between chemicals in the food production chain and possible side effects," said Pope. "Historically, the organization was restricted to running this analysis once a month. Given that there's a time value to safety-related information and reports, month-old data is not going to be as effective as more recent data, especially if there could be public health risks at stake." [1]

Now the organization can customize information retrieval calls on those millions of texts across the entire food chain, honing in on the most relevant information before download. As search functions crawl the Web, smart filters with embedded extraction rules filter out the irrelevant content. "This customer found out that only about 10 percent of the data they previously stored was what they were interested in," said Pope. "By narrowing down the data store and analysis to that critical 10 percent, they can now report much more frequently and deliver better and more timely alerts of emerging contaminants or other safety risks, for government agencies to take action."

## Smart Filters Determine Where to Keep What You Capture

In addition to identifying the most relevant nuggets of information from the available universe of information, smart filters can help determine where to store this data. Is it highly relevant? Then you'd want to have it readily accessible in an operational database type of storage. Or is it lower relevance? If so, it can be stored in lowercost storage, such as a Hadoop cluster.

Now organizations have a way to analyze data up front, determine its relative importance, and use analytics to support automated processes that move data to the most appropriate storage location as it evolves from low to high relevance, or vice versa.

## Capture and Correlate Data on the Fly

Often it's not a matter of storing the data somewhere, but how to manage it in flight, for instance, when capturing website activity to optimize the online customer experience. "We may be capturing deep and broad information about a person or product from the Web or other sources – getting complete and accurate, detailed data on everything they view, everything they do and everything that happens, timed to the millisecond," said Pope. "Once we bring in that data from online applications, we want to be able to tie it to other data sources. We might want to tie it to the customer relationship management system, or to an in-store promotion or contact center script. So the big data challenge is two-pronged: There's a need for extremely high efficiency in processing data into insight, and speed in delivering that insight to the point of action."

## From Hindsight to Insight to Foresight

"Raw data has the potential to do a lot of things, ranging from static reporting about what happened in the past to predictive insight about what will happen in the future," said Pope. "Business intelligence (BI) helps keep your business running this year; business analytics help you keep running your business three to five years from now." Most companies that think they have analytics actually just have operational reports that tell them about what has happened in the past. Such hindsight reports are important to an organization, because they describe the current pulse of the organization and inform decisions to react to it. For instance, you may need to know how many people have downloaded articles that mention your company, how customer sentiment about your brand has changed in social media, and which keywords drive the best prospects to your website. "A proactive report, on the other hand, not only gives you that operational view of what happened in the past or present – such as how many website visitors downloaded which articles – but also gives you a prediction into the future – what visitors will most likely want to download next week. You gain foresight to help determine which content to generate, how to optimize the website design and so on."[1]

Is your organization using the data for hindsight as well as foresight? And is it using all the data it could to its best advantage? If we can assume that (A) more data can lead to more insight and hence is better than less data, and (B) analytics provides more forward-looking insight than point-in-time reporting, then the business value the organization gets from its data can be conceptualized in four quadrants.

## New Thinking About Data and Model Management

In an on-the-fly, on-demand data world, organizations may find themselves having to rethink how they do data preparation and how they manage the analytical models that transform data into insight.

## Evolve from Being Data-Focused to Analytics-Focused

"In the typical IT-focused organization, application design is driven by a data focus," said Pope. "This is not a slight on the IT organization, just that applications are designed for a known outcome that you want to deliver to the organization over and over again. That approach is great for automating repetitive delivery of a fact or a standard report, but it isn't adaptable for developing new insights. If the data sources change, you would have to change all the models and applications as well. "In an analytic organization, on the other hand, application design is driven by an analytics focus. End users are looking to the IT infrastructure to deliver new insights, not the same thing over and over. These new discoveries may arise from any type of data (often combinations of data), as well as different technologies for exploring and modeling various scenarios and questions. So there must be recognized interlinks between data, analytics and insights – and applications must make these connections accessible to users. With an analytics approach, you can add new data sources on the back end without having to change the application."

## Consider That Data Preparation Is Different for Analytics than for Reporting

Different analytic methods require different data preparation. For example, with online analytical processing (OLAP) reporting, you would put a lot of effort into careful data cleansing, transformation through extract-transform-load (ETL) processes, dimension definition and so on. However, with query-based analytics, users often want to begin the analysis very quickly in response to a sudden change in the business environment. The urgency of the analysis doesn't allow time for much (if any) data transformation, cleansing and modeling. Not that you'd want to, because too much upfront data preparation may remove the data nuggets that would fuel discovery. For example, if you're trying to identify fraud, you wouldn't want a data cleansing routine to fix aberrations in names and addresses, since those very inconsistencies help spot potential fraud. For many such cases, you want to preserve the rich details in the relevant data that could reveal facts, relationships, clusters and anomalies.[3]

## Manage Models as Critical Information Assets

The proliferation of models – and the complexity of the questions they answer – call for a far more systematic, streamlined and automated way of managing the organization's essential analytic assets. A predictive analytics factory formalizes ongoing processes for the requisite data management and preparation, model building, model management and deployment.

A predictive analytics factory closes the analytical loop in two ways, by:

- Providing a mechanism to automatically feed model results into decision-making processes – putting the model-derived intelligence to practical use.
- Monitoring the results of that intelligence to make sure the models continue to add value. When model performance has degraded – for example, due to customer behavior changes or changes in the marketplace – the model should be modified or retired.

## Use All the Data, if It Is Relevant

Depending on your business goal, data landscape and technical requirements, your organization may have very different ideas about working with big data. Two scenarios are common:

- In a complete data scenario, entire data sets can be properly managed and factored into analytical processing, complete with in-database or inmemory processing and grid technologies.
- Targeted data scenarios use analytics and data management tools to determine the right data to feed into analytic models, for situations where using the entire data set isn't technically feasible or adds little value.

The point is, you have a choice. Different scenarios call for different options. "Some of your analytic talent has been working under self-imposed or system-imposed constraints," said Pope. "If you need to create subsets using analytics on huge data volumes, that is still valuable – if you're doing it in a smart, analytically sound way. But when you do predictive modeling on all your data, and you have the infrastructure environment to support it, you don't have to do all that work to find that valuable subset."[1]

## How to Get Started with Big Data Analytics

Determine the Analytical Maturity of the Organization Pope outlined a four-stage hierarchy that describes an organization's maturity level in its use of analytics for decision making:

- The Stage 1 organization is analytically naive. Senior management has limited interest in analytics. Good luck with that.
- The Stage 2 organization uses analytics in a localized way. Line of business managers drive momentum on their own analytics projects, but there's no enterprise-wide cohesion, infrastructure or support.
- The Stage 3 organization has analytical aspirations. Senior executives are committed to analytics, and enterprisewide analytics capability is under development as a corporate priority.
- A Stage 4 organization uses analytics as a competitive differentiator. This organization routinely reaps the benefits of enterprise-wide analytics for business benefit and continuous improvement.

## Consider an Analytics Center of Excellence

A center of excellence is a cross-functional team with a permanent, formal organizational structure that:

- Collaborates with the business stakeholders to plan and prioritize information initiatives.
- Manages and supports those initiatives.
- Promotes broader use of information throughout the organization through best practices, user training and knowledge sharing.

Several different types may exist within a single organization. For example, a data management center of excellence focuses on issues pertaining to data integration, data quality, master data, enterprise data warehousing schema, etc. A traditional business intelligence (BI) center of excellence focuses on reporting, querying and other issues associated with distributing information to business users across the organization. In contrast, an analytics center of excellence focuses on the proper use and promotion of advanced analytics, including big data analytics, to produce ongoing value to decision makers at both an operational and strategic level. Forming an analytics center of excellence will not solve all the problems and challenges that may exist in the information environment today, but it will lead the way toward alignment – shaping the analytic evolution from project to process, from unit-level to enterprise-level perspective. [4]

# SAS® HIGH-PERFORMANCE ANALYTICS

SAS High-Performance Analytics enables organizations to quickly and confidently seize new opportunities, make better choices ahead of the competition and create new value from big data. It will handle your most difficult challenges and quickly generate high-impact insights.

With SAS High-Performance Analytics you can:

- Get the timely insights needed to make decisions in an ever-shrinking window of opportunity. Processing that once took days or weeks now takes just minutes or seconds, enabling faster innovation.
- Discover precise answers for complex problems.

Seize opportunities for growth that otherwise would remain unrecognized, and achieve better organizational performance.

- Optimally use and manage IT infrastructure resources to leverage big data and accommodate future growth while providing superior scalability and reliability.

## Challenges

- Increasing volumes and varieties of data. Exploding data volumes hinder the completion of key analytic processes in a timely manner.
- Excessive data movement, and unnecessary data proliferation. Organizations struggle to determine what data should be stored where and for how long, what data should be used in analytical processing and how it should be prepared for analysis.
- Overwhelmed and poorly deployed IT resources. More requests for analytical processing mean longer waits for answers and unpredictable response times.
- Analytical processing complexities. The growing number of analytical models and data refreshes that are needed require an on-demand pool of distributed and parallel processing resources. Otherwise, it simply takes too long to get results.

## How SAS® Can Help

Organizations are constantly seeking more effective ways to make decisions, relying increasingly on facts derived from a variety of data assets. But difficulties arise when data volumes grow ever-larger and there are hundreds or thousands of decisions to make each day.

Whether you need to analyze millions of price points, recalculate entire risk portfolios in minutes, identify well-defined customer segments or make attractive and targeted offers to customers in near-real time, SAS can help.

The scalability of SAS to handle huge volumes of data is unsurpassed. And SAS Analytics is considered best-in-class by both our customers and industry analysts. These advantages, combined with highperformance analytics, enable you to quickly exploit high-value opportunities from big data, while making the most of your existing investments or the latest advances in analytics infrastructure.

## Benefits

- Immediately capture value and gain competitive advantage by exploiting big data, including existing information and new data collected from other sources, such as mobile devices and social media.
- Achieve incredibly fast response times and gain rapid insights to identify optimal actions and make the best decisions.
- Use more granular data and more complex analytical algorithms to produce new insights quickly, solve your most difficult problems, act confidently to seize new opportunities and better manage risks.
- Improve collaboration and productivity among your analytic and IT groups.
- Ensure data quality, improve data governance and enhance resource use by reducing data movement and redundancy.
- Quickly meet ever-changing business demands with flexible and dynamic workload balancing and high availability.
- Incrementally grow and optimize IT infrastructures to support faster time to value in a cost-effective manner.

## Business Value

- Highly accurate and precise insights that lead to superior decisions.
- Near-real-time insights at the point of decision or embedded in business processes.
- The ability to act quickly and confidently to seize new opportunities and effectively manage risks.

## *IT Value*

- Superior performance, scalability and reliability.
- Optimal resource usage.
- Better data governance.

## Components

SAS Grid Computing enables you to automatically leverage a centrally managed grid infrastructure to achieve workload balancing, high availability of computing resources and parallel processing. Multiple applications and users can share a managed grid environment for better use of hardware capacity, while making incremental IT resource growth a possibility.

SAS Grid Manager allows individual SAS jobs to be split up, with each piece running in parallel across multiple SMP machines in the grid environment using shared physical storage. It enables organizations to create a managed, shared environment for processing large volumes of data and analytic programs. This makes it a perfect solution for managing multiple SAS users and jobs while enabling efficient use of IT resources and lower-cost commodity hardware.

SAS In-Database processing is a flexible, efficient way to get more value from increasing amounts of data by integrating select SAS technologies into your databases or data warehouses. It uses the massively parallel processing (MPP) architecture of the database or data warehouse for scalability and better performance.

Using SAS In-Database technologies, you can run scoring models, some SAS procedures and SQL queries inside a database. Moving relevant data integration, analytics and reporting tasks to where the data resides reduces unnecessary data movement, promotes better data governance and provides faster results. SAS Scoring Accelerator takes SAS® Enterprise Miner™ models and publishes them as scoring functions inside a database. This exploits the parallel processing architecture offered by the database to achieve faster results. SAS Scoring Accelerator interfaces are currently available for Aster Data, EMC Greenplum, IBM DB2, IBM Netezza and Teradata. [2]

SAS Analytics Accelerator for Teradata is designed for users of SAS Enterprise Miner, SAS/STAT® and SAS/ETS® who want to build predictive and descriptive models for executing directly within the database environment. In-database analytics shortens the time needed to build, execute and deploy models, improving productivity for both analytic professionals and IT staff. They also help tighten data governance processes by giving analytic professionals access to consistent, fresh data.

SAS® In-Memory Analytics enables you to tackle previously unsolvable problems using big data and sophisticated analytics. It allows complex data exploration, model development and model deployment steps to be processed in-memory and distributed in parallel across a dedicated set of nodes. Because data can be quickly pulled into the memory, requests to run new scenarios or new analytical computations can be handled much faster and with better response times.

SAS High-Performance Analytics (available for EMC Greenplum and Teradata) is the only in-memory offering on the market that processes sophisticated analytics and big data to produce timesensitive insights very quickly. SAS HighPerformance Analytics is truly about applying high-end analytical techniques to solve complex business problems – not just about using query, reporting and descriptive statistics within an in-memory environment. For optimal performance, data is pulled and placed within the memory of a dedicated database appliance for analytic processing. Because the data is stored locally in the database appliance, it can be pulled into memory again for future analyses in a rapid manner. SAS High-Performance Analytics addresses the entire model development and deployment life cycle. Unlike other offerings, SAS High-Performance Analytics can perform analyses that range from descriptive statistics and data summarizations to model building and scoring new data at breakthrough speeds.

SAS Visual Analytics is a highperformance, in-memory solution that empowers all types of users to visually explore big data, execute analytic correlations on billions of rows of data in minutes or seconds, gain insights into what the data means and deliver results quickly wherever needed. Giving multiple users the ability to dynamically examine huge volumes of data simultaneously, combined with SAS software's powerful high-performance analytics, provides organizations with an unprecedented way to tap into big data and identify new and better courses of action more quickly. Users can easily spot opportunities for further investigation and analysis, and then convey visual results to decision makers via Web reports or the iPad.

## SAS® In-Memory Industry Solutions

SAS High-Performance Markdown Optimization is part of the SAS Revenue Optimization Suite. It analyzes massive amounts of data in parallel and enables retailers to identify and implement optimal pricing strategies. Retailers can quickly determine which products to mark down, how much to mark them down, and when and where to adjust pricing to maximize revenues.

SAS High-Performance Risk delivers faster risk calculations. Global market volatility and economic uncertainty require financial services firms to be quick and agile. SAS High-Performance Risk helps rapidly answer complex questions in areas such as market risk, counterparty exposure, liquidity risk management, credit risk, stress testing and scenario analysis.

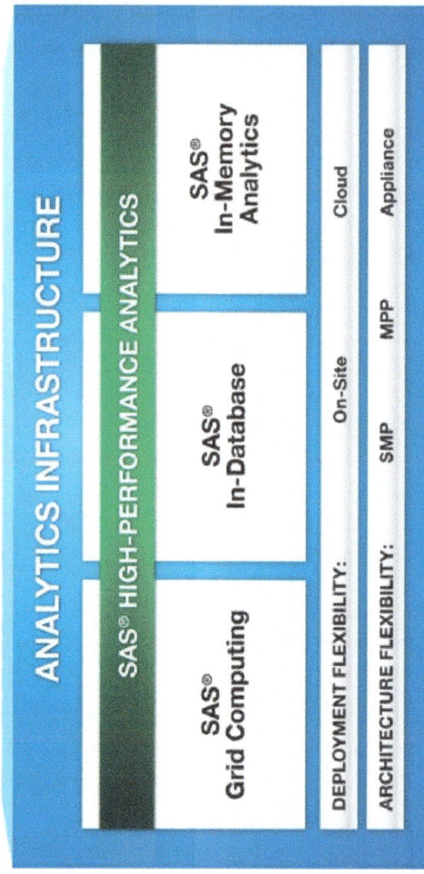


**Figure 2:** SAS® High-Performance Analytics – Key Components

## CONCLUSIONS

Big data technologies – such as grid computing, in-database analytics and inmemory analytics – can deliver answers to complex questions with very large data sets in minutes and hours, compared to days or weeks. You can also analyze all available data (not just a subset of it) to get more accurate answers for hard-to-solve problems, uncover new growth opportunities and manage unknown risks – all while using IT resources very effectively.

Using a combination of advanced statistical modeling, machine learning and advanced linguistic analysis, you can quickly and automatically decipher large volumes of structured and unstructured data to discover hidden trends and patterns. Whether you need to analyze millions of social media posts to determine sentiment trends, enrich your customer segmentation with information from unstructured sources, or distill meaningful insights from millions of documents and diverse content sources, big data technologies redefine the possibilities.

## REFERENCES

1. From Big Data to Meaningful Information - Webinar: kmworld.com/Webinars/487-From-BigData-To-Meaningful-Information.htm, David Pope, Principal Solutions Architect, SAS ® High-Performance Analytics
2. SAS High-Performance Analytics: www.sas.com/hpa
3. SAS white paper, Big Data Meets Big Data Analytics: www.sas.com/reg/wp/corp/46345
4. Thomas H. Davenport and Jill Dyche, "Big Data in Big Companies," May 2013.

CHAPTER 4

# SAS ENTERPRISE DATA INTEGRATION SERVER - A COMPLETE SOLUTION DESIGNED TO MEET THE FULL SPECTRUM OF ENTERPRISE DATA INTEGRATION NEEDS

Silvia Bolohan and Sebastian ciobanu

**Keywords**: Metadata, data cleansing, data integration, ETL, ELT

## INTRODUCTION

What does SAS® Enterprise Data Integration Server do?

SAS Enterprise Data Integration Server, featuring DataFlux® technology, is a powerful, configurable and comprehensive solution designed for managing big data. It can meet a wide variety of data integration requirements, from small tactical projects to strategic business initiatives.

- Access virtually all data sources.
- Extract, cleanse, transform, conform, aggregate, load and manage data.
- Support data warehousing, migration, synchronization, federation and provisioning initiatives.
- Support both batch-oriented and real-time master data management solutions.
- Create real-time, reusable data integration services in support of service-oriented architectures and data governance.

Why is SAS® Enterprise Data Integration Server important?

It enables organizations to efficiently manage data integration projects on an enterprise scale in a timely, cost-effective manner and meet the high data quality expectations of information consumers.

For who is SAS® Enterprise Data

Integration Server designed?

It is designed for organizations in all industry sectors that are implementing one or more data integration projects, dealing with changing business landscapes and business-driven IT initiatives, trying to meet regulatory requirements, or implementing data governance.

## SAS® ENTERPRISE DATA INTEGRATION SERVER

### Product overview

SAS offers the only comprehensive enterprise data integration environment that is built from the ground up to meet the full spectrum of enterprise data integration needs. Instead of linking and managing technologies from different vendors, SAS Enterprise Data Integration Server provides a collaborative design environment promoting object reuse and sharing, administrative controls, wizard-driven design process workflow, and ease of use and maintenance. This flexible, reliable solution can access data from virtually any system in

**Citation:** Silvia bolohan and Sebastian ciobanu, SAS Enterprise Data Integration Server - A Complete Solution Designed To Meet the Full Spectrum of Enterprise Data Integration Needs, http://www.dbjournal.ro/archive/7/7_5.pdf.

any form, transform and cleanse data even in real time, and handle data migration, synchronization and federation projects all through a versatile services environment that is easy to deploy and maintain.

## Interactive data Integration Development Environment

A graphical user interface (GUI) simplifies and speeds projects with wizards, extensive built-in transformations and powerful productivity enhancements, all while providing a single point of control for managing complex enterprise data integration processes. SAS Data Integration Studio is easy to learn and use. It provides a collaborative environment that lets you build reusable processes to speed data integration development both now and in the future. It automatically captures and manages standardized metadata from any source, and enables you to easily display, visualize and understand enterprise metadata and your data integration processes.

## Connectivity and Data Access

Most organizations struggle with accessing the plethora of data sources (legacy, relational, flat files, XML, cloud data, text, etc.) that are necessary to support analytical systems. SAS Enterprise Data Integration Server provides connectivity to virtually all types of data sources and types, operating systems and hardware environments using both native access and open standards. It also supports the reading and writing of data from message queues and the sending and receiving of data to and from Web services.

## Metadata Management

SAS provides a shared metadata environment that is both independent (for data integration) and part of SAS' comprehensive platform. Technical, business, process and administrative metadata is stored and managed in a way that leverages and facilitates reuse of existing table definitions, business rules and more. Navigational tools help users understand how the data was derived and where it is stored and used. Shared metadata provides a consistent definition across data sources to speed integration projects, simplify design and reduce maintenance costs.

## Data Cleansing and Enrichment

There is an increased awareness, driven by compliance mandates and data breaches, of how data quality and data governance can directly affect the bottom line. This puts increasing pressure on IT to address potential data quality issues. SAS Enterprise Data Integration Server provides a single environment that seamlessly integrates data quality within the data integration process, taking users from profiling and rules creation through execution and monitoring of results. From data de-duplication (for example, within database marketing applications) to cleaning up data (for example, before storing in a data warehouse), SAS provides an enterprise approach that lets you develop and share a library of data rules and processes between projects and across the entire data integration solution. Organizations can transform and combine disparate data, remove inaccuracies, standardize on common values, parse values and cleanse dirty data to create consistent, reliable information.

## Extraction, Transformation and Load (ETL) and Extraction, Load and Transformation (ELT)

Loading data warehouses and data marts within their allotted time windows, quickly building analytical marts for special projects, and creating extract files for reporting and analysis applications are tasks IT organizations face each day. SAS Enterprise Data Integration Server includes an intuitive point-and-click Design Editor window that allows developers to easily build logical process workflows, quickly identify the input and output data stores and create business rules in metadata, enabling the rapid generation of data warehouses, data marts and data streams. Users can also choose to have many transformations and processes take place inside a connected database, data warehouse or storage system. This is referred to as ELT, push-down or in-database processing, and can substantially speed up overall processing times by reducing unnecessary data movement. SAS Enterprise Data Server uses visual SQL push-down to select the optimal processing approach.

## Migration and Synchronization

Moving data from system to system is a constant activity in most organizations. Mergers and acquisitions result in multiple, overlapping systems containing information that often needs to be synchronized and ultimate migrated. Moving legacy data during upgrades and conversions is an on-going process, as is the movement of data into and out of ERP systems.

SAS Enterprise Data Integration Server provides the capability to migrate, synchronize and replicate data across different operational systems and data sources. The point-and-click process design editor makes it easy to document migration and synchronization processes in workflows that can be reused and modified for other projects. Powerful data transformations are available for altering, reformatting and consolidating information during these processes.

You also can build a library of reusable business rules ensuring that bad data is never spread from system to system. In this way, information delivered across all applications, systems, environments and geographies is up-to-date, consistent and accurate.

### Data Federation

Organizations today have data stored and scattered in and across numerous data sources. Often what's needed is fast access to the most current operational data to support real-time analytics and reporting needs. SAS Enterprise Data Integration Server provides the ability to query and use data across multiple systems without the physical reconciliation or movement of source data. The logical semantic layer shields business users from the complexities of the underlying physical data. By avoiding unnecessary data replication and movement, it is possible to quickly and cost-effectively deliver up-to-date data that is consistent and accurate.

## Master Data Management Support

SAS Enterprise Data Integration Server includes data-mastering capabilities that provide a basis for implementing master data management projects that enable you to identify, standardize and correct common master data such as customer and product data. Unsurpassed data access, profiling, enrichment, clustering and consolidation to clean, standardize and enhance data, and an intuitive development environment that is adaptable to each organization's technologies and standards, increase productivity and produce more rapid results.

## SOA and Message Queue Integration

Organizations are challenged to improve operational efficiency, streamline processes and be more agile. Using a service-oriented architecture (SOA) approach helps IT ensure that various applications can communicate with each other to better meet changing business requirements. SAS Enterprise Data Integration Server delivers easily maintained data services that enable developers to build sophisticated data services once and deploy them across the enterprise for reuse. Message queue integration is another way to reduce maintenance, integration costs and bridge new technologies.

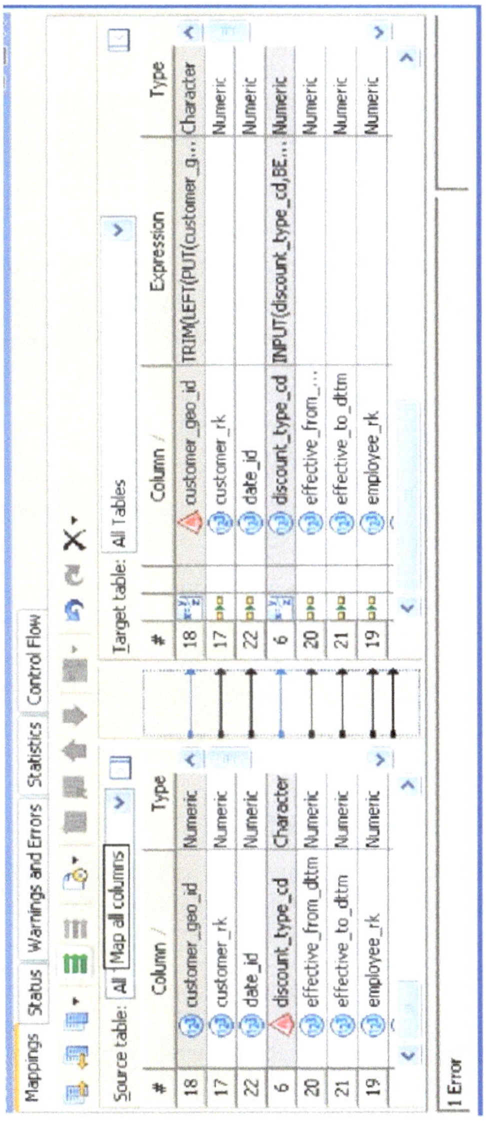


**Figure 1:** Default mapping rules chart

Using SAS Enterprise Data Integration Server, you can access message queues in batch or real time without the need for custom programming. Integration developers simply treat message queues as any other source and target. [1] With SAS Enterprise Data Integration Server, you can define the propagation of information from table to table in your transformations. This shows an example of the default mapping rules being applied when mapping numeric to character columns, and character to numeric columns. This also shows the intelligence of the mapping display that uses color to indicate the presence of a transformational expression between source and target. Default mapping rules are predefined but can be extended to meet business-specific needs.

## KEY FEATURES

### Interactive data integration development environment

- An easy-to-use, point-and-click GUI uses an intuitive set of configurable windows for managing data integration development processes.
- A visual, end-to-end process designer lets developers quickly build and edit processes.
- Drag-and-drop functionality eliminates programming.
- Wizards make it easy to access source systems, create target structures, import and export metadata, and build and execute ETL process flows.
- The multiple-user, multiple-level design environment supports collaboration on large, enterprise projects.
- Role-based permissions show users only what they are authorized to see.
- Customizable metadata tree views let users display, visualize and understand metadata.
- Dedicated GUI for profiling data to identify and repair source system issues while retaining the business rules for use in other ETL processes.
- Interactive debugging and testing of jobs during development and full access to logs.
- Check-in/check-out of jobs, related tables and objects; and job status viewing.
- Audit history lets designers see which jobs or tables were changed, when and by whom.
- Ability to distribute data integration tasks to nearly any platform and to connect virtually any source or target data store.
- Integration with third-party vendors Subversion and CVS provides enhanced version and source control features such as archiving, differencing and rollback.
- Job status and performance reports provide the ability to track metrics such as CPU use, memory, I/O, etc.
- Automated job deployment allows the use of common

scripting languages to deploy SAS Data Integration Studio batch jobs in an automated manner.

- Enhanced SAS code import capabilities give current SAS users an easy way to import their SAS jobs and SAS code into SAS Data Integration Studio. Includes logging and error checking.
- Command-line job deployment for deploying single and multiple jobs.
- Enhanced data integration job orchestration (process flow).
- The ability to surface in-database scoring models within SAS Data Integration Studio.
- Enhanced connectivity to Aster Data, EMC Greenplum, Hadoop and Sybase IQ databases with the ability to push down more processing to the databases. [2]

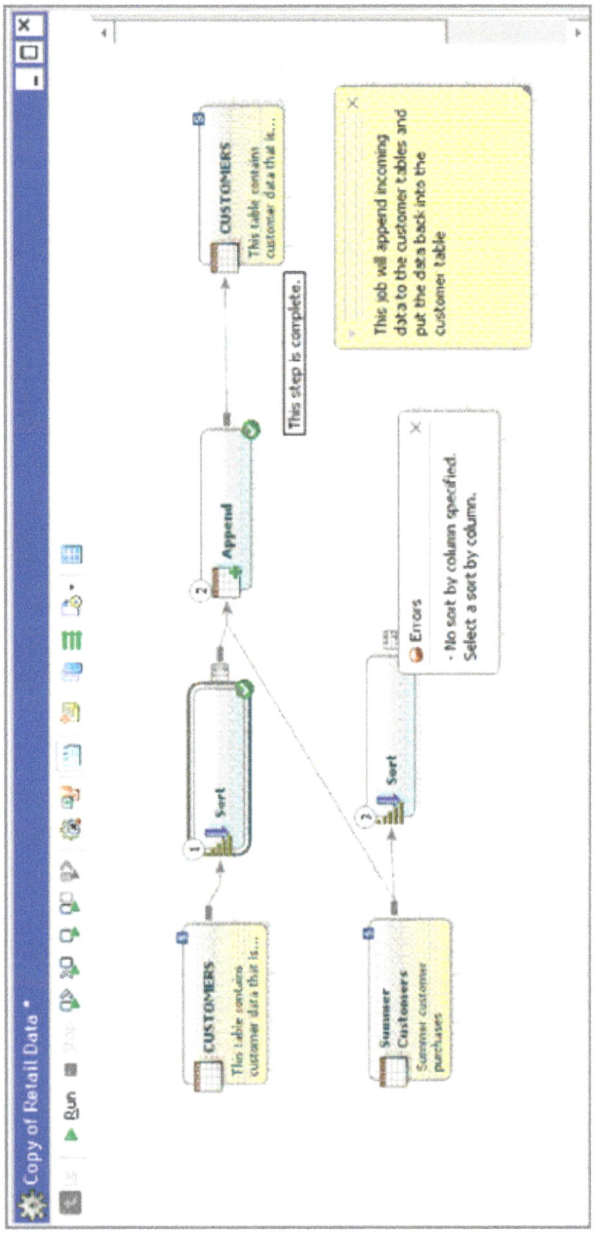


**Figure 2:** Retail Data Chart SAS Enterprise

Data Integration Server includes an easy-to-use and informative GUI. You build jobs by dragging and dropping data objects into the diagram area. You can add transformations such as sorts, joins and loads from a library and draw arrows to connect the objects together. Self-documentation is provided using annotated data, and yellow notes containing further information can be added by users.

## Connectivity and data access

- Provides connectivity in batch or through message queues in real time to more data sources on more platforms than any other solution.
- Data access engines are available for enterprise applications, nonrelational databases, RDBMSs, data warehouse appliances, PC file formats and more.
- Specialized table loaders provide optimized bulk loading of Oracle, Teradata and DB2.
- File reader/writer available for Hadoop file system (HDFS).
- Support for Hadoop's MapReduce, Pig and Hive within flows.
- Data movement capabilities to and from
- A complete and shared metadata environment provides consistent data definition across all data sources.
- Native access methods deliver the best performance and reduce the need for custom coding.
- Support for message-oriented middleware, including WebSphere MQ from IBM, MSMQ from Microsoft, Java Message Service (JMS) and Tibco's Rendezvous.
- Support for unstructured and semi-structured data to parse and process files.
- Access to static and streaming data for sending and receiving via Web services.
- Expanded support for MPP databases: AsterData nCluster, EMC Greenplum and Sybase IQ, enabling more ELT pushdown and support for bulk-load utilities.
- Native support for SQL-based processing.

## Metadata management

- Metadata is captured and documented throughout transformations and data integration processes, and is available for immediate reuse.
- Sophisticated metadata mapping technologies for quickly propagating column definitions from sources to targets, and for creating automated, intelligent table joins.
- New metadata search tool.
- Impact analysis for assessing the scope and impact of

making changes to existing objects such as columns, tables and process jobs before they occur.

- Ability to determine the path, processes and transformations taken to produce the resulting information.
- Data lineage (reverse impact analysis), which is critical for both validating processes and building user confidence in data.
- Change analysis for metadata change discovery, comparison, analysis and selective propagation.
- Multiple-user collaboration support includes object check-in and check-out.
- Promotion and replication of metadata across development, test and production environments.
- Wizard-driven metadata import and export.
- Wizard for metadata column standardization.
- Metadata-driven deployment flexibility so that process jobs can be deployed for batch execution, as reusable stored processes or as Web services.

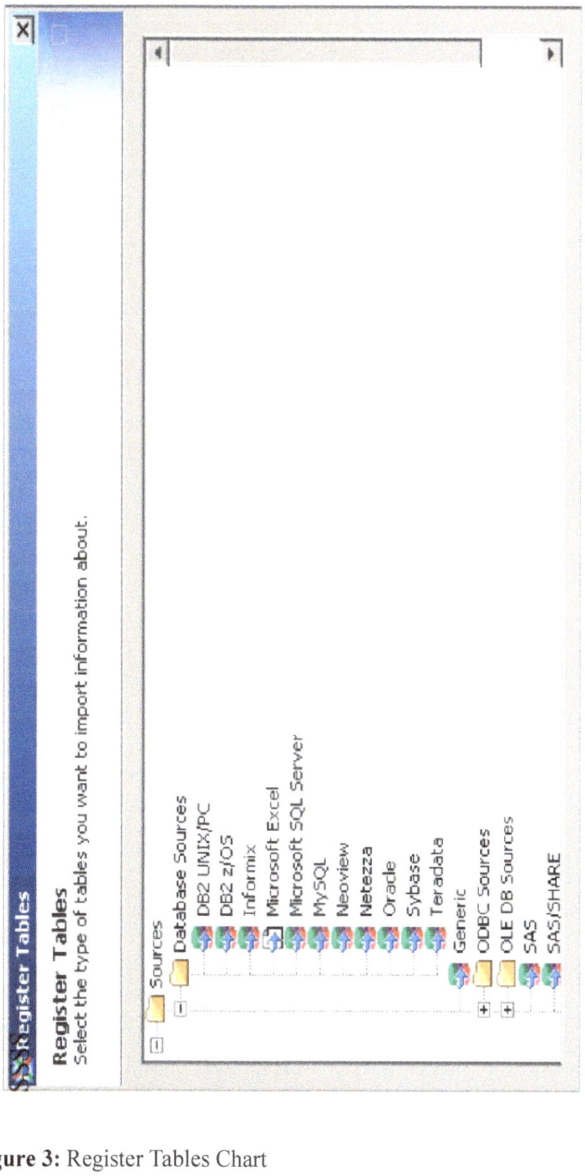


**Figure 3:** Register Tables Chart

The Register Tables wizard makes it easy to access data from many different systems, as well as read and manage metadata from external sources.

## CONCLUSIONS

From legacy systems to ERP applications to data stored in Hadoop, data from virtually any hardware platform or operating system can be accessed, cleansed and processed. New source systems can easily be added and security is managed centrally. This saves time, shortens learning curves and gives decision makers the complete information they need.

Another conclusion is that a common repository enables the centralized storage, management and reuse of work based on user authorizations, reducing both development and maintenance time. A GUI environment that is easy to use provides a standard interface for building and documenting work. Collaboration is encouraged and manual coding is available when needed. New team members can get up to speed quickly on work done by others, which is important when documentation is inadequate or missing.

A huge benefit of this tool is that you can manage security and administration at all levels. Reusable templates make it quick and easy to provide role-based authorizations and administrative privileges at the user, department or enterprise level.

SAS processes data fast! Organizations can take advantage of a grid-enabled load-balanced, multithreaded parallel processing architecture that can quickly trans-form and move data between different platforms and systems. SAS also supports zero data movement by using SQL pass-through into popular database appliances, including Oracle, DB2, Teradata, Netezza, SQL Server, AsterData and Hadoop.

Consistently getting correct data when and where it is needed provides increased confidence in the accuracy and timeliness of operational and business information. Data quality auditing tools monitor the quality of data in processes and source systems. Users can see where data originated and how it was transformed. Optional enrichment components can add value and ensure everyone receives the best possible data. Deliver consistent, trusted and verifiable information.

SAS offers the only comprehensive enterprise data integration solution that is built from the ground up to meet the full spectrum of data integration needs. It eliminates the piecemeal approach of linking and managing technologies from different vendors and provides lower overall cost, reduced risk and faster results.

## REFERENCES


1. SAS Data Integration Studio 4.4: User's Guide, http://support.sas.com/documentation/c dl/en/etlug/65016/HTML/default/viewe r.htm#titlepage.htm
2. Base SAS 9.3 Procedures Guide, http://support.sas.com/documentation/c dl/en/proc/63079/HTML/default/viewer .htm#titlepage.htm

CHAPTER 5

# DATA ENTRY IN SAS® STRATEGY MANAGEMENT

David Shubert

## INTRODUCTION

Using SAS Strategy Management in SAS is an excellent way to keep up with the various goals and directions of the organization but has historically been unpleasant to use when inputting raw data. In SAS Strategy Management version 5.4 the data-entry system has been completely redesigned to facilitate this task. The primary users of the system will discover a much-improved HTML5 user interface, extensive validation to insure data integrity, and integration with SAS Workflow Studio to allow for a user-defined system of approval before committing data to the application. In replacing the previous system this new functionality provides data-entry users greater accuracy, managers with an enhanced approval process, and modelers with a quick and simple way to create data entry forms.

## REVIEWING THE PREVIOUS DATA ENTRY SYSTEM

Before examining this new system it is instructive to consider the previous data-entry system included with SAS Strategy Management. It started with a form creation wizard that allowed the modeler to create a form. The modeler indicated which scorecards and elements for which data was to be collected, which metric attributes were to be used, and what period was involved. This wizard was long and not particularly intuitive, especially when specifying period information.

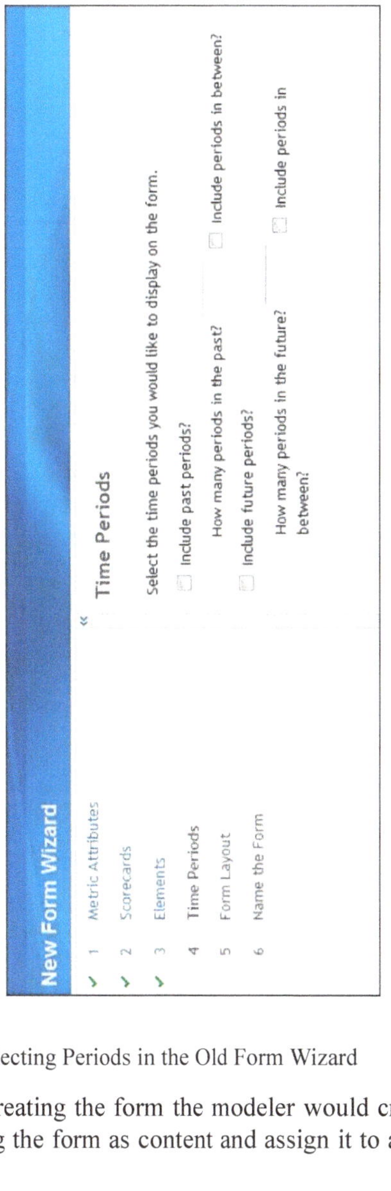


**Figure 1:** Selecting Periods in the Old Form Wizard

After creating the form the modeler would create a SAS portlet using the form as content and assign it to a number of

**Citation:** David Shubert, Data Entry in SAS® Strategy Management, http://support.sas.com/resources/papers/proceedings13/052-2013.pdf.

data-entry users by using SAS® Management Console to give those users access. Then the modeler would have to notify the users that the form was ready to use using email or some other method of communication.

The users would then begin to enter data by logging into the SAS® Information Delivery Portal and adding the form to their portal page. The form offered very little data validation. The validations were mostly as crude as checking for a nonblank entry or a value not interpretable as a number. This was implemented in JavaScript so at least the user did not have to submit the whole page to the system in order to get some validation, however there were other validations that required submission. The page of values could not be saved before submitting them to the system and once again the user had to notify the correct individual that they were finished.

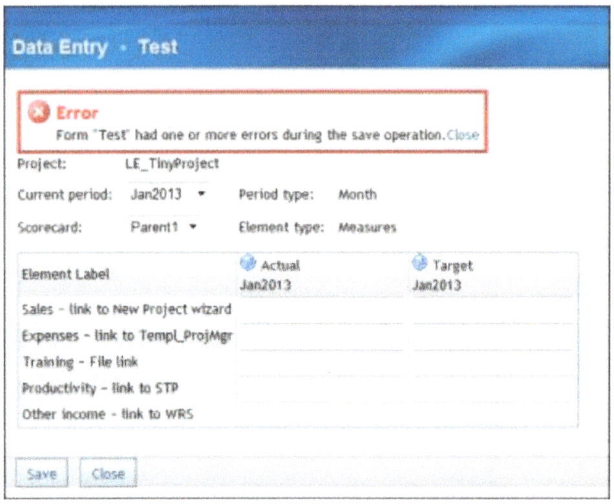


**Figure 2**: Data Submission Error in the Old Form Wizard

If the above seemed bad enough consider the situation presented to managers. Initially the system offered no opportunity for the manager to verify that the data entered was correct according to organizational standards. Instead it was simply written out to the SAS ® Strategy Management database and immediately reflected in all scorecards that used the data. Later the option of writing the data out to a temporary location (the WDE application option) was added. This allowed a user with the correct privileges to see a button that submitted all the data changes to the permanent database after that user had reviewed them.

Taken as a whole, the data-entry system was far from a polished and effective technique for data input to any application.

## DATA ENTRY METHODS IN SAS STRATEGY MANAGEMENT

The SAS Strategy Management application has come a long way as far as data-entry methods. It began with the Web user interface in the SAS Strategy Management Builder where the user could select a scorecard and element, then select a metric attribute and period to finally enter a numeric or text value. However to do all of this required many mouse clicks to enter a single value. A single SAS Strategy Management project often contains many scorecards each with many elements, and the time it took to enter data into all of them became prohibitive. Over the years the SAS Strategy Management development group has added various other methods of entering data into scorecards.

### The Batch Maintenance Facility

One method was the Batch Maintenance Facility (BMF). As the name implies this is a batch oriented process that was added to SAS Strategy Management version 2.3. A user can invoke a macro inside a SAS client to read data into or out of the SAS Strategy Management application. This macro can be very effective for SAS Strategy Management "power" users such as consultants and data modelers. However, BMF is not web-based, requires users with Modeler privileges, and is inherently technical in nature.

### Bulk Edit

The ability to add data in bulk or "Bulk Edit" was added to the Web application. This is web-based and allows the user to add values to a group of scorecards and elements at one time. Furthermore the user interface is reasonably intuitive. However, bulk edit also requires users with Modeler privileges and it forces the user to add the same value to every object in the group.

### The Import Feature

Starting in SAS Strategy Management version 5.3, the Import feature was added. Implemented as a hybrid approach between a batch process and an interactive Web-based process, this feature leverages BMF to read Excel spreadsheets and SAS datasets for input. Also it allows the user to map columns in the input data to SAS Strategy Management objects. The Import feature is more user friendly to less technical SAS Strategy Management users and it can be run from either the Builder or scheduled as a batch process. However the Import feature also requires that the user have Modeler privileges. Import also involves some degree of interaction with an administrator in order to set up the data source. Finally someone must learn the required format of the input spreadsheet or SAS data set.

All of the above methods have their place depending on certain kinds of tasks performed by the organization. But they all require advanced user privileges meaning that the person that enters the data has to be a Modeler or Administrator. Most companies might consider forcing all data entry through what is usually a relatively small number of people a bottleneck. The more common paradigm is to assign data entry to individuals that do not model the data themselves. Furthermore none of the above methods have any system of data approval inherent in the method. The data is immediately written into the SAS Strategy Management database. Again, it is a more common paradigm to have other individuals check the work before committing it. Finally, all of the above methods require that the user involved take on the responsibility of any notifications to any and all interested parties. Notification to these parties is crucial and requiring the user to perform this should not be necessary.

## INTRODUCING THE NEW DATA-ENTRY SYSTEM

In order to deal with the needs of a modern enterprise, SAS Strategy Management has redesigned its data-entry system and is introducing it in SAS Strategy Management 5.4. The basic concepts are still there. It starts with the creation of a data-entry form by a Modeler which is then incorporated into a portlet used by data-entry users. But the entire implementation has been rebuilt from the ground up. Take a tour of the new system and its features.

### User Interface

The new user interface has been created in HTML5 using the Dojo open source JavaScript library. It provides for a more modern and stylish appearance as seen in the screen capture below:

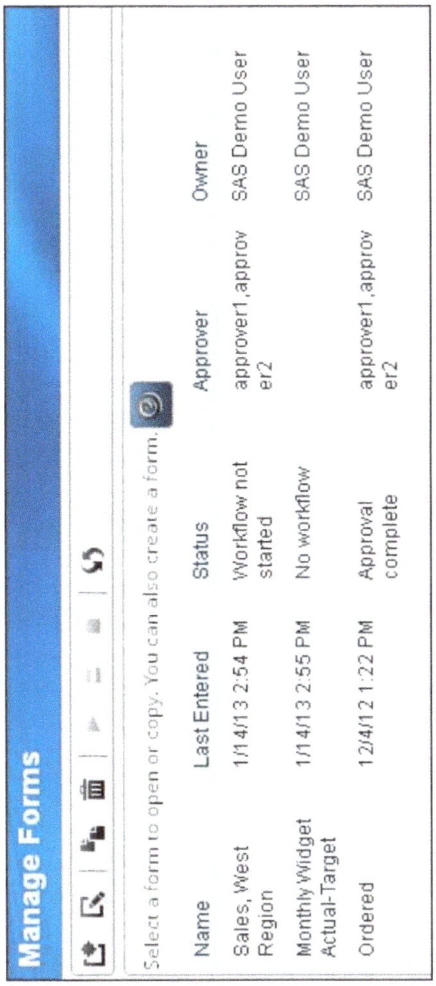


**Figure 3:** New Data-Entry System User Interface

Supported in Internet Explorer 8, 9, and above, FireFox 3.6 and above the new user interface offers a more visually appealing design. Additionally it makes use of Ajax-style server calls. This means that as you interact with the various controls data is fetched from the server without performing a time-consuming page refresh, that irritating holdover from the early Web application days. Data validations are performed almost instantly as you move out of a text field. You do not have to click a Submit button and wait for the page to return with updated values.

**Figure 4:** Data Validation

The entire user experience is enhanced making what can be a tedious and involved task much less painful and

### Rules-Based Data Validation

Another huge improvement comes in the area of data validation. As described earlier the old data-entry system had very rudimentary validation checks performed. Some were implemented in JavaScript so that the user did not have to submit the entire form to the system for validation, however some of the checks did require submission. When you consider that some forms may have over a hundred or more text fields you can imagine how difficult submitting the form over and over could be.

SAS Strategy Management 5.5 introduces rules, a new system of data validation that the user can associate with each metric attribute numeric and text value. The rules feature is implemented in HTML5 and Dojo. When you visit the Manage Rules page, you discover the ability to create a named data validation rule.

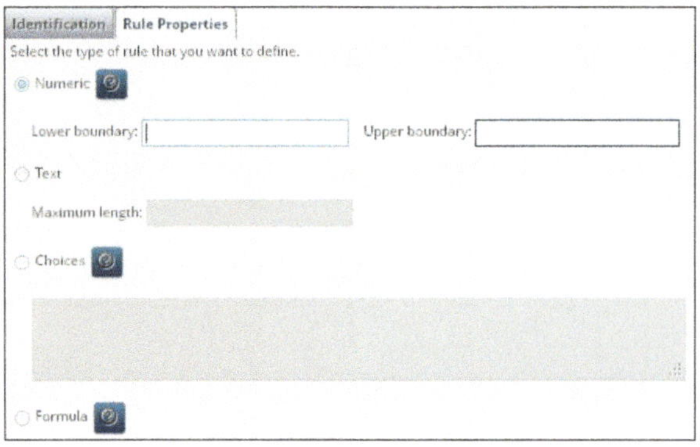


**Figure 5:** Rule Definition

Here the Modeler has the ability to define a data validation rule for the input values of a form. Notice that you can specify that the value is numeric or text along with a numeric range for numbers and a maximum length for text. Another possibility is Choices. This provides the Modeler with the ability to restrict the entered value to one of a discrete list of selections. The data-entry user will see a dropdown with the values entered here. Finally the rules feature leverages the considerable power of formulas for data validation. The Modeler can basically create almost any kind of validation, even the ability to compare the entered value with the value contained in some other SAS Strategy Management object. For maximum usability, the Modeler can specify a custom error message to explain why a potential entered value has failed validation because of a formula.

After specifying what the validation is the Modeler gives it a name which can be descriptive of what kind of validation is performed. Every metric attribute value whether numeric or text can have a rule assigned to it. This association is done in the SAS Strategy Management Builder on the Edit Metric Attributes page. More than one metric attribute can use a rule so the Modeler can define a core set of rules to be used by any metric attribute in the project.

When the form is displayed to the data-entry user the rules come into play. Because the user interface is using HTML5 the data validation occurs without submitting the page back to the server. Instead when the user's focus leaves the text field the data is checked. If it fails validation the text field is outlined in red and the appropriate error message is displayed (see Figure 4).

## Using Column Definitions for Column Selection

Another improvement is how the columns of metric attributes are selected for the form. In the new data-entry system, you select which metric attributes you want included by adding its column selection, not the attribute itself. As you may know the system of column selections in SAS Strategy Management allows a user to decide aspects of how each metric attribute column is displayed. You can determine the order of display, what date range is used, and whether the user can change the value. This functionality has now been extended to the data-entry system and makes it consistent with the way you view the table in the SAS Strategy Management Builder.

## WORKFLOW

The biggest enhancement to the data-entry system is the incorporation of workflow. Workflow is related to Business Process Management and when used here it is a subset of BPM that "emphasizes static routing and administration of human tasks." The SAS® Web Infrastructure Platform Database on which SAS Strategy Management runs, comes with a suite of workflow services and applications. SAS Strategy Management has integrated this feature into the data-entry system. The Modeler now has the option of attaching a predefined workflow pattern to the form. This opens up a whole new world for data entry with the ability to define precisely which users enter data into the form and which users approve the entered values. Notifications, if desired, are automatic. No more relying on the users to send email indicating that they are done. The form can be designed to be used once or restarted automatically after it has completed. Also, there exists the option to automatically perform other custom jobs of the Modeler's choosing during the workflow cycle.

### Integration with SAS Groups and Roles

Workflow is tightly coupled with the SAS Web Infrastructure Platform groups, users, and roles paradigm. SAS Strategy Management already makes use of the Modeler and Data Entry groups. With SAS Strategy Management 5.4 comes the introduction of a new group called the Data Entry Approver group. Like the Data Entry group, it has limited permissions compared to the Modeler role and that is by design. Most companies want users in these groups to see and alter only specific parts of a project. The data-entry system enables the Modeler to assign members of the Data Entry group to enter the data and members of the Data Entry Approval group to approve the data after it is entered.

### Workflow Templates

As mentioned above, the SAS Web Infrastructure Platform includes a workflow application. The application is called SAS Workflow Studio version 1.2 and it was used to design two workflow "templates" that are shipped and installed with SAS Strategy Management. These templates define the workflow cycle and can be thought of as a set of instructions. Visually they look like a chart of boxes and arrows. The boxes represent tasks and the arrows (really vectors) represent the path taken to the next task. The templates are designed separately from the software that runs the templates. Below is an example of a template in SAS Workflow Studio.

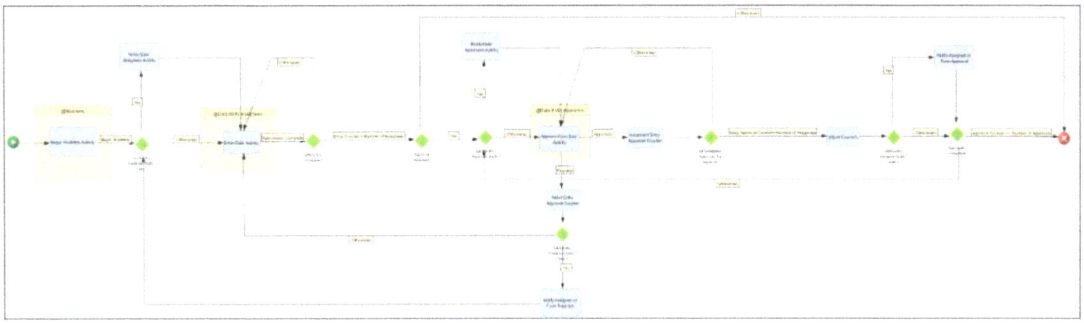

**Figure 6:** Workflow Template for Ordered Approval

## Attaching Workflow to a Form

When the Modeler creates the form he decides whether or not to use workflow with the form. If so he must provide some information that is passed to the Workflow service and determines which paths the template will take. This is done in the form wizard. Key parts of that information are lists of users who are to input the form data and lists of users who are to approve that data. After the form is created and the Modeler has selected a workflow template to use with it he must start the workflow by clicking a button on the Manage Forms page. This tells the Workflow service to begin an instance of workflow based on one of the templates.

At this point the Workflow service takes over. If the Modeler has opted to notify the data entry users that the form is ready for use the users receive a SAS alert notification with a message telling them that the form is ready for input. The type of notification depends on how the user has configured alerts in his portal. If email is desired he gets an email. If he wants the message in a Shared Alerts portlet then the message arrives there. All notifications are handled this way and are completely the responsibility of the Workflow service.

Then the Workflow service decides what is appropriate for each user to see. After the workflow instance is started and optional notifications are sent out the only users that can see the form in a portlet are the data-entry users selected when the form was created. If a data approver creates a portlet with the form he will only see a message telling him that it is not his time to see or interact with the form. This can become even more granular depending on which template was used to create the form. One of the templates enables the Modeler to define an ordered list of approvers with only one approver able to approve the form at a time. Using that template means that only the appropriate approver sees the form in his portlet, other approvers see a message indicating it was not their turn to approve.

All during this process the entered data is deposited into a temporary table, not into the SAS Strategy Management database. Data-entry users can enter data and save it without indicating that they are ready for it to be approved, a useful feature when you has significantly large forms to fill out.

When the data-entry user is done he submits his work. The Workflow service receives it and determines what happens next. If all the data-entry users are finished the service makes the form visible to the appropriate approver or approvers. When the approver views the form he is allowed to look at the entered data but not change any of it. The approver now has the option of accepting all the changes from all data-entry users, or accepting one or more data entry user's changes while rejecting another user, or rejecting all users' changes. The approver also can pass any desired comments to rejected data-entry users though the SAS Comment service.

If all changes are approved the Workflow service optionally notifies all data-entry users of success and the form is complete. However, if any rejection occurred the erroneous data-entry user is optionally notified and the form is returned to him in order to make corrections. He can refer to the comments made by the approver to make any necessary changes and resubmit the form, in which case the form goes back to the rejecting approver for a second attempt at approval.

After a form is completely approved by all approvers the data is then transferred into the SAS Strategy Management database. At this point the temporary data is discarded.

The Modeler can return to the Manage Forms page at any time to view a table of existing forms and associated statuses. Forms with workflow have a status value that reflects the point in the process the form is at. Of course the Modeler is not required to attach workflow to every form. SAS Strategy Management still preserves the older functionality where a form simply writes entered data immediately into the SAS Strategy Management database.

By default, the entire process described happens on a one-time basis. However the Modeler has the option to make this a recurring process when creating the form. Selecting this option means that when the form finishes final approval and the data is written to the SAS Strategy Management database the workflow cycle automatically restarts. This feature enables the Modeler to set up a company process that occurs on a regular basis and not have to restart it every time the process finishes. To allow greater control the Modeler can elect to stop any workflow cycle immediately and discard all data entered through it or to allow a recurring process to finish the current cycle and then stop.

Using the SAS Workflow service opens up some additional possibilities for the Modeler to add arbitrary functionality through modification of the workflow templates. By using SAS Workflow Studio you can check out one of the installed templates, make a small change, check it back in, and add some new process to be performed when a certain action is taken in the workflow cycle. For example refer to the section of one of the templates below:

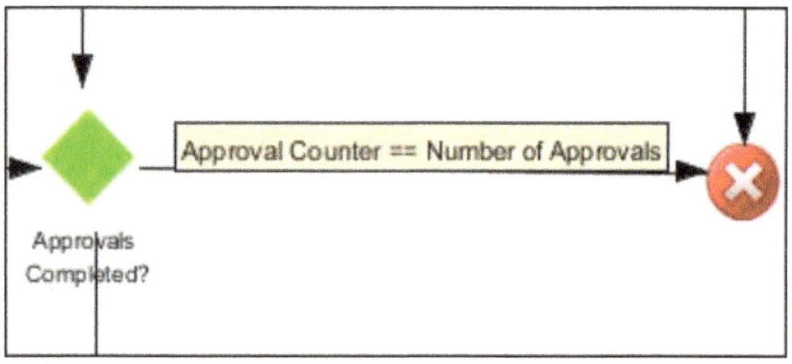


**Figure 7:** Altering a Workflow Template

The red circle with an X (the termination node) indicates where the workflow cycle terminates. Notice that there are lines with arrows pointing to it. One of the arrows has the label Approval Counter==Number of Approvals. This line originates from a green diamond that represents a decision gate labeled Approvals Completed?. This is the path that the workflow travels when all of the approvers have approved the form.

Suppose that you have a SAS stored process that performs some analytics on the data entered by the data-entry users that you would like to have automatically started when the form is completed. You can insert just such a task in between the Approvals Completed? decision gate and the termination node by using SAS Workflow Studio. You can add all sorts of such tasks to the template: call a web service, send email, invoke SAS code, and send an HTTP request. You do need to be careful so that the original data-entry process is not broken. Fortunately the Workflow service enables you to version your change to the template. If you do break something you can have the service revert to using the original template.

## AN EXAMPLE OF USING THE NEW DATA ENTRY SYSTEM

To examine the data-entry system in detail, this example describes creating a form and using it to input data. First, this example makes the following assumptions about an existing template:

- Template: Company Financials
- Project: 2013 Sales
- Element Type: Measures and Perspectives
- Metric Attributes: Actual, Target, and Performance

Here is the Project 2013 Sales setup:

- Scorecards: Europe, United States, Asia, Australia, South America
- Grandchild scorecards for Europe: France, Spain, Italy
- Elements: Green Widgets, Red Widgets, Blue Widgets
- Metric Attributes: Actual, Target, Performance

This setup presents a SAS Strategy Management table view like the one below:

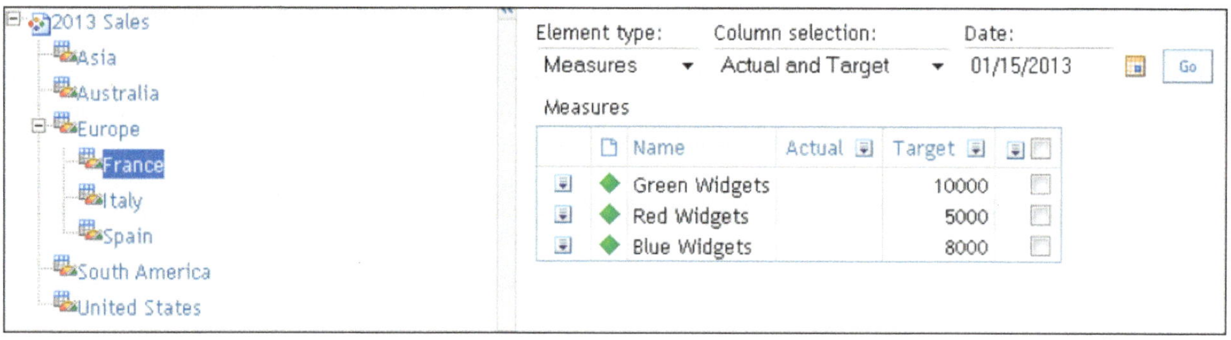


**Figure 8**: Table View of an Example Project

Now suppose that our company has just got the actual sales figures for their European region for January 2013. The manager has two interns available to input the figures. Given that they are interns and relatively new and inexperienced, the manager knows that someone needs to confirm that the input data is correct before any report goes to the Chief Financial Officer. The manager has a more experienced office worker and an assistant manager available to double-check the figures. The manager goes to Amy, the SAS Strategy Management Modeler for the office, and tells her to set things up. It's late in the day Friday but the manager wants the interns to get started Monday. Amy groans. She had wanted to leave on time today to start her weekend. Oh well

## THE DATA-ENTRY FORM WIZARD

Amy begins by logging in to SAS Strategy Management, navigates to the 2013 Sales Project, selects Manage Forms and creates a new form. She gives it a name and description but decides to forego adding any named link on the form (one of the form options available).

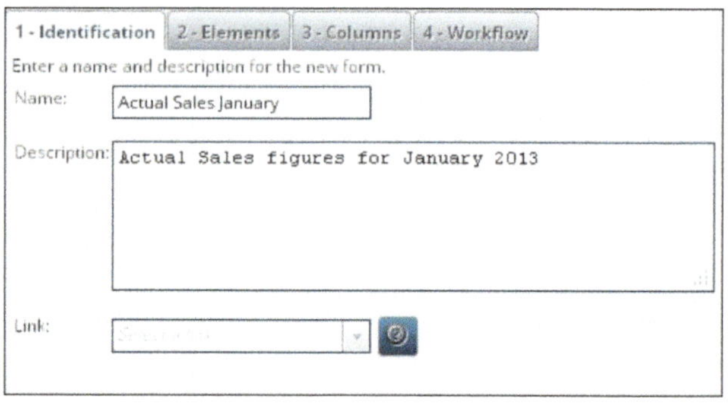


**Figure 9**: Data-Entry Form Wizard: Identification Tab

Now she selects the Elements tab and notices that the

change is instantaneous with no waiting for the page to refresh. "That's nice and quick!" she thinks to herself, "Maybe I can leave work on time today." The sales data is a Measure so she selects that from the drop-down list. All of the scorecards are displayed and since she is setting up a form for Europe she selects those scorecards.

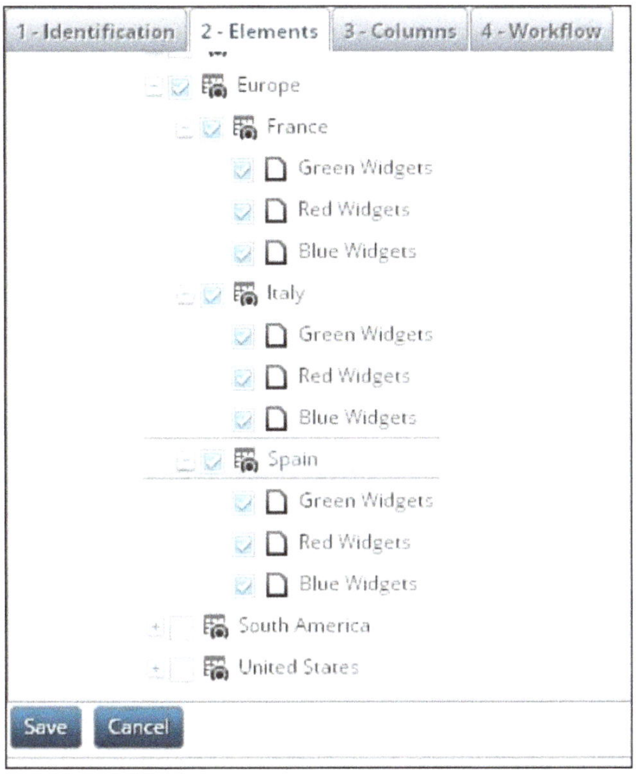


**Figure 10:** Data Entry Form Wizard: Elements Tab

Next Amy advances to the Columns tab and sees that things have really changed here. Instead of seeing a large table of available metric attributes with checkboxes for selecting a metric attribute's numeric value, text value, and read only status she sees only a drop-down list with column selections. "What's this? I am supposed to pick a column selection here?" she thinks. Amy knows that the relevant columns that need to appear on the form are the Actual column for the input data and the Target column (which in this case has already been filled in). The Actual column matters to all form users. The Target column is of interest primarily to the approvers, and no one should make any changes to the Target data.

She saves the work she has done on the form so far and navigates to the Column Selections page in the Builder. Since there is no default column selection that has what she wants she creates a General column selection, names it Actual and Target, and clicks the checkbox indicating that it is to be shared with all users. She then adds the two metric attributes to the display list and decides that the current date for each attribute should be what displays in the form. Finally she clicks the Allow Data Entry checkbox for the Actual attribute and leaves the one for Target unchecked. She has made the Target column read only – exactly what she wants.

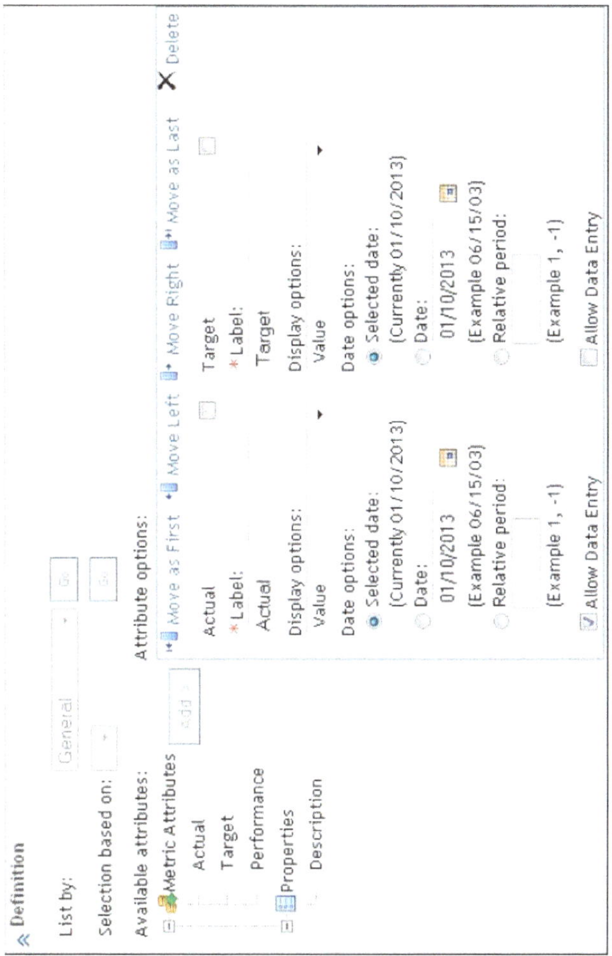


**Figure 11:** Creating a Column Selection to Use with a Data-Entry Form

She saves this column selection, reopens her form, and looks at the Columns tab again. Yes, the new column selection "Actual and Target" is there so she selects it. Now the columns in the form will work just as they do in the Builder.

Now Amy moves to the Workflow tab. She knows that her manager intends for the two interns, Frank and Kathy, to input the data. She also knows that Ellen is to check their work and Bradley, the assistant manager for European Sales, needs to give the final approval. So Amy selects that the form have a workflow and clears the No workflow required check box. Her manager did not say anything about this process happening over again next month so she does not check that option but remembers it in case management decides to repeat the process.

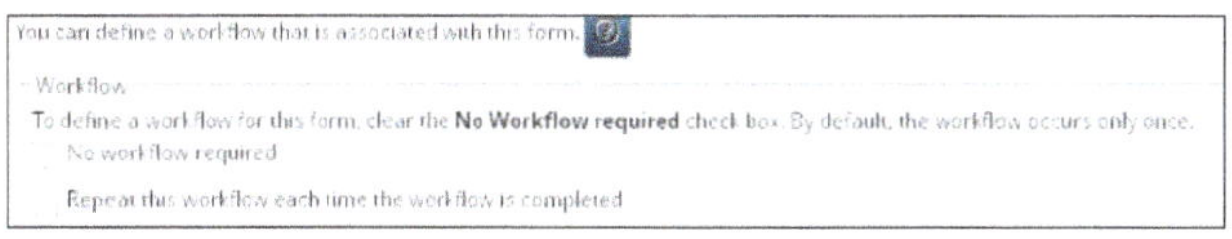


**Figure 12:** Data Entry Form Wizard: Workflow Tab Part 1

Next she considers how to assign Frank and Kathy as data-entry users. Both of them are set up as members of the Data Entry group only. She wants them to be notified when it is time to start so she clicks the Send notification that a form is available for data entry check box. Then she looks at the list of Data Entry group users and selects Frank and Kathy from the drop-down list. The work has been divided up between them so both have work to do. Amyclicks the All users must submit the form check box because of this division of labor.

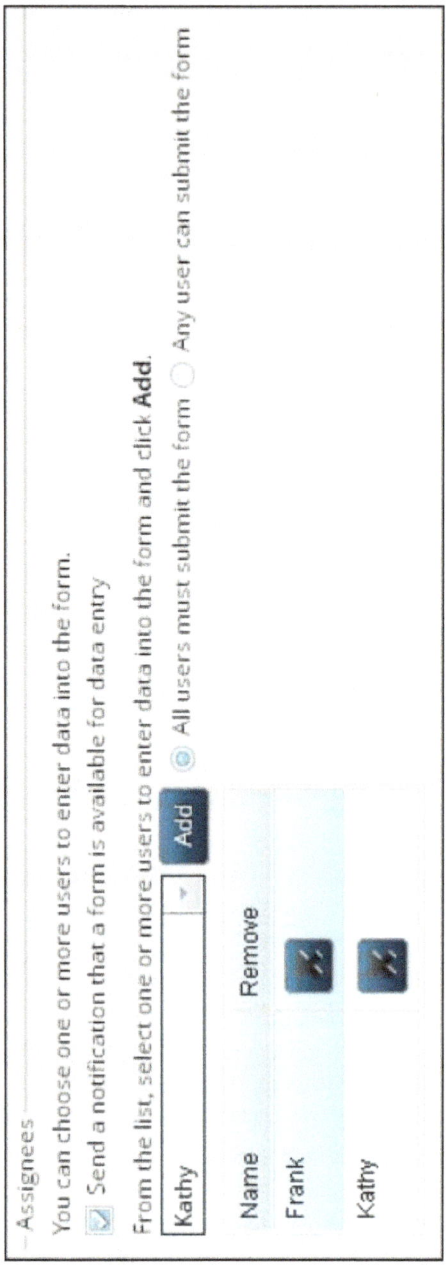


**Figure 13:** Data-Entry Form Wizard: – Workflow Tab Part 2

Now Amy knows that Ellen needs to see the form first and approve both Frank and Kathy's changes before the form is passed to Bradley. This kind of form is referred to as an "Ordered Approval" in SAS Strategy Management. It is chosen by selecting the Each user must approve the form in the assigned order radio button.

She wants Ellen and Bradley to be notified when it is their turn to approve so she checks the notification box for approvers and then adds them. As you can see, Amy added Ellen first and Bradley second and this order is respected when the form is passed to the approvers.

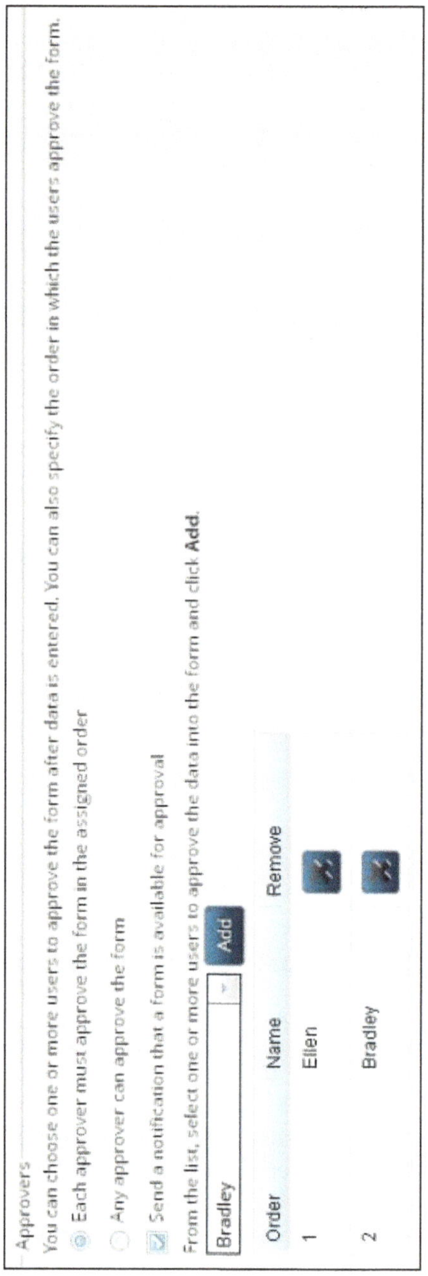


**Figure 14:** Data Entry Form Wizard: Workflow Tab Part 3

The form is done and Amy clicks the Save button to save it. She can come back at any time before she starts the form workflow and modify these settings.

## SETTING TEMPLATE AND PROJECT PERMISSIONS

Amy next needs to create the portlet that contains this form. Before she does so she realizes that Frank and Kathy need to be able to make changes to data in the project so she needs to update the permissions. First she goes to the Properties page of the template and enables Frank, Kathy, Ellen, and Bradley to be able to see the template. Then she goes to the Project Properties page and gives Frank and Kathy write permission to the project.

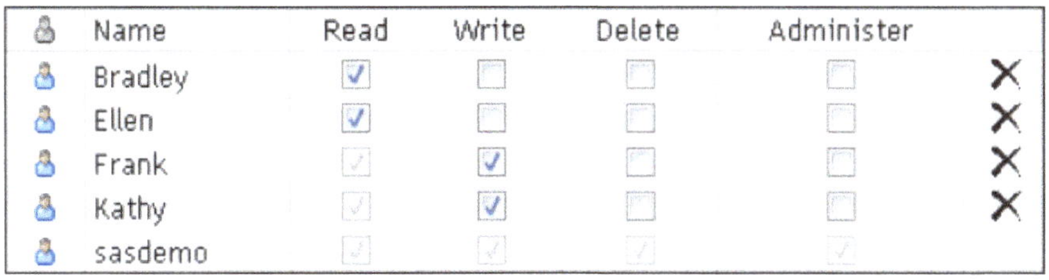


**Figure 15:** Project Permissions

## CREATING THE PORTLET

Creating the portlet requires logging into the SAS Information Delivery Portal. After doing so Amy adds the new portlet by using the Edit Page Content option and sets up the portlet as you see below:

**Figure 16:** Adding the Portlet

As you can see the portlet type is Performance Data Entry. The rest of the entries are for the name and other information. The Location selection bears some explanation. Strategy Management Data Entry Portlet Admin Group is a special group installed with SAS Strategy Management that facilitates expanding the visibility of the portlet to the Data Entry and Data Entry Approvers users. Those users now can search on "January European Sales Data" to find the portlet in order to add it to their own portal page.

After Amy has done this she needs to specify some information to the portlet. She clicks the Edit Portlet button and the following page appears:

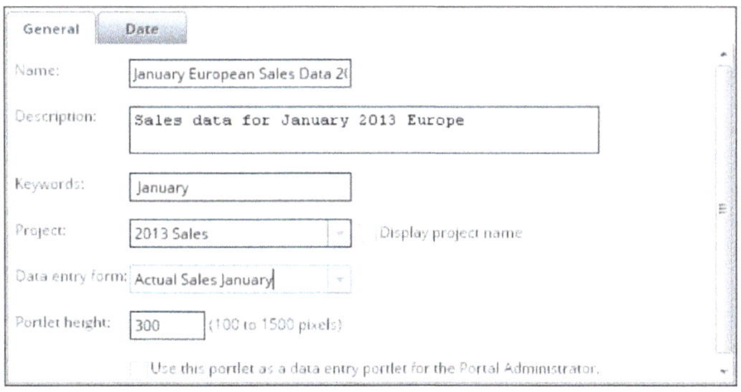


**Figure 17:** Portlet Properties: General tab

Amy needs to indicate what project and form to use along with some descriptive information. She does this on the General tab along with the desired height of the portlet. If Amy was going to be one of the data-entry users herself she would select the Use this portlet as a data-entry portlet for the Portal Administrator check box. After entering the above information she clicks the Date tab.

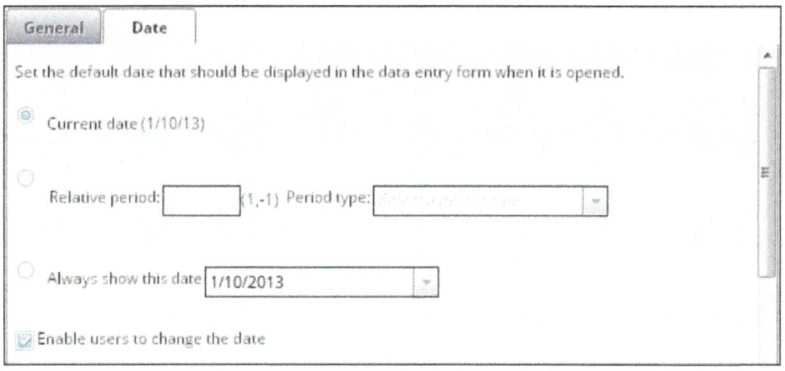


**Figure 18:** Portlet Properties: Date Tab Step 1

Amy wants the value for the current date to appear when the portlet is displayed so she selects Current Date. She wants the users to be able to adjust the date of the portlet so she selects the Enable users to change the date check box to make a date control appear on the portlet.

The date section has one more setting available:

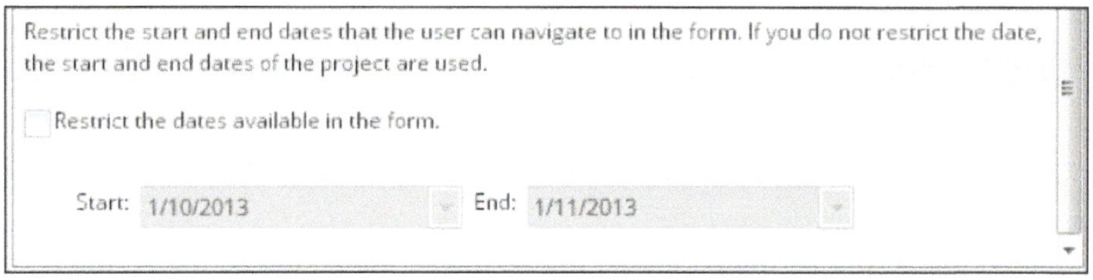


**Figure 19:** Portlet Properties: Date Tab Step 2

She can elect to control the range of the dates in which users can change the date. This is useful if there is some data from a previous or future period that you do not want the data-entry users to see. Amy has no such need in this example so she does not select the option.

Amy then saves the form and the page changes to the portal page. She notices that nothing displays in the portal area except a message:

You are not a data enterer or data approver for this form

This makes sense. Amy should not be allowed to enter data into the form as she is not a member of either of the relevant groups. However she still can click Edit portlet to modify the settings of the portlet. At this point the form and the portlet are ready and all she has to do is start the workflow. But that is to be done next week. "This didn't take long at all!" Amy thinks to herself. She can go ahead and leave for the day.

## STARTING THE WORKFLOW

Monday comes and it is time to start the form's workflow. Amy navigates to the "Manage Forms" page to see her newly created form. All she has to do now is start it by selecting the form from the list and clicking the "Start" button.

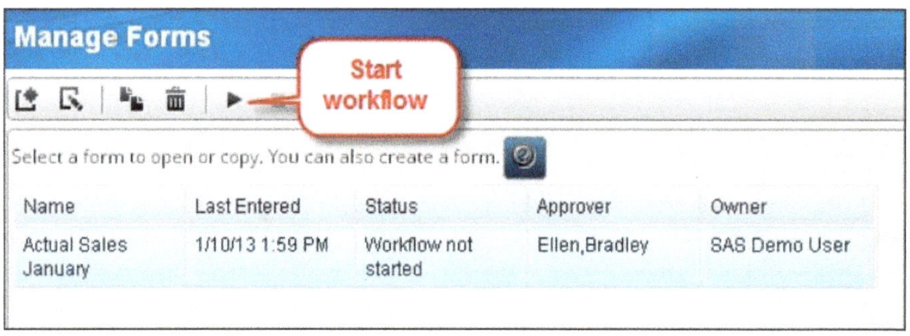


**Figure 20:** Starting the Workflow

After doing so the Workflow service begins the workflow instance and she sees the message indicating the workflow started successfully.

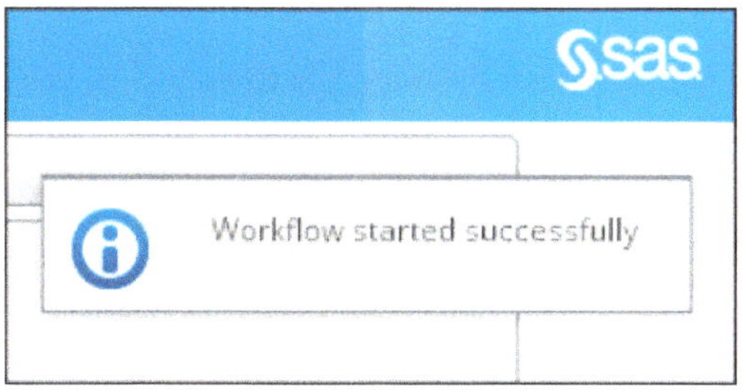


**Figure 21:** Workflow Started

At this point Amy is done. The Workflow service will handle everything from this point. Because she selected the option for the data-entry people to be notified immediately Frank and Kathy get an Alert, an email, or both depending on how they configured receiving SAS Alerts.

## PERFORMING THE ACTUAL DATA-ENTRY AND APPROVAL

When Frank or Kathy logs in to the Portal they will see something like this (assume that both have added both the Shared Alert and Data Entry portlet to their Portal page):

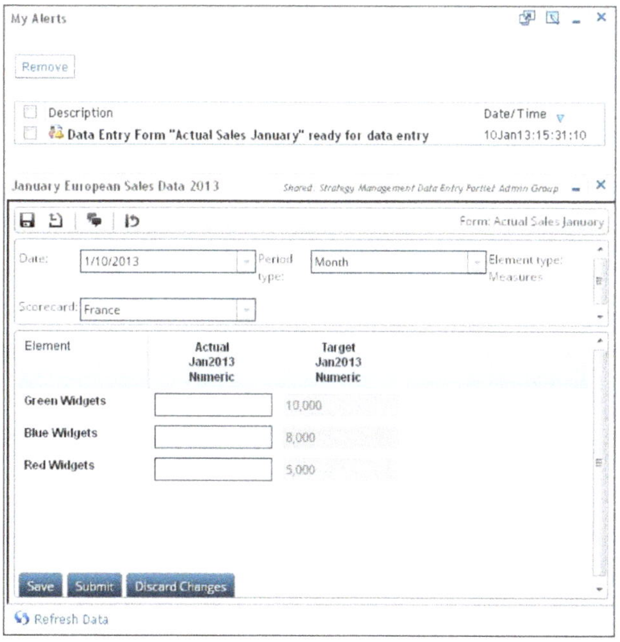


**Figure 22**: Data-Entry User's Portlet

In this case Frank has a message in his Alerts portlet. Today's date is January 10, 2013 and as per Amy's setup that is the date of the data he sees. She has allowed him to see the Target values but notice that they are read-only, just as she intended. Frank can adjust the date, the scorecard he is entering data for, and the period type. Frank can save his work, discard all his changes, or submit the entire form to the approvers based on the buttons he clicks.

Frank and Kathy have divided up the data-entry job so that Frank enters the figures for France and Kathy enters the data for Italy and Spain. Frank begins to enter data. At one point he inadvertently types a negative sign before one of the values. As he tabs out of the text field an error message appears:

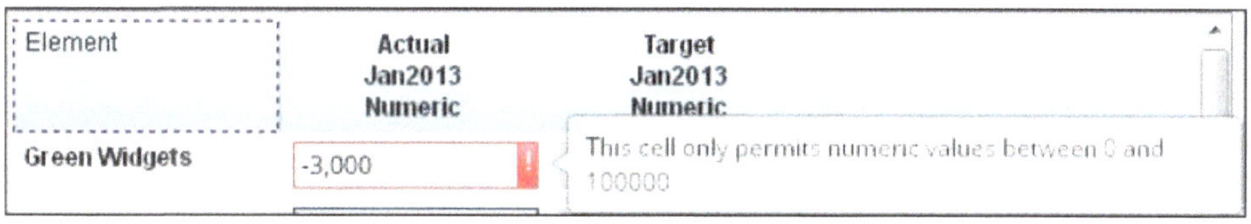


**Figure 23:** Data-Entry Error and Resulting Message

This happened because Amy set up a Named Rule for the Actual values. As per the company's business rules, Actual sales cannot be less than zero. Amy added a ceiling of 100,000 figuring that such an entry was highly unlikely. And sure enough Frank incorrectly adds too many zeroes to another figure:

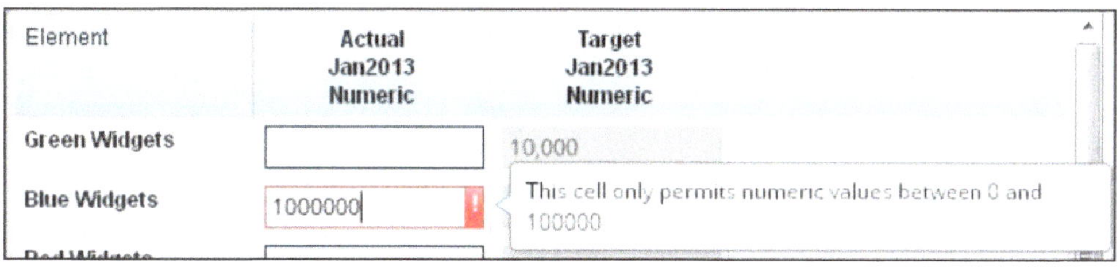


**Figure 24:** Another Data-Entry Error

After Frank finishes entering the figures he submits the form. When he does so the portal area displays the following message:

The form has been submitted. There are no further actions available at this time.

Kathy goes through a similar experience, enters the data, submits it, and sees the same message. At this time the data-entry portion of the cycle is finished. The Workflow service notifies Ellen that she can start to approve the form data. Why only Ellen and not Bradley as well? Because Amy configured this form to use Ordered Approval workflow and Ellen is supposed to approve the form before Bradley ever sees it.

Amy's manager asks her about the status of the January figures. She logs into SAS Strategy Management and looks at the Manage Forms page:

| Name | Last Entered | Status | Approver | Owner |
|---|---|---|---|---|
| Actual Sales January | 1/10/13 4:23 PM | Awaiting approval | Ellen,Bradley | SAS Demo User |

**Figure 25:** Form Status

The Status column clearly indicates to what point the workflow has progressed. She tells him the data-entry team has finished their work and now we are waiting on the form data to be approved.

Now Ellen receives an email telling her the form is ready to be approved. She logs on to her portal page and sees the following:

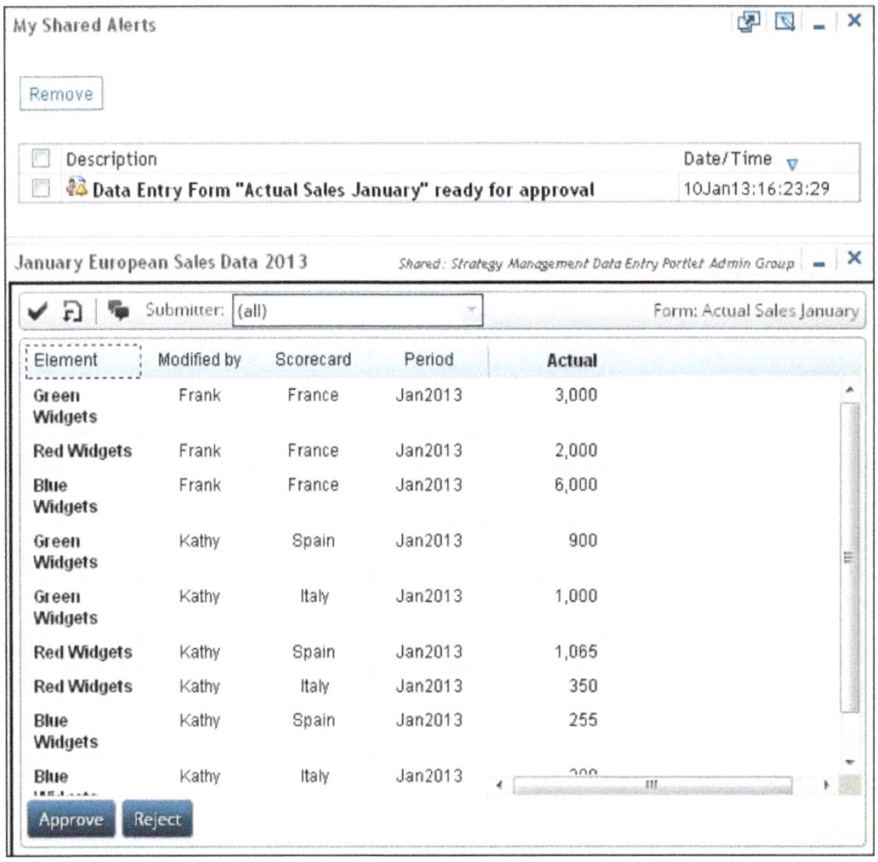


**Figure 26:** Approver's Portlet

By default Ellen sees all changes made by the two interns. She can choose to see only Kathy or Frank's changes by using the Submitter drop-down list. She cannot change any of the data as it is read-only. Ellen sees no issue with the data entered by Frank, but Kathy got the numbers for Spain wrong. Ellen accepts Frank's data but rejects Kathy's data requiring Kathy to re-enter it. Ellen adds a comment for Kathy to read by clicking the Comment button next to the Submitter drop down list.

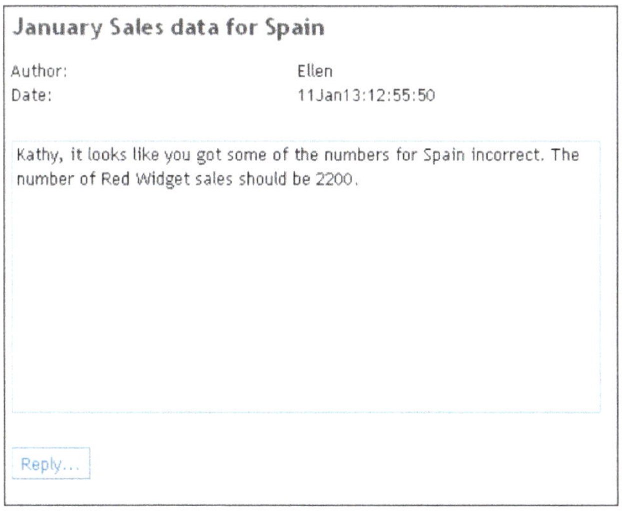


**Figure 27:** Using the Comment Service

Ellen changes the Submitter drop-down list to Frank and clicks the Accept button. She sees a message asking her to confirm this choice.

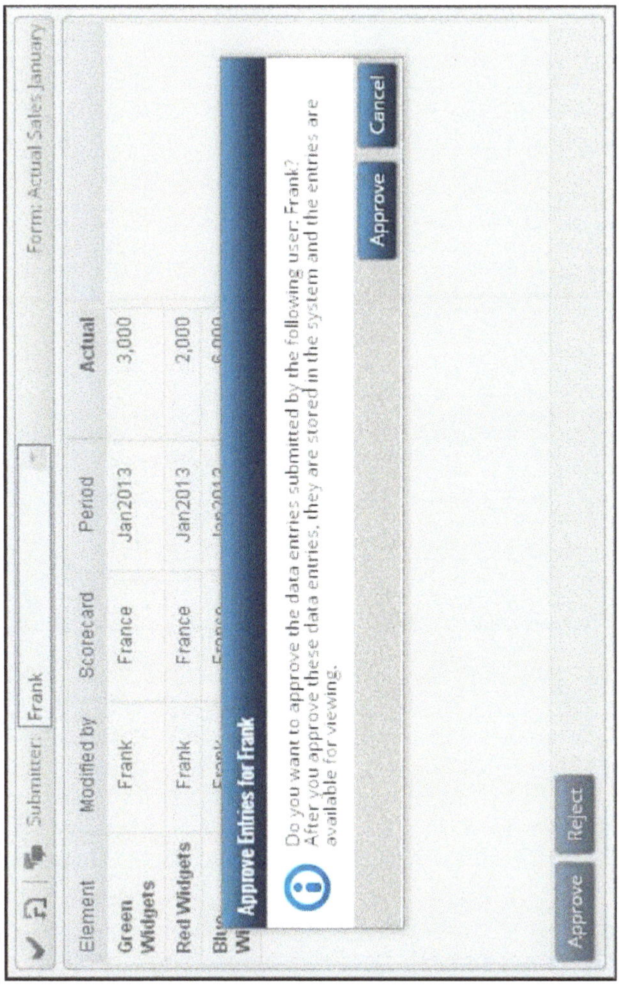


**Figure 28:** Accepting Frank's Data Entries

Now Ellen changes the Submitter drop-down list to Kathy and notices that the choice for Frank is now greyed out and not selectable. She chooses Kathy and clicks the Reject button.

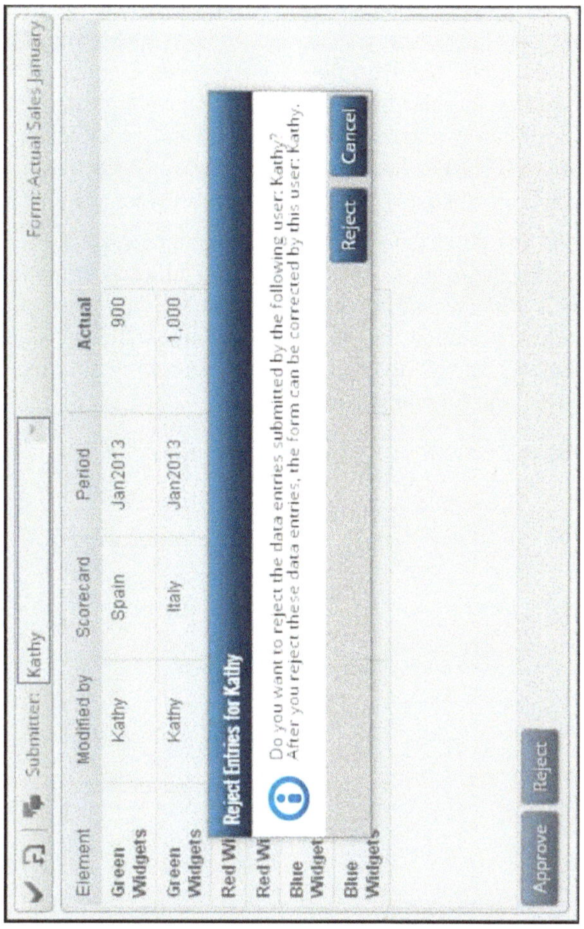


**Figure 29:** Rejecting Kathy's Entries

The portlet area now contains a message indicating that the workflow cycle has moved back to the data-entry process. Because Kathy was the user whose data was rejected, she receives a notification and her data-entry portlet is viewable again. She can read Ellen's comment to determine what she needs to change. She does so and corrects the number of Red Widgets accordingly. Notice the alert she received for rejection:

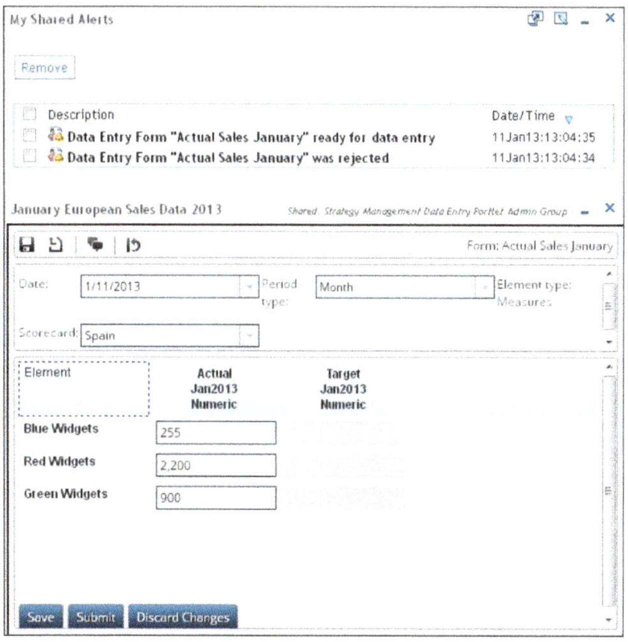


**Figure 30:** Kathy Makes Corrections

After Kathy submits this correction Ellen is notified again. She checks Kathy's data and finds no other errors. Ellen approves it and the Workflow service sends a notification to Bradley that it is his turn to approve the data. A typical manager Bradley quickly glances at the combined entries for Kathy and Frank, figures Ellen has done the real work in validating it, and approves all changes.

At this point the workflow cycle completes. Amy sees a status that the form is now approved and informs her manager. Soon it will be time to enter the February data and Amy is considering setting up the form to automatically restart, minimizing her involvement with the process and letting her leave on time for many Fridays to come.

## CONCLUSION

We have discussed the new data-entry system to a fair degree of depth. With this system the enterprise can leverage the correct category of employee to perform the data-entry task while assigning the approval process to a different level of personnel. With a more efficient user interface more work can be done in less time. Robust validation that is completely configurable preserves the integrity of one of the organization's most important resources: company data. With the ability to incorporate a workflow to guide the business process this data-entry system becomes a polished and valuable tool as a part of SAS Strategy Management.

CHAPTER 6

# SAS® BI DASHBOARD: INTERACTIVE, DATA-DRIVEN DASHBOARD APPLICATIONS MADE EASY

Scott Sams

## INTRODUCTION

Using SAS® BI Dashboard to build a Dashboard Application will save you time vs. building the application from scratch. Using the Dashboard Builder, you can assemble your application and interactions without having to write any code. If you decide to use custom code, you can expand the power of your application by writing custom Stored Processes to provide data and process user input.

Saving time is crucial. One group built a reporting application using custom Flash programming and it took six weeks to build. The same application was built using SAS® BI Dashboard and it took only a few days.

If you have existing SAS® code, you can leverage it with the BI Dashboard Stored Process data provider, allowing you to put a "pretty face" on your data with graphs and tables.

## EXAMPLE DASHBOARD APPLICATIONS

To give you an idea what is possible with BI Dashboard, we will present examples from several Dashboard Applications solving real business problems.

**Figure 1:** Customer Smart Meter application. This application uses the following techniques discussed in this paper: Navigation bar, Status messages, Embedded help, Time frame control, Custom filtering.

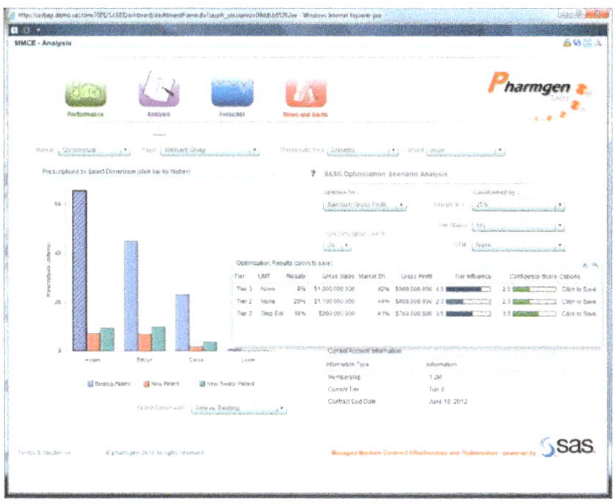


**Figure 2:** Market Optimization. This application uses high-level

---

**Citation:** Scott Sams, SAS® BI Dashboard: Interactive, Data-Driven Dashboard Applications Made Easy, http://support.sas.com/resources/papers/proceedings13/061-2013.pdf.

"data entry" to save user input for later use in the application.

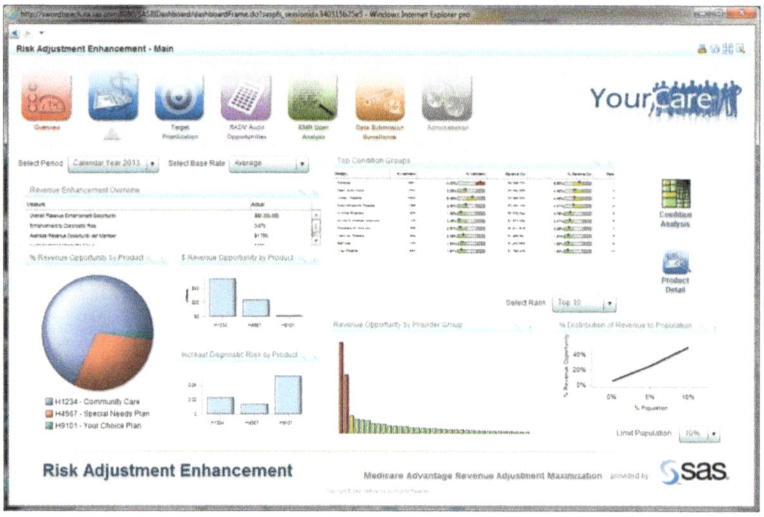


**Figure 3:** Revenue adjustment maximization. This application uses custom filtering/paging.

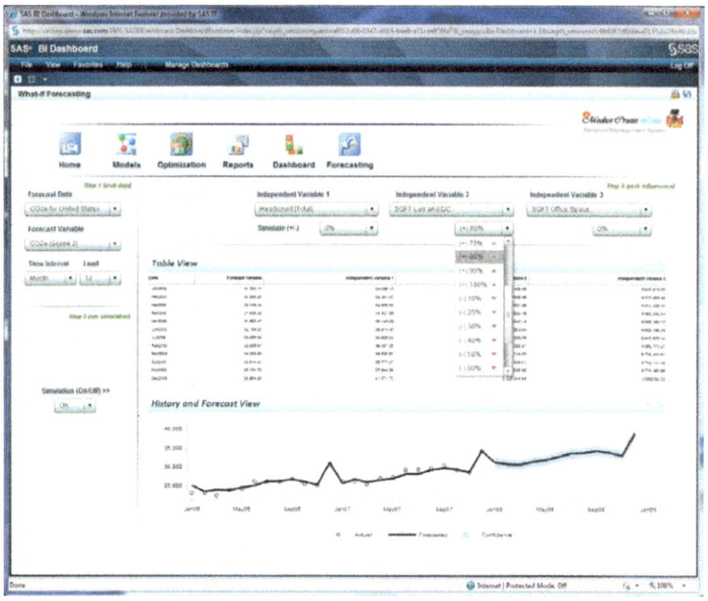


**Figure 4:** Forecasting and "what-If" analysis. This application uses dynamic prompts with a gauge as an input control to run forecasts

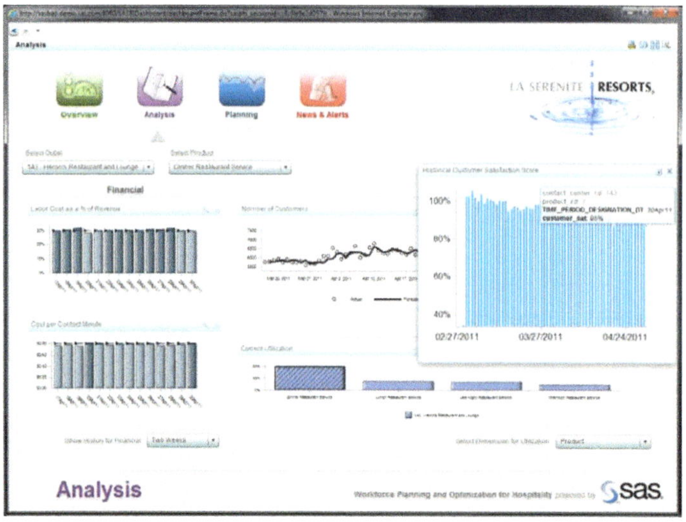


**Figure 5:** Financial reporting dashboard. This dashboard uses multiple drill downs and time frame control.

## GENERAL DASHBOARD APPLICATION TECHNIQUES

### Powering Dashboard Applications with the Stored Process Data Provider

The Stored Process Data Provider gives you powerful control over processing user input and organizing data to display. You can collect user input and run advanced analytic forecasts and display the results in a graph directly in the dashboard.

The idea is to create a Stored Process that takes one or more parameters. These parameters are used to generate a single dataset that will be returned to BI Dashboard. You can then display this dataset using any of the BI Dashboard visualizations.

### Dashboard Parameter Passing

For some applications, you may want one dashboard to select or filter through options. Then you may want to pass the current set of parameters to another dashboard for further exploration. This is accomplished through the Linking Dialog. In 4.31M2, you can link an Indicator to another Dashboard and pass parameters that the Indicator knows about.

### High-Level "Data Entry" And Processing

Any time a user clicks on an indicator, your application can pass information to a Stored Process. This information can be stored in a dataset for later use in the application. For example, you can present a table of "leads" that is generated by a forecast. When the user clicks on a particular lead, you can save that lead in a table of "interested leads" for that user, which can be displayed on another dashboard for them to explore at any time. You can also have a stored process to delete the lead when the user clicks the row on that table.

### Delayed Interactions

Sometimes, you can have a large number of parameters that would be passed to an indicator for display. Normally, every time a user makes a selection in a prompt, that parameter is sent to the indicator, and the indicator is refreshed. This might be undesirable. To prevent this, create two versions of your dashboard: one with everything and one with just the prompts. On this "prompt" dashboard, all of these prompts will go to a single "Custom Graph" indicator. This hidden indicator is powered by a stored process that has one job: to record all the parameters it receives into a dataset, then return it. When the user clicks on this image, it links to your "main" dashboard and passes all the parameters it has been keeping track of. The main dashboard will then load and all the prompts will be populated, as well as the indicator of interest.

### Building Drill down Explorations

Drill downs in BI Dashboard are very flexible. You can drill down by using the Linking Dialog to pass parameters to another Indicator, even one based on completely different data. You need only decide on which parameters to use in the drill sequence.

### Using Cascading Prompts

Cascading prompts are a powerful and common technique. It is possible to design these using interactions with BI Dashboard. The key consideration with cascading prompts is that the cascade sequence could be "ragged" and therefore all prompts "below" the current one need to be refreshed when a selection is made. Each prompt needs to send a copy of the interaction to each of its "children" in the hierarchy (which includes the indicators displaying the data). The last prompt in the hierarchy only sends one interaction to the target indicators. The picture below illustrates this better. While it might look daunting at first, it will make sense when you understand what is happening. This hierarchy is: Country->State->Year->Quarter. Note: for the third level of the hierarchy (Year) we are using a graph instead of a Dynamic Prompt. A "prompt" doesn't have to be a menu!

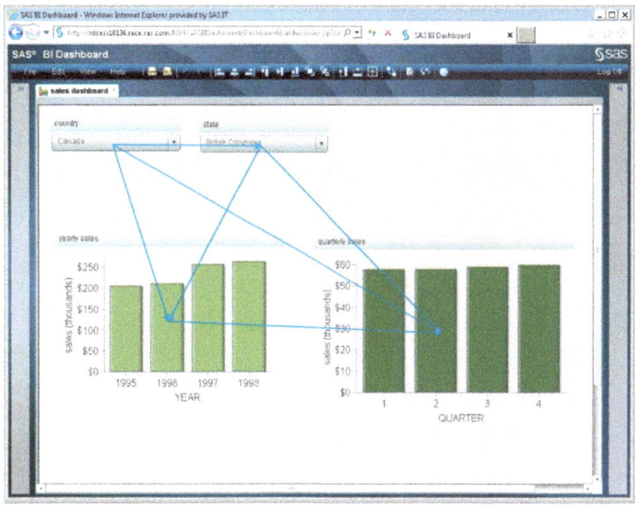


**Figure 6:** Interactions view of the cascading prompt example

### Building Comparison Dashboards

A useful new feature in 4.31M2 is the ability to apply default parameters to an indicator. With this feature, it is easy to set up comparison dashboards to compare indicators using the same data model, but with different parameters. For example, if you have a Stored Process that takes the parameter Year, you can create two identical indicators that pass different default parameters to the same Indicator Data. This way you could compare 2012 sales with 2011 sales side by side on a dashboard. This can also greatly simplify dashboard design, as different indicators can share the same Indicator Data. Building comparison dashboards is simple: once you create your "master" Indicator, you just change the parameters and do a "Save As..."

## SPECIFIC TECHNIQUES

### Minimal Decoration Mode

In the example screenshots in section 2, you will notice that the dashboard application runs in its own window, without extra decorations, looking like a real "standalone" application. To do this, create an .html file with JavaScript to launch a new browser window without decorations, and load a special URL for BI Dashboard that hides its decorations (like when used in the Portal), and load whatever dashboard you like. You need to know the SBIP URL, which you can copy from the browser's URL bar after you click 'Manage Dashboards' on the dashboard you are viewing. The JavaScript to launch this looks like:

```
<body
onLoad="window.open('http://<SERVER>:8080/SASBIDashboard/Director
?_directive=PortletDisplayDashboard&dashboard=<SBIP_URL>&frameWid
th=800&frameHeight=600', 'BI Dashboard',
'width=800,height=600,toolbar=no,location=no,menubar=0,status=no,
directories=no,menubar=no,scrollbars=no,resizable=no')">
```

## Application Navigation Bar

A navigation bar makes the collection of dashboards look like a real application. If you are using minimal navigation mode, it is an essential technique to change dashboards. Each "button" is a separate image with a link to a different dashboard. To make things easy, it is best to build the navigation bar first and to save this in a "template" dashboard so it will be easy to create the other dashboards based off it. Once you have created your other dashboards, it will be more work to make changes to the navigation bar, since you would have to edit all the dashboards. On each dashboard, you can mark the "current" navigation point somehow, either with another image, or change out the image for the current "button." You could also disable the link for the current "button" image.

## Status Messages

You can use the Dynamic Text indicator to create simple status messages. Your message has the opportunity to change whenever a user loads that dashboard. You just need to create the data behind it and generate your message. Another use for a status message is within an interaction. The Dynamic Text indicator can be the recipient of any interaction and the message can change any time one of those interactions occurs. A third usage is to display a title, e.g. "2010 Sales" above a graph. The year would change whenever you change the "year" prompt.

## "Alerts" Indicator

You can make your own "Alerts" indicator with the SparkTable indicator. The data behind the indicator can be custom generated from a Stored Process or come from a table that is updated externally. You could also make a "news feed" indicator that links to external URLs.

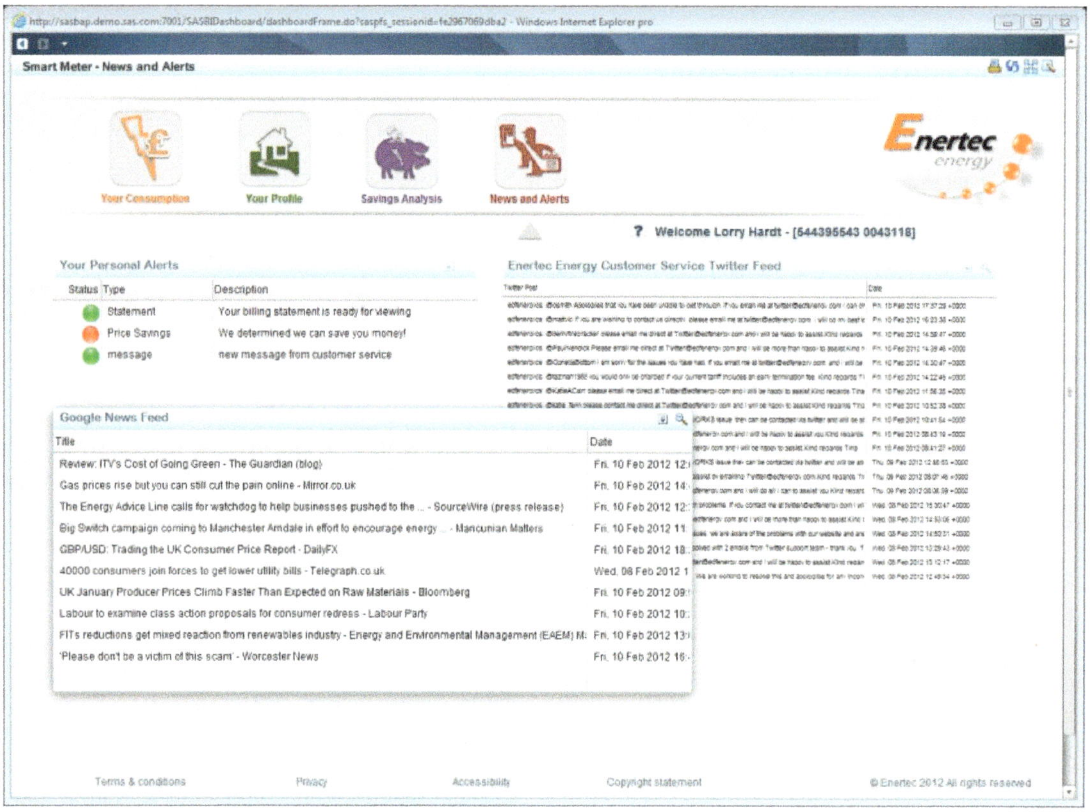


**Figure 7:** Custom "alerts" indicator built using SparkTable

## Embedded Help

You can provide help to your users several ways. First, you could simply position static instructions using the Text decoration.

Second, you could position a "question mark" image and link it to either an external URL that provides help, or to a Custom Graph Indicator, which could load an image URL of nicely formatted text and images. With this method, your help will appear in a "pop-up" window inside the application which looks more seamless.

The third method is to use static text with a link to help, just like using an image.

**Custom Paging**

You can use a Dynamic Prompt to page results on a SparkTable, e.g. "1-100, 101-200, 201-300, >301" etc. The data for the Dynamic Prompt would need to know the number of rows in the target table, and output the intervals. The Stored Process for the target would take a "page" parameter that would determine which rows to show.

## Custom Filtering

Sometimes, you may want to have a complex filter and not rely on a single parameter. It is possible to create a Dynamic Prompt with a series of custom "where clauses" that could be used to apply a custom filter for the target. Each where clause would be for a commonly used filter, like: "Top 10 Revenue" or "15 Most Profitable." The entire "where clause" gets passed as a single parameter to the Stored Process, which would use the clause to subset the data. The nice thing about this approach is you can save your where clauses in a separate table and add new filters easily.

## Controlling a Time Frame

When using time data, there are several things you may want to control: the interval size (Day, Week, Month, and Year) and the start and end date. Your Stored Process would aggregate the data differently for each interval size, and limit the results based on the start and end date.

You could use a Dynamic Prompt to change the interval size. There a few options for the start and end date. You could have two Dynamic Prompts to independently set these values. Or you could use a "Chart With Slider Prompt" if you wanted to select a value by dragging a slider on a "big picture" graph. You could also use a "window" parameter, such as the number of weeks/months/years, and just have a start date.

## OTHER 4.31_M2 ENHANCEMENTS

## Easier Building of Prompts

Prior to 4.31M2, you had to select a Range when creating a Dynamic Prompt, even if you were not going to use it. Now, the Range is not required so you can build simple prompts quickly. You can add a Range later if you change the type to "Prompt with gauge."

A second feature is the ability to display a label for the prompt. Previously, you would have to create a separate Static Text object and play with the alignment. Now, it is much easier to create great looking forms that line up.

## "All" Option for Prompts

There is now an option to include an "All" marker at the end of the prompt that will pass all the values in the menu to the target. This works automatically when using InformationMaps, but when using a Stored Process, you need to use the right code to take advantage of it.

The easiest way is to use the %_eg_WhereParam macro, generated using SAS Enterprise Guide®. You should be able to get a copy of this from a Stored Process generated by EG. In this example, yearPrompt will contain either a single year, or multiple years when "All" is selected. The macro automatically generates the where clause portion and can detect single vs. multiple values.

```
WHERE %_eg_WhereParam(t1.year, yearPrompt, IN, TYPE=N)
```

e.g.: this would resolve to:

```
WHERE t1.year in (2008, 2009)
```

## Multi-Select Interactions

You can now use multi-select on graphs and tables for interactions by holding down the control key. This can be used for comparisons to quickly compare, e.g. different regions.

To take advantage of multi-select in Stored Processes, use the same %_eg_WhereParam macro. Then your Stored Process can handle single or multi-select with the same code.

## BOOKMARK A DASHBOARD WITH THE CURRENT PARAMETERS

The Dashboard Viewer application has a new feature for users to bookmark a dashboard with all the current parameters applied. (Normally, when you load a dashboard in 4.31 the prompts will be reset to whatever value you selected last.) This enables users to create "favorites" for comparisons, e.g. "2008 Sales" and "2009 Sales" or to bookmark commonly viewed selections, e.g. "U.S. Sales" and "Europe Sales."

## Automatic Lookup of Parameter Names in the Linking Dialog

Building links to Indicators and Dashboards just got easier in 4.31M2. Previously, you would have to know the exact name of all the parameters to pass. Now, those parameter names are automatically fetched, so it is much quicker to build links and less error prone.

## Designing Dashboard Applications for Optimal Performance

1. Reduce the number of indicators on a single dashboard.
   a. You can spread your information across several dashboards and use a navigation bar to assist users.
   b. If possible, make one query do as much work as possible. For example, if you want to display a KPI for five regions, don't make five KPI indicators. Make a single KPI and have your query fetch all the regions you need.
2. Return only the data you need in your queries. Instead of doing a "Select *" pick only the columns you need for the graph/table.
3. Use client side filters where appropriate. If the total number of rows in the table is reasonably small (<200) make your query return all the rows and use a client side filter.
4. Make sure you are using the latest hotfix for fastest performance.
5. Configure data caching on the midtier. This may not be appropriate if your application processes user input and needs to refresh the data.

## CONCLUSION

Building Dashboard Applications with SAS® BI Dashboard saves development time and produces great-looking interactive applications with your data. The techniques and examples explored in this paper will give you an idea what is possible for your business problems, and help you get started creating custom Dashboard Applications.

## ACKNOWLEDGMENTS

Special acknowledgments and thanks go to John Green's team, especially Keith Renision and Carlos Sebastiani. They have been producing lots of pre-sales solutions for big customers using BI Dashboard and custom Stored Processes. They chose SAS® BI Dashboard because it looks good, has great functionality and flexibility, and it saves them time. What they have done with the product was more than we imagined possible!

# CHAPTER 7 APPLICATIONS OF SPATIAL DATA USING BUSINESS ANALYTICS TOOLS

Anca Ioana Andreescu, Anda Velicanu, and Daniela Mitroescu

**Keywords**: Spatial data, business analytics, SAS system, map charts

## INTRODUCTION

Historically speaking, since the '70, methods of statistical calculation and data processing have begun to change with the introduction of integrated statistical packages. They allow users to perform one or more statistical procedures on a single set of data stored in a file format standard. Processing and data management have been hardly started and cumbersome and mapping packages were missing from the standard system [1]. Given the growing necessity of representing geographical distributed information we will discuss in the paper how analytics tools deal with geographic data and allow graphical descriptions based on this data.

## SPATIAL DATA STRUCTURE

The spatial data (geographical data) emerged from the need to work and process geographical data like points, lines, polygons, three-dimensional geometric objects representing real world objects. Spatial locating this data can be bi-or tri-dimensional, depending on its type and the information available. Such a two-dimensional level can indicate the latitude and longitude coordinates or x and y coordinates of a given finite area and a three-dimensional level can specify latitude, longitude and height / altitude or the x, y and z coordinates in a given finite area. Examples of spatial objects are cities, buildings, rivers, touristic points of interest etc. This article will mainly deal with issues regarding bi-dimensional spatial databases.

**Citation:** Anca Ioana andreescu, Anda velicanu, and Daniela mitroescu, Applications of Spatial Data Using Business Analytics Tools, http://www.dbjournal.ro/archive/6/5_Andreescu_Velicanu_Mitroescu.pdf.

Spatial objects consist of points, lines, surfaces, volumes and objects of higher dimensions that are frequently used in computer aided design applications, cartography, GIS, etc. They are described by spatial attributes (length, configuration, perimeter, area, volume, etc.) and by nonspatial (common) attributes (the creating date, ownership, membership of a superior structure, etc.). The values of spatial attributes of these objects represent spatial data.

Objects in the real world can be divided into two categories: discrete objects (a house) and continuous fields (rainfall or altitude). Geographic data represent real world objects (roads, soil, elevation) by storing data with two or three measurable dimensions relative to a Cartesian coordinate system or latitude-longitudinal system.

Spatial data can be divided into point data and regional data. The point data is completely characterized by its location in a multidimensional space. It can come directly from measurements or can be rendered in order to be more easily stored and retrieved. Regional data is characterized by location (a fixed point in a region) and destination (a line in 2D or a 3D surface).

Spatial data are also those of a certain rank (e.g. "Cities in Europe"), approaches data (e.g. "Three close lakes in Romania"), junction data (e.g. "Pairs of cities in Romania located at 50 km of each other ").

Spatial data structure is specific for storing, querying and processing the geometric information. This allows us to provide the necessary information for a database management system (DBMS) so that it can follow the spatial data model. In general, a geographic data structure must allow the representation of three components:

- data on the geography of objects (points, lines, polygons);
- date on objects' attributes (name, description);

- images (used usually as background maps or as symbolic representation of objects – e.g. a green cross for pharmacies, a triangle for campsites, a tree for forests etc.).

Raster and vector data models based on spatial data representation are considered to be dual by [2].

The two main models used for storing such data - raster and vector - are detailed in [3]. Raster model is based on partitioning the areas and the vector model works with points, lines and polygons that describe the geometry of a spatial object. [4] identifies five levels of significance for the representation of real world entities in data structures that can be implemented in the computer:

- entities level;
- objects level;
- conceptual level;
- raster and vector level;
- data structures level (implementation level).

The difference between entity and object, shown by [4], is that entities can be seen as phenomena that have no clear physical boundary, while the objects are defined by dimensional attributes (length, width, volume).

At a conceptual level, the objects acquire attributes such as distance, coordinate system, and topology. Raster or vector level determines how objects are represented as spatial data. The implementation level depends on the DBMS through which spatial data is stored according to available data structure and the specialized spatial database (SDB).

Table 1 presents a comparative analysis of both data types, in terms of characteristics such as storage, operations' implementation, compatibility with relational databases, updating and analysis capabilities.

**Table 1:** Comparative analysis of raster and vector data

| Data | Storing space | Implementing overlapping operations | Viewing capabilities | Compatibility with relational databases | Updating | Analysis capabilities |
|---|---|---|---|---|---|---|
| Raster | Big | Easy | Images | Little | Difficult | Reduced |
| Vector | Small | Difficult | Graphics | Large | Easy | Many |

In the table above it can be noticed that using raster data has advantages like easy implementation of overlapping operations, methods of rendering images, while using vector data requires less storage space, methods of rendering graphics, large compatibility with relational databases, ease to update and many analysis facilities.

As illustrated in paper [5], creating a professional looking Map Chart in SAS Enterprise Guide is a simple process that has gotten easier with each release of the software. As long as data that can be joined to a map dataset, high quality maps can be created. It only requires one task and two datasets in the simplest form.

The coordinate system, also called spatial reference system, is another important notion when talking about spatial data. The coordinate system is a mean of allocating the coordinates to a location and establishing relationships between sets of such coordinates. This allows interpreting a set of coordinates as a representation of a location in the real world. Each spatial data has an associated coordinate system. The coordinate system can be:

- with a geo-reference (geodesic, depending on a certain representation of Earth);
- without a geo-reference (Cartesian, not depending on a certain representation of Earth).

If the coordinate system is geodesic, then it has an associated default unit of measurement (e.g. meters), but can have automated transformation of data into other units (e.g. miles). Spatial data can be associated with Cartesian, geodetic (geographical), projected or local coordinate system.

Cartesian coordinates are those which measure the position of a point along the axes that are perpendicular in the origin, representing two-dimensional or threedimensional space. If a coordinate system is not explicitly associated with geometry, it is assumed that the geometry is in Cartesian coordinate system.

Geodetic coordinates are longitude and latitude, closely related to spherical polar coordinates and are defined relative to a certain geodesic data.

Projected coordinates are plane Cartesian resulting from performing a mathematical mapping from a point on the Earth's surface onto a plane. There are many such mathematical mappings.

Local coordinates are Cartesians in a non-geodetic coordinate system. They are often used for CAD (Computer Aided Design).

When performing operations on spatial data a Cartesian model or a curvilinear pattern must be used, according to the coordinate system associated with the data. In SAS Enterprise Guide the coordinate system can be defined after the spatial data is imported from a database or a data file (xls, html etc.).

For systems that store and process spatial data in spatial databases it results in a number of advantages, primarily due to their specialization (dedicated system). Thus, the general advantages of working with geographic data are shown in [6]:

- precision in representing the data and processing it;
- creating and using specific libraries (information structuring, using standards, interchanging information);
- possibility to update information;

- quick access to information (due to flexible organizing criteria and to fast working speed of the equipment);
- easily, precise and unlimited reproducing of graphic material (paper copies can be obtained quickly and also spreadsheets and scale drawings can be done considering the user's choice);
- adaptability to evolution of informatics technologies.

If data to be used is not yet in digital format, there are several techniques by which spatial information can be obtained. Thus, maps can be digitized or drawn with the mouse for collecting the coordinates of various items. Scanning with electronic devices can also help convert the lines and points on a map into digital data.

Entering data into the system is requesting the largest amount of time resource. Each occurrence of objects in a map and spatial relations between them must be specified.

Editing the automatically retrieved information can also be difficult. Electronic scanners record the map patterns with the same accuracy with which they retrieve important elements from the map. For example, such a pattern can lead to connecting two lines that should not meet. Such unwanted information be edited or removed from the data file.

## PRODUCING MAP GRAPHS WITH SAS ENTERPRISE GUIDE

Being one of the largest software producers for statistics and business analytics in the world, SAS paid particular attention to the representation of spatial data in its solutions. SAS Enterprise Guide is the Graphical User Interface (GUI) that helps to exploitation and dynamic publication in a Microsoft Windows client application. SAS interface is the preferred solution for business analysts, programmers and statisticians.

SAS means analysis and data management, a series of procedures and programming capabilities. An important feature offered by SAS statistical processing of cartographic data based on geographically and able to juggle with these statistics to obtain cartographic works. Map coordinates are stored in tables provided to streamline the process. So, in order to create a map, the user needs tables for storing the owned information that will be implemented through a mapping process. Further, the imported data are joined (intersection) in Enterprise Guide with the coordinates provided by the system, and this will generate the final mapping product. SAS offers users the possibility to choose the type of map produced from a variety of devices widely available, simple maps, maps with parameter chosen by the user, the possibility to redefine the geographical regions, the possibility to choose maps colors [7].

The following paragraphs will present the process steps necessary to create a cartographic work. The analyzed data are actual values of macroeconomic indicators, studied for the countries of the international economic organizations, the Organization for Economic Co-operation and Development (OECD).

The first step is to import tables containing data. Different formats of tables can be imported, including xls, mdb, csv and html. In the example, we have chosen to import tables in mdb format. To create a parameter map with all the values we need in a single table of indicators including Gross Domestic Product (GDP), Net Domestic Product (NDP) and UNEMPLOYMENT, so the tables imported have been joined. To join two or more tables Query Builder tool have to be used and one can choose the type of join (manually or automatically).

To create a map using SAS Enterprise Guide 4.2, we need to get the geographic coordinates owned by the system in the map library. A join was made between the imported table, which contains indicators for each country, and the table with the coordinates of the system. Next, a map is created for the data we get by processing imported tables. As settings we can choose the type of the map (Choropleth, Riser and Prism), data sources, appearance, titles and other properties. To set up a map with a parameter that can be chosen at runtime, a variable that will contain the list of indicators was created. Creating a map in SAS Enterprise Guide 4.3 is even easier than in version 4.2 of this product. Briefly, the key element to create a Map Chart is to making sure your data and the map file have a commonly named variable on which to join. As mentioned before, earlier versions required to use the Query Builder task to join your data to the shape or map file. In 4.3, this is done automatically. In order to create a basic Map Chart, the user must only provide data with a geographic variable and an analysis variable [5].

In figure 1 is presented a two-dimensional (choropleth) map chart which indicates levels of magnitude or response levels of the corresponding response variable by filling map areas with different colors and patterns. For each OECD country, one level of the Gross Domestic Product for the year 2008 is described using various shades of the same color. An example of a 3D map chart can be found if figure 2. This is a riser map graph having riser appears to be standing on each geographical area. The height of the riser is proportional to the value of the chart column for that geographical area. The same information as in figure 1 is represented in this chart.

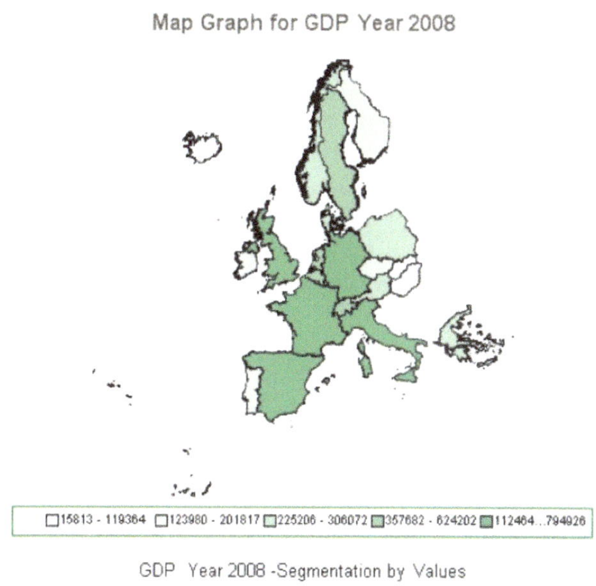


**Figure 1:** Choropleth map chart

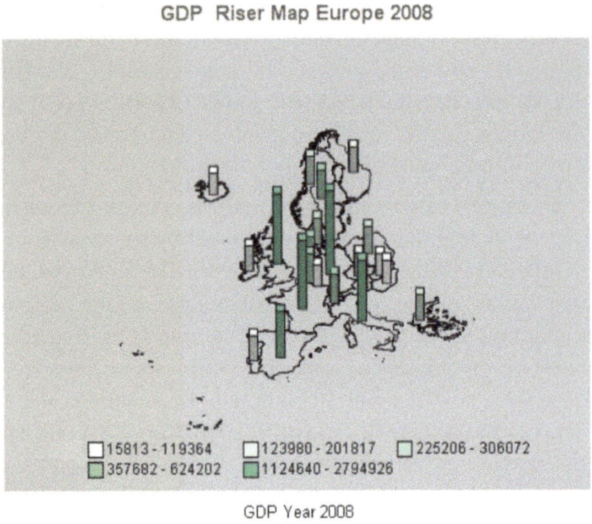


**Figure 2:** Riser map chart

## EXTENDED FEATURES OF MAP GRAPHS IN SAS

Map graphs produced by SAS Enterprise Guide are static and their lone purpose is to display information. New features within SAS/GRAPH allow for the creation of maps with dynamic features like drill-down areas, pop-ups and animation. This implies writing SAS code for achieving such features.

```
*** Section 1 - create a format to
display county name;
data county_fmt (keep=fmtname start
label)
/ view=county_fmt;
retain fmtname 'countyname';
set romanian_dens
rename=(ID=start county_name=label));
run;
proc format cntlin=county_fmt;
run;

*** Section 2 - set graphics and
output options;
goptions reset=all
device=activex
xpixels=700
ypixels=500;
ods listing close;
ods html file = 'c:\romania.html';
title 'ROMANIAN POPULATION
DENSITY By COUNTY, 2006';
footnote j=r 'Pop-ups in Map Graph';

*** Section 3 - define graph
parameters;
proc gmap data=romanian_dens
map=maps.romania;
id ID;
choro density / levels=all nolegend;
format ID countyname.;
label ID = 'COUNTY';
run;
```

Starting from the examples illustrated in [7], we demonstrate the use of the ACTIVEX device driver that enables a number of facilities, including the ability to pop-up information associated with each map area. In this regard, two data sets will be used to create a map graph which will display the population density for all Romanian counties. The first (named romanian_dens), containing the response data set, has three variables: ID – identification number for a county, County_name and Density – the density of population per square kilometer in the year 2006, information retrieved from [8]. The second data set (named Romania) is the Romanian shape file provided by SAS system and located in the map library.

The SAS code from the program below generates a map graph of the Romanian population density in the form of an html type file.

The following paragraphs explain how the SAS language features were used in the source code presented above.

In Section 1, the data step creates a user format (county_fmt) that will be used in proc gmap command to display information associated with each Romanian county. This will be done starting from the romanian_dens data set (specified in the set command). The keep flag determines whether or not a variable is written to the output data set. The specified variables will be the only variables in your output data set [9]. The view option tells SAS to compile, but not to execute, the source program and to store the compiled code in the input DATA step view that is named in the option [10]. Retain flag is used to prevent fmtname variable from being reset to missing at the top of the data step. This makes it a vital tool for passing information from one observation to another.

An important feature of SAS language is the ability to create user-defined formats starting from a specially constructed SAS data set. This can be done using the proc format option cntlin= (control in) that permits the user to name the data set (or data view in our case) which will be used. Control input data set require a minimum of three variables, named ftmname (the format name), start (a single value that will be formatted) and label (information to be displayed) [11].

Section 2 has the roles of resetting the graphics options to default values, selecting the JAVA device driver and setting the image size. Also, using the Output Delivery System (ods) a html file is generated and characteristics of this output type (title and footnote) are being defined.

Section 3 involves the actual construction of the graph through the gmap procedure. The GMAP procedure produces two-dimensional (choropleth) or three-dimensional (block, prism, and surface) maps that show variations of a variable value with respect to an area [12]. The only type of map graph that SAS can create using only code, not Enterprise Guide tasks is the surface graph type. Main parameters of gmap proc are response data set (data), map data set (map), variable that determines the color intensity of the geographic areas (id) and type of graph (choro, in the presented example). In the resulting map, as it can be seen in Figure 3, information about each area (the value of the ID variable and the value of the variable in the CHORO statement) appear in pop-up box as the mouse cursor is moved over the map. In addition, the user could alter the appearance of the map if the right mouse button is clicked anywhere on the map surface.

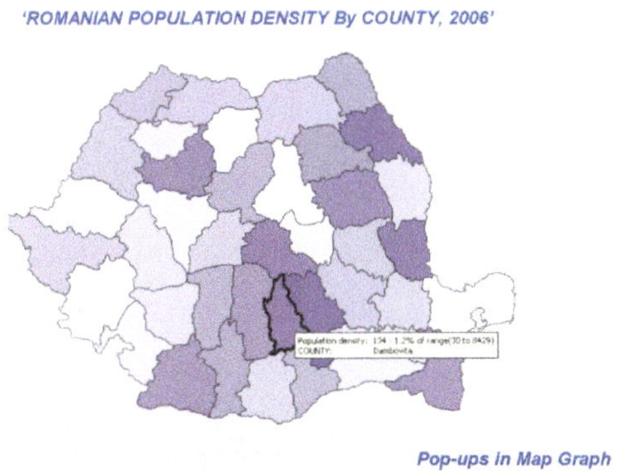


**Figure 3:** Map chart with pop-up features

## CONCLUSIONS

The possibility to represent spatial data in statistics and analytics software tools is an important characteristic in the context of the new economy, mainly due to globalization and geographic distribution of organizational units in various economic areas. SAS software offers big support in this regard, by letting users to manipulate different kind of spatial data and to create map graphs. Besides the support offered through the map library, additional maps can be found on the SAS Maps Online page available at [13]. Besides this, a connection with professional spatial analysis tools can be made using, for example, SAS Bridge for ESRI to access ArcGIS files.

## REFERENCES

1. G. B. Meehan, Statistical Mapping Capabilities and Potentials of SAS, Institute for Research in Social Science, University of North Carolina, 1982
2. D. Peuquet, Representations of Geographic Space: Toward a Conceptual Synthesis, Annals of the Association of American Cartographers, Nr. 78 (3), 1988, pp. 375-394.
3. Geographic information system http://en.wikipedia.org/wiki/Geographic_ information_system#Data_representation
4. R. McMaster, L. Barnett, A spatialobject level organization of transformations for cartographic generalization, Proceedings of the International Symposium on Cmputer – Assisted Cartography Auto-Carto 11, 1993, pp. 386-395.
5. S. R. Thompson, Easier than You Think: Creating Maps with SAS Enterprise Guide, SAS Global Forum 2011, Las Vegas, Nevada, USA, http://support.sas.com/resources/papers/ proceedings11/311-2011.pdf
6. M. Băduţ , Soluţie pentru proiectarea si administrarea întreprinderilor - O tripletă de încredere: MicroStation - MicroStation GeoGraphics - PlantSpace, PC World Romania, nr 7, 1997, pp. 12
7. M. Zdeb, Creating Maps with SAS/GRAPH- Drill Downs, Pop-Ups, and Animation, SUGI 29 Conference Proceedings, Montréal, Canada, 2004, http://www2.sas.com/proceedings/sug i29/toc.html
8. Density of Romanian population, http://enciclopediaromaniei.ro/wiki/Index:Jude%C5%A3e#cite_note-2
9. An Introduction to SAS Data Steps, http://www.ssc.wisc.edu/sscc/pubs/4- 18.htm
10. DATA Step Views, http://support.sas.com/documentation/ cdl/en/lrcon/62955/HTML/default/viewer.htm#a001278887.htm
11. R. Cody, Learning SAS by Example: A Programmers Guide, SAS Institute Inc., Cary, USA, 2007
12. SAS GMAP Procedure, http://support.sas.com/documentation/cdl /en/graphref/63022/HTML/default/viewe r.htm#overview-gmap.htm
13. SAS Maps Online, http://support.sas.com/rnd/datavisualizat ion/mapsonline/

# INDEX